L.S.E. Studies on Education
from the Higher Education Research Unit
of the London School of Economics
and Political Science

Tessa Blackstone

A FAIR START:
THE PROVISION OF
PRE-SCHOOL EDUCATION

ALLEN LANE THE PENGUIN PRESS

To Tom, Benedict and Liesel

Contents

Appendix 7. Smelser's model of structural differentiation   206

Foreword

This book deals with a topic which is becoming of increasing importance in public discussion about educational policies. For this reason it was decided to include it in the series 'LSE Studies on Education' although, unlike the other books in the series so far, it does not arise from research carried out in the LSE Higher Education Research Unit. It was written for a doctoral thesis partly under my supervision and, since its conclusion, Dr Blackstone has been linked with the Unit as a consultant. These points apart, we were keen to include the book in our series because of the importance of the topic and the combination of statistical, historical and sociological approaches used in studying it.

The book describes the growth of pre-school education in England and Wales during the twentieth century. It begins by identifying the nineteenth-century origins of the education of children under 5, and continues with a description of the growth of provision up to 1965. It attempts to identify the political, economic and demographic factors which have affected the supply of nursery education, and to consider some of the wider social changes relating to the structure and functions of the family and the roles of its members, which may explain the growing demand for it. This is followed by a cross-sectional analysis of provision, which measures the number of places available in 1965 and tries to explain the variation in supply from one area to another. Finally it describes decision-making on nursery education in four local authorities, in an attempt to identify some of the unique historical factors affecting the extent of provision which would not emerge from a statistical study at the national level.

C. A. MOSER
Director of the Unit

Author's Preface

Many people have helped me with this study, and I should like to mention some of them by name here, and to thank all the others who at one time or another have given me advice, information, ideas or encouragement.

My first debt is to the University of London for providing me with a studentship which enabled me to spend one year working full-time on the study. Having begun graduate studies as a part-time student without a grant of any kind, its financial worth and the opportunity it gave me to spend more time on my research was appreciated.

In writing Chapters 2–4, I drew on the resources of several different libraries, but I should like particularly to thank the librarians at the Department of Education and Science. The Nursery School Association gave me permission to use their library where I found literature about pre-school education which is otherwise unavailable in one collection. Various other organizations helped me to gather the material for these chapters including the Pre-school Playgroups Association, in particular its secretary, at that time Mrs Hannah Corbishley, and the Save the Children Fund, particularly its Playgroup Organizer, then Miss Joan Pearse. Miss Fitzgibbon of the Inner London Education Authority supplied me with many leads which I might otherwise have left unexplored.

I am especially grateful to my colleague Bleddyn Davies, and to his research assistant, Mrs Valerie Williamson, who relieved me of the onerous chore of collecting much of the data for the independent variables in Chapter 6. Equally I owe a great deal to the statisticians at the Department of Education and Science who provided me with unpublished data on maintained nursery schools and classes. For data on independent nursery education I must thank all those Medical Officers of Health who sent me information about their areas. The data on the present provision of pre-school education was collected for the year 1965, but in the five years since then relatively few changes have taken place because there has been no major expansion of maintained nursery education. As a result of the urban programme, there is now rather more nursery provision in areas of social need than in 1965, and the growth of independent provision has continued, so that the overall figures for private facilities are now higher.

For giving me the opportunity of studying the way decisions are taken about nursery education at the local level, I should like to thank the Chief Education Officers of Burton-on-Trent, Hertfordshire, Kent and Smethwick.

In Burton, Mr N. T. Clamp, the Deputy Education Officer, also helped me, as did Mr Ridger, Assistant Education Officer in Hertfordshire, and Miss Calveley, at one time Nursery Schools Organizer in the county. Mr W. E. Moore, Assistant Education Officer in Kent and his assistant, Mr Adrian Harrison, put up with more irritating requests for information, which was hard to obtain, than most people could have tolerated. I am very grateful for their patience. I want particularly to thank Mr Percy Muncey, Assistant Education Officer for Hertfordshire, now retired, who gave me so much of his time. Two Labour councillors who had campaigned for nursery education, Mrs Chadwick of Burton and Mrs Hale of Hertfordshire, also helped me.

Joyce Groves took on the unenviable task of typing the manuscript, for which I am grateful. I should like to thank Dr Celia Phillips and my father, G. V. Blackstone, for commenting on earlier drafts and Professor Asher Tropp for his help as my supervisor initially. Dr Percy Cohen who replaced him, provided me with many stimulating ideas, and I am most grateful to him. I owe a great deal to Professor Claus Moser, my other supervisor, without whose encouragement and interest, I should never have completed the thesis on which this book is based.

Finally I want to thank my husband Tom Evans, who has accepted with such good grace the implications of the changing role of wives and mothers described in this book. By sharing both the intellectual and domestic tasks that faced me, he has made the study possible.

TESSA BLACKSTONE

1. Introduction

This study originated in an interest in the reasons for the gap between the social demand for nursery education and its supply. Although the size of this gap had never been measured, since there was no reliable data on demand and the data on supply had not been fully assembled, circumstantial evidence suggested that it was growing. The supply in the maintained (state) sector was not increasing at all, although, partly to compensate for this, new forms of independent nursery provision, such as pre-school playgroups, were emerging. The increasing demand for nursery education was highlighted by letters to newspapers from frustrated parents who had been unable to obtain places for their children. Waiting lists for accommodation had grown disproportionally to the places available. Nursery education is not unique in this respect; the supply of several other social services is insufficient to meet the demand, but, largely due to growing middle-class pressure for the extension of nursery provision, the gap became more obvious than in many other services. It seemed important to investigate the particular circumstances that had led to it, and various questions came to mind. Why had provision developed so slowly? Why were some areas better supplied than others? What were the causes of the growing demand? This book provides some tentative answers to these questions. In order to answer them it has been necessary to obtain information on the nature and extent of the different kinds of pre-school education, and the way the supply varies from one area to another. Much of the study is therefore descriptive.

To begin with, it is necessary to define pre-school or nursery education. Pre-school education is undergone by the young child before reaching school age and starting compulsory education. He attends an establishment outside his own home regularly in order to participate in educational activities. The type of establishment he may attend varies in staffing, financing and administration. In spite of this institutional variety, such establishments have one common characteristic: their prime aim is to educate the child. If this is not their prime aim they cannot for the purposes of this study be defined as providers of nursery education. For this reason, services whose prime aim is care and protection of young children, rather than education, are excluded. The most important example of this are day nurseries which are designed 'to meet the special needs of children whose mothers are constrained by individual circumstances to go out to work, or whose home conditions are unsatisfactory from a health point of view, or whose mothers are incapable for some good reason of undertaking full care of their children' (Ministry of Health, Circular 221, 1945). Of course, these institutions are not without an educational function. They are equipped with educational apparatus, and the children's timetable is frequently planned to satisfy social and educational needs. Thus a manifest function of care and protection may be supplemented by a latent function of education. In the same way, the nursery school or class caters for the needs of working mothers, as well as for the education of their children. Nevertheless, in spite of certain limitations and difficulties arising from the exclusion of care institutions such as day nurseries, it is justified insofar as this study is concerned with conscious efforts to provide facilities for the *education* of young children and the social forces behind these efforts.

The education provided at the pre-school stage is usually informal: teaching reading, writing or arithmetic is rarely undertaken. There is an emphasis on education through play, which is mainly free and unorganized, although some time may be devoted to more formalized games. The child is given various materials which he learns to manipulate, and is encouraged to express himself through new media by way of play. Many establishments for pre-school education also aim to develop the child's personality towards self-reliance, independence and cooperation. Those who are responsible for such establishments hope that play with other children will encourage the child to cooperate in a group situation, and that part of the day spent away from his mother and home will help him to become independent and prepare him for his entry into compulsory schooling.

The main aim of this study is to explain the growth of pre-school education in England and Wales since the beginning of this century. In doing this its emphasis lies rather in describing in detail the nature and development of the supply of this service, than in measuring the extent and considering the nature of the demand. However, any attempt to explain the growth of a social service must consider both facets, and the distinction made is one of emphasis. The question of why parents want this experience for their children is fundamental in considering how it is supplied, in what quantity and why. The framework in which these questions are considered is first a historical analysis of the development of pre-school education in England and Wales from 1900 to 1965 and includes the nineteenth-century antecedents. The second half of the study describes the extent and nature of provision in 1965 and analyses the variation in provision between local authority areas. This is followed by a study of decision-making with reference to nursery education in four local authorities since the war.

The historical chapters attempt to identify some of the political, economic, social and demographic strands which have stimulated or impeded rates of growth. Since historians of education have neglected nursery education, the establishment of various forms of pre-school education is described in detail. A few specialized studies concerned solely with its growth and its content do exist, but there has been no comprehensive British study on the history of pre-school education since the mid-1930s and those works did not have a sociological approach. Chapter 2 considers the various strands in the origins of pre-school education in the nineteenth century, including the ideas of the continental reformers and Robert Owen, the establishment of Froebel's kindergartens and the large-scale provision for children under 5 in the infant schools. Chapter 3 traces the development of the idea of publicly maintained schools for children prior to compulsory schooling, considers the effects of the First World War, of the 1929 Labour government, the decline in the birth rate and the Depression. Chapter 4 continues with the effects of the Second World War, the post-war shortage of teachers and school buildings and the growth of private nursery education. Having considered the growth of pre-school education over time, Chapters 5 and 6 describe variation in pro-vision cross-sectionally. Chapter 5 provides detailed figures of the number of nursery places of different types available in the maintained and independent sector in 1965 and presents additional data on, for example, the proportion of part-time to full-time places and the size of nursery schools. Up till now, most information of this kind has been based on guesswork. The description in Chapter 5 provides a basis for the analysis in Chapter 6, which describes the types of local authority with high and low provision, and attempts to account for some of the variation in provision by identifying possible deter-minants of the number of places available, such as the proportion of married women working in different areas. Chapter 7 was written to try to improve understanding of the influences on the development of nursery education by tracing decisions on pre-school education in two county boroughs and two administrative counties. In this way, the effects of historical factors can be investigated, which might not otherwise be obvious in tracing changes at the national level, nor in a statistical analysis. It also reveals more starkly the problem of limited resources that faces the providers of such services.

The Theoretical Framework

The availability of resources for the social services in general and for educa-tion in particular has been vital in determining the levels of expansion that nursery education has achieved. But it is necessary to look beyond this and consider what shapes priorities in spending. This study contends that there are broad underlying social changes in the family in an advanced industrial society, which have led to a demand for extra-familial institutions to educate young children. The pressures generated by these changes are only partly conceded as legitimate grounds for action in providing extra-familial agencies, since traditional values and attitudes concerning the family command power-ful adherence. These attitudes act as a barrier to the acceptance of the need for universal pre-school education and have led to the low priority given to expenditure on nursery education.

Much has been written about the changing structure and functions of the family with the advance of industrialization. The well-known changes which the family has undergone during the last sixty years will not be discussed, nor the extent to which these can be directly attributable to the process of industrialization, or the degree of universality of such changes. However, various examples of these changes and studies illustrating them will be quoted. There has been a tendency to explain them in terms of industrialization and urbanization, which need not be disputed, but we have not explained all that happens today by simply sticking these all-embracing labels on them. Many myths surround the sociology of the family, a number of which have been perpetrated about the family of fifty years ago, about which we know little. No detailed studies were done of the family at the time. As Goode has suggested, we still do not know precisely where the impact of industrialization on the family occurs (Goode, 1963–4). He suggests that there has been a weakening of role obligations in the family, although no one has shown precisely why this weakening takes place. However, it is perhaps possible to indicate some of its consequences, one of which has been the growth of outside agencies as aids in the socialization of the young child.

The development of such agencies can be analysed not simply in terms of historical description and speculative and empirical studies on changes in the family as a social organization, but also within the context of a theoretical framework, which should aid explanation and interpretation. The model of change developed by Smelser, which he terms structural differentiation, can be used for this purpose (Smelser, 1959). This model is described in more detail in Appendix 7 but references will be made to it at various places in the book.*

Limitations

The study is limited by being confined to England and Wales. Research comparing the development of pre-school education in a number of countries would lead to a better understanding of the factors which determine both provision and demand. The pattern appears to be similar in most Western industrial societies: only a small proportion of children obtain this kind of education; the supply does not meet the demand; and many places are provided by organizations or individuals outside state schemes. Nevertheless, although these generalizations are broadly applicable to most industrial societies, there are variations in the extent of provision. A higher proportion of children obtain pre-school education in the urban areas of Eastern European countries than in the towns of Western Europe. The most important exception to the general pattern of haphazard and limited provision is the USSR. In the urban areas of European Russia a high proportion of children

* Those readers who do not wish to read the whole of this theoretical appendix should turn to paragraph 1, p. 209, which summarizes the role of the model in the study.

attend nursery schools. An analysis of the historical traditions, ideological leanings and political and economic conditions behind such provision would be of interest. It would provide further insight into the causes of the chequered development of nursery education in Britain by pointing to the pre-conditions for its development in a society where it has been adopted more extensively, and with less ambivalence. The difficulties of such international comparisons have been well documented in studies of other social phenomena such as industrial conflict and social mobility. These difficulties are compounded in the case of nursery education by the fact that compulsory elementary schooling begins at varying ages in different countries. However, it is a matter of regret that it has only been possible to study nursery education in one society.*

This limitation does have the advantage of allowing a more detailed consideration of the historical background to the development of the institution under scrutiny, and of the relationship of this institution to other institutions in the wider society. Floud and Halsey have criticized sociologists writing on education for failing to conceive of educational institutions, and to consider their nature (see Floud and Halsey, 1900). They suggest that these are institutions functioning in close relation to the wider social structure, but in partial independence of it. The nature of this partial independence is unclear. Possibly such institutions function independently of the wider social structure in the sense that they may initiate certain changes or act as barriers to such changes. The extension of the nursery school, for example, may initiate the large-scale employment of women with young children. Educational institutions tend to be conservative in their roles, in that they reflect rather than modify other aspects of the social structure. Even when they do successfully initiate change, the concept of partial independence seems somewhat misleading. This study is concerned with the interdependence of educational institutions with economic, demographic, political and ideological factors.

In describing different rates of growth at different periods and indicating some of the barriers to growth, three theoretical questions will be touched on: first, the role of ideas in promoting educational change; second, the extent to which new social policies are formulated in response to changing social needs; and third, the application of Smelser's model of structural differentiation to the change described. These questions will be referred to in unfolding the story of nursery education and establishing the facts about provision, past and present. But the major aim is to describe the growth of nursery education in England and Wales since this has not been done before. Chapters 5 and 6 on the statistics of nursery education in 1965 and the variation in provision form the section of this study which is most confined to the presentation of factual data. However, even this section is not limited to studying local authority variations *per se*. It also aims to discover whether any of the factors indicated by a study of provision over time appear significant

---

* For a short study of provision in Western Europe see Blackstone, 1970.

in a cross-sectional picture of provision. The local authority has been chosen as the unit of analysis since many decisions about the provision of pre-school education are made at this level, and it is the only level at which data are available. In trying to identify the factors which determine the level of provision as well as describing the variation from area to area, the purpose is to find out, as far as is possible, whether the forces which appear to lie behind the extent of provision at various periods are replicated in the distribution of provision from area to area. This is also relevant to the theoretical questions raised above, particularly the second concerning the response to social needs. Do areas with more obvious needs have better provision? The major problem is to isolate variables which provide valid indices of the operation of the forces described in Chapters 2, 3, and 4, on the history of pre-school education. This cannot always be done; for example, there are no data on regional or area differences in the structure of the family. It is therefore difficult to quantify the extent to which the need for extra-familial agencies varies as a result of such differences.

The study concludes with an attempt to weight some of the factors considered earlier, in the light of the three different kinds of evidence: at the macro level; historical and statistical; and, at the micro level, a description of decisions in selected local education authorities. It also describes briefly the current emergence of new issues in the pressure for pre-school education, and makes some suggestions for future policy. In weighting the influences the conclusion indulges in speculation; more rigorous testing of some of the hypotheses and assertions presented here awaits further research.

2. The origins of pre-school education

One of the apparent differences between industrial societies and other social systems is the level of prestige allocated to children as a distinct social group within the wider society. The status position of children is not constant; it varies from time to time and place to place. The classification of human beings into age categories, such as adults and children, or the aged, the mature and the young, also varies. The concept of the child has acquired added significance in the industrial society. It has also extended its boundaries to include a greater age range than in the past. The pressure to raise the age of criminal responsibility and the extension of special treatment to young offenders are manifestations of this. The juvenile courts exist to deal with young offenders against the law. Special forms of treatment are applied to all those found guilty of an offence under the age of 17, and offenders are not sent to prison before the age of 21.* The exclusion of young people from the labour market is another manifestation. The extension of the period of compulsory schooling is both an expression and a cause of the widening concept of childhood. The disappearance of the child as an active participant in the productive forces of the economy is probably the most fundamental and significant of the changes. The early entry into the labour force of the majority of the child population is prevalent in all pre-industrial societies. The years of childhood are regarded increasingly as different in kind to those of adulthood; the child is something more than a youthful copy, a smaller edition of its elders. Childhood is a separate stage marked by special forms of dress, special hours for rest, legitimized types of leisure and even particular kinds of food. Accompanying this increasing differentiation of childhood from adulthood, are a series of attitudes, which tend to idealize this stage of man's life, and to demand special care and conditions for those at this stage. Bossard and Boll have expressed this development succinctly in terms of

* The existing differentiation of children by the law with reference to criminal behaviour is regarded as inadequate by a considerable section of informed opinion. The Ingleby Report (1960, para. 65) recommended modest change. 'Its basis [the change] is a recognition that ideas and practices of ordinary criminal jurisdiction are unsuitable for dealing with children, and that a similar unsuitability attaches to any ordinary civil procedure. What is needed is a special jurisdiction designed for the particular purpose, and not a modified version of something that is essentially meant for adult courts.' They recommended that the minimum age of criminal responsibility should be raised to 12 with the possibility of it becoming 13 or 14 at some future date. There have been more far-reaching and radical recommendations, such as that children ought not to be brought before any form of criminal court, but should be the subject of some form of social welfare agency.

legislative change. 'The drawing of precise lines identifying certain age groups and assigning them legal status has become increasingly frequent in modern culture chiefly because of various types of social legislation based on age distinction.' They continue that 'the more recent legislation has advanced the ages by one or more years to protect children from being treated as adults too soon' (Bossard and Boll, 1963, p. 577).

A new philosophy has grown up which maintains that the needs of the child ought to be given consideration before all others. The child belongs to the most privileged age range in the advanced industrial society, and demands are constantly made that its rights should be respected. Sacrifices made by adults on behalf of children do not receive scorn on the grounds of undue sentimentality, but are applauded as virtuous acts of unselfishness. Frequent references will be made to how child-centred our society is — a characteristic it shares with other industrial societies.

The accorded status of the child is high: he is essentially virtuous and unmarked by the evils of adult society. Some evidence for this has been indicated by Martha Wolfenstein in her analysis of the portrayal of children in films in four cultures: France, Britain, Italy and the United States. An analysis of a large number of films produced in these four countries revealed very few examples of children presented as malign or evil characters. On the contrary, the common characteristic of the child in the films from all four countries was 'his nobility and his function as a touchstone of virtue' (Mead and Wolfenstein, 1955, p. 278). This view contrasts strongly with the image of children that emerges from studies of late eighteenth- and early nineteenth-century literature, which was dominated both in England and the United States (Miller and Swanson, 1958) by the Puritan Calvinistic conception of the infant as a depraved individual whose will cannot be broken. Susannah Wesley gave the following advice in a letter to her son:

In order to form the minds of children, the first thing to be done is to conquer their will and bring them to an obedient temper . . . the subjecting of the temper is a thing which must be done at once, and the sooner the better . . . the parent who indulges it does the devil's work; makes religion impracticable, salvation unobtainable . . . (John Wesley, 1823, p. 263).

Similarly, a New Englander wrote in 1834, 'No child has ever been known since the earliest period of the world, destitute of an evil disposition however sweet it appears' (Mead and Wolfenstein, 1959, p. 159). A relaxation of such attitudes and a higher status for the child was concomitant with growing interest in children. This has been recorded by Robert Sunley.

Between 1820 and 1860 . ,. the American public showed a markedly increasing interest in the importance of children and in child-rearing problems. For the first time in the United States a substantial body of literature appeared on the subject, ranging from practical advice on infant care to elaborate theories on the moral training of children. The child-rearing literature suggests some of the reasons for this increasing concern over the upbringing of children: a greater emphasis on the child as the extension of parental ambitions and as the representative of the parent's status in society; a growing belief in man's power to control the environment and direct the future, including the moulding of the child; a new need for personal direction, as established patterns of child rearing were being disrupted in the rapid shift to industrialisation and urbanisation (in Mead and Wolfenstein, 1955, p. 151).

This analysis can be applied to Britain and other industrial societies. During the twentieth century the trend has continued and intensified into child-centredness. The role of the child as an extension of parental ambitions has become applicable to a far larger proportion of the population, as the possibilities for social mobility have improved. The revaluation of the child has contributed to the family's growing difficulty to cope alone with the early socialization of young children, since the need for high standards of care and education is recognized, yet cannot be perfectly fulfilled, hence the process of structural differentiation occurs.

With the extension of the concept of the child has come a subdivision of childhood into more than one age-set. Such groupings are not an entirely new phenomenon, nor are they unique to the industrial society. Cultural anthropologists have noted their existence in primitive societies and studied their structure and function in detail. Initiation ceremonies frequently mark the move from one age-set into another, however they usually mark the leaving of childhood and entry into adult status. A number of distinct age-sets below the age of initiation is less common. Ruth Benedict has defined the phenomenon of age-sets in the following way,

Age graded cultures characteristically demand different behaviour from the individual at different times of his life and persons of a like age grade are grouped into a society whose activities are all oriented toward the behaviour desired at that age. Individuals graduate publicly and with honour from one of these groups to another (Benedict, 1938, pp. 161–7).

The extent of this age grading is more limited in industrial societies and does not have the same significance as in some pre-literate cultures, nor is it much applied to the adult members of the society. However, it does seem to be applicable to children at present. In twentieth-century Britain, until very recently final acceptance of the individual as an adult has not taken place till he has reached 21 years of age. Below this age there are obvious though informal sub-divisions, which are moulded chiefly by the structure of the educational system, in part by the physical and psychological growth of the child, and in part by other factors such as the legal age of marriage. Childhood, it appears, is divided into three main periods: the period from infancy to compulsory school age, hence the frequently used term 'the under-5s', never 'the under-4s' or 'the under-6s'; the period from 5 to 12 or 13 years old, which is marked by primary school education, and ends with the onset of puberty*; and the period known as adolescence, which can perhaps be sub-divided into two stages, consisting of teenagers up to the age of 16 and young people from the age of 17 to 21, the majority of whom have started work, and some of whom are already married.

These three periods do not have the rigidly defined qualities of an age grade in a primitive society. The classification is thus of a subjective kind, and undoubtedly there is blurring at the boundaries of the groups. It would be interesting to obtain information from a large sample of individuals, to discover if and how they would classify people by age. This would provide more extensive evidence of this form of social differentiation. There are very different expectations about the way children in different age groups should behave, and there are differences in the status appropriated to the different age groups. As the child approaches adulthood, during the period of adoles-cence his accorded status appears to fall. There is a conflict in social attitudes towards the adolescent with a condemnation of juvenile crime, youthful affluence and overspending, and a disdain towards 'teenage' culture (see Musgrove, 1964), and yet a recognition of greater pressures and stresses placed on this age group, which are believed to be outside their control, and an admiration for their growing knowledge and their acts of charity as volun-tary social workers. It is when this stage is reached that the dangers of the application of the concept of status to an age grade are revealed. There are too many internal differences within the grade to allow the simple application of such a concept. However, the dangers seem less when it is applied to the young child and it is hard to dispute that he occupies a position of high regard. Musgrove suggested that the adolescent is a recent socio-psychological invention, created by modern social attitudes and social institutions. He implies that because adolescence is invented in this way it is a myth. It is unclear whether he means by this that, because society imputes age-based limitations to people and then reifies them, adolescence is a myth, or that the characteristics assigned to the period of adolescence do not have their roots in reality, and are therefore mythical. If he means the latter his argument may have some validity, but if he means the former the term myth is surely unsuitable. The role of a social definition of age rather than a biological one is very apparent in the allocation of roles and statuses. Thus the existence of the 'under-5s' is moulded by the attitudes and beliefs of adults about the special care and protection needed by this group, and by the institutional fact that there is no universal agency outside the home to take responsibility for it. This differentiates it from other age groups.

The origins of the concept of pre-school education are to be found in the acceptance of a definite stage of childhood before compulsory school age is reached, and a child-centred attitude which holds young children in high regard and sees them as sufficiently important to make special arrangements

---

* There is no commonly used term to describe children of this age. W. A. L. Blyth has suggested the midlands of childhood.

for their care and education. These are two of the vital preconditions to the growth of early education outside the home. The third necessary precondition is the belief that it is in the interests of the child for him to spend some time outside his own home. The existence of this form of education is therefore confined to the century since 1850, and has only reached significant proportions in the twentieth century. The nature of the definition of pre-school education precludes its development before that of school education. Universal elementary education was not introduced in Britain until W. E. Forster's Act of 1870, and did not become compulsory till a later Act in 1880. During the next thirty years large numbers of children between the ages of 3 and 5 were admitted to the infant schools, although attendance was not compulsory till the age of 5. It was not until 1905 that the suitability of the infant school for the child under 5 was questioned officially, and not until 1908 that the concept of the nursery school was introduced and given official recognition (Board of Education, 1905, 1908). This involved the notion of a separate and special kind of education for children before they start compulsory schooling. It is with this innovation and its later development that this study is concerned. However, it is necessary to trace back the events and attitudes which led to this change. 'Educational policy like all social policy is rarely single-minded. To understand the final compromise of policy means taking the main strands of ideas and influences which have been woven into it. . . .' (Glass in Halsey, Floud and Anderson, 1961).

There were various pioneer efforts to educate young children during the eighteenth and nineteenth centuries both in Britain and on the Continent and there have been attempts to provide a theory on which to base this education since Comenius published *The School of Infancy* in 1630. Comenius did not advocate the removal of children under 6 from the home and the care of their mothers. His educational theory was designed for the use of mothers in the home. Indeed, as Raymont has pointed out, 'in all ages, and all civilised communities until quite recent times, the proper and indeed the only place for young children was assumed to be the home, and the natural educators were assumed to be the parents, especially of course the mother for whom a nurse might deputise' (Raymont, 1937, p. 2). There have always been individual critics of the home and family as the source of children's early education. Plato advocated that children should be removed from their homes at an early age, and placed in the care of individuals with specialized training in the care and education of children. Strindberg wrote of 'the family, the hell of the child, the home of all social vices' (Ellis, 1922, pp. 30–1). However, such schemes and such invective play no part in the development of pre-school education. There appear to be no examples, amongst those who have advocated nursery schools, of the belief that institutions for early education should replace the home. Much emphasis is placed on the necessity for maintaining close relations between home and school. This emphasis and the reasons behind it will be discussed later. Early education outside the home is not seen as a replacement for socialization within the home but as an adjunct of it.

The publication of Rousseau's *Émile* initiated a revolutionary change in education. Although he and the other Continental pioneers were not solely or even largely concerned with the education of young children, children of an early age were included in their schemes and they influenced later work which was specifically designed for children under school age. The revolution that Rousseau brought about was in the attitude towards the child and the process of learning (see Rusk, 1933). He can be regarded as the first of the child-centred educationalists. He stressed the necessity to view the acquiring of knowledge from the child's point of view; the child was to develop 'naturally'; formal instruction was to be discouraged and freedom and learning by experience were considered vital. The need to learn from nature was central to his educational philosophy. He himself never attempted to put his theories into practice by founding experimental schools, but in Germany and Switzerland there were a number of attempts to do this.*

None of these institutions, and the other less well known examples of the Nature School, made a significant move forward in the extension of schooling to large numbers of children. They were isolated and usually short-lived experiments. Nor did they even have a direct influence on the later provision of mass education. Other factors outside the sphere of educational theory and experimentation played a more vital role here. They did, however, have a lasting effect on the content of education advocated by certain schools of thought, and their influence has been particularly apparent in the realm of pre-school education. It was to them that Froebel owed some of his ideas, and it is to Froebel that every student of pre-school education must at some point return. It is not proposed to discuss the details of his educational philosophy, nor to consider the advantages and disadvantages of his methods and his curriculum. His educational theories were dominated by the mystical philosophy of the German idealism of his day. Much of what he wrote was harmless nonsense, as was his use of mystical symbolism in the apparatus he designed for his pupils. However, he was the first person to formulate a comprehensive theory of pre-school education, with a detailed method of carrying it out, and his writings (Froebel, 1826) still provide the basis for many of the activities in pre-school agencies today and indeed in the early

---

* The most important was that of Pestalozzi, during the last decades of the eighteenth century, and the first decades of the nineteenth. He accepted Rousseau's theories and elaborated them further, basing his own theory on the notion of '*Anschauung*', which can be translated by 'observation by the senses'. This, he thought, was the basis of our knowledge. Thus self-activity was to be encouraged, and the senses developed. His approach was new, in that he stressed that teaching should be undertaken in terms of the pupils' needs; children were not to be forced but taught according to their stage of development. He denied the necessity for repression or the need for an authoritarian approach. His schools were successful, and he also set up an institution for training teachers in his method. See Pollard (1956) for a more lengthy description of the work of the Nature School.

years of compulsory schooling. Like Pestalozzi, he stressed the importance of training through the senses. He greatly respected the child and believed in his rights as an individual. 'Every human being, even as a child, must be recognised, acknowledged, and fostered as a necessary and essential member of humanity, and so the parents should feel and recognise themselves responsible as fosterers to God, to the child, and to humanity' (Froebel, 1889, p. 53). He was opposed to training children to be subservient and subordinate. 'Unlike most of his contemporaries and many of his successors, he says that the real object of training is to establish self-control, not servile obedience' (Raymont, 1937, p. 299). Perhaps his most important innovation was his approach to play. He was the first person to perceive the significance of play for the young child and its role as part of the educational process. 'The plays of childhood are the germinal leaves of all later life, for the whole man is shown and developed in these . . . play is not trivial, it is highly serious and of deep significance.' His writings were a source of inspiration to John Dewey and other members of the progressive school.

Froebel did not confine himself to the development of a theoretical system for early education; he had a great deal of practical experience with small children. He maintained that early education based on organized play cannot be carried out exclusively by the child's mother. Thus in 1837 he set up the first kindergarten in Blankenburg. In 1840 a second was founded, and by the year of his death, in 1852, approximately twenty kindergarten were in existence. He also began to train students, mostly young women, to teach in kindergarten. After his death the number of kindergarten did not increase rapidly, although they did spread from Germany to other European countries, including England. The work of Froebel and the Nature School had a lasting and more important impact in terms of the revolutionary methods of pedagogy which they proposed, than in terms of the direct implementation of pre-school education; the role of their ideas was central to the way pre-school education developed. Nevertheless the small number of kindergarten founded in the second half of the nineteenth century form one of the major strands in the origins of pre-school education in England and Wales, but there is another entirely different strand which it is necessary to trace in this search for origins.

The industrial conditions of the late eighteenth and early nineteenth century focused attention on the needs of what were termed 'the infant poor'. A few people recognized the necessity of rescuing such children from the degrading conditions in which they lived and worked. These pioneers pushed through legislation providing limited protection for the 'little slaves' from exploitation by parents and employers, and a few more mostly at a later period saw the necessity for positive provision to care for working-class children. The difference between this strand and that represented by Froebelian kindergarten is fundamental. The latter developed from concern with education and became identified with a small sector of the middle class, who set up privately run institutions out of the conviction that their children needed something which the home by itself could not give. The two strands share this conviction: the home is inadequate, therefore an alternative must be found. In every other respect the two strands differ. For the purpose of convenience, the first strand will be termed the working-class need and the second the middle-class need. It seems reasonable to identify their origins in terms of social class. They differed first in the sequence of events, which brings about a recognition of these needs. In the middle-class strand the need was not initially recognized, because of a realization of inadequacy, which was then followed by the seeking of a remedy. The 'remedy' preceded the discovery of the need, and indeed played a vital role in highlighting its existence. Thus a new educational theory came into being, which pointed to problems which had previously received little consideration. How might the young child's social and educational development be enhanced? The early Froebelian kindergarten indicated the possibilities of extra-familial communal activity, of guided and organized play as aids to the development of the young child. This appealed to a small section of the liberal-minded bourgeoisie, and a sprinkling of intellectuals, as the deficiencies of life in the nursery became plain to them. The numbers affected in this way by the kindergarten idea were small. This fact is an illustration of the limited efficacy of an educational idea in promoting change. It was not till other changes in the middle-class family's situation had come about that the kindergarten and other forms of pre-school education were popularized. As with the working-class origins, the expression of dissatisfaction with the family's role has been a necessary precursor to the educational remedy. Secondly, they differed in terms of the relationships between those playing the vital roles in initiating this change. In the middle-class strand the change was brought about by parents for their children, although the parents did not usually run the extra-familial agency themselves but paid someone else to do so. The working-class needs were not initially recognized by parents and the agencies were created by organizations or individuals outside the family. The latter might have taken the form of large-scale state intervention and provision, as in post-revolutionary Russia (see Fediavevsky and Smith Hill, 1936), it might have taken the form of working-class organization such as the cooperative movement but, like so many of the endeavours to aid the family in an increasingly industrialized Britain, it took the form of middle-class philanthropy. Lastly, the two strands differed in their aims. The philanthropist was largely concerned to save the child from moral and religious debasement,* an ambition shared by many of those members of the middle classes concerned to provide education for older children, and also to protect the

* 'By taking children at an early stage out of the reach of contamination on the streets, and removing them from the no less baneful influence of evil example at home, we may lay such a foundation of virtue as is not likely to be shaken . . .'. (S. Wilderspin, *The infant system for developing the intellectual and moral power of all children from one to seven years of age,* 1840, p. 38.)

health of the child. Samuel Wilderspin, in a plea for the establishment of infant schools, tried to point out the value to the community of such aims and thus convert more to the cause of institutions for the care of young children.

Surely those persons who disapprove of educating the poor at all will see the propriety of keeping, if possible, their children safe from accidents, and preserving the lives of many little ones who would otherwise be lost to their country, from thus falling a prey to surrounding dangers. Poor parents frequently return from their labours and find to their mortification that one, or probably two of their children are gone to a hospital; *which of course makes them unhappy and unfit for their work* [my italic] (Wilderspin, op. cit., p. 86).

It would be cynical to suggest that all those actually involved in attempts to cater for the needs of the working-class child were doing so in order to ensure that their parents would be less molested in their daily toils in mill or factory; but the form of Wilderspin's plea does indicate contemporary attitudes: many advocated the infant school as a means for preventing juvenile delinquency. 'All who feel in duty bound to preserve their generation, are, we think, bound in conscience to encourage and extend this new and most important scheme [Wilderspin's infant school] for the prevention of juvenile delinquency, and for the promotion of the best interests of society' (*Wesleyan Methodists Magazine*, 1823). The middle-class parent, on the other hand, was concerned with educating his child.

Some of the original attempts to mitigate the evils of industrialization and provide for the working-class need are traced in the following paragraphs. A number of the earliest and best known examples of these took place on the Continent in France and Germany. In Paris in the mid eighteenth century *'garderies d'enfants'* were set up. These were little more than shelters for children and were not exclusively for younger age groups, but in 1789 Count Oberlin, a Lutheran pastor working in Alsace, set up a school at Waldbach primarily for young children, whose mothers were working in agriculture. This was an exception to the rule that the origins of pre-school education are to be found in the conditions created by industrialization. The classical conception of the effects of the growth of large-scale industry on the family was expressed as follows: 'With the Industrial Revolution came the growth of cities, little adapted to child life. Coupled with these conditions was the breaking up of homes and the drawing of mothers into industry' (Ogburn, 1950, p. 241). The effect of the Industrial Revolution on the home as a child-caring institution was great, but its enormity has been exaggerated, and there has been a tendency to over-generalize. It is not possible to give an account of the history of industrialization, and the mechanisms at work here (see Pinchbeck, 1930). It must suffice to say that the working-class home had never been a suitable environment for the socialization of young children, by today's standards, whether the parents were involved in agriculture, domestic industry or both. Oberlin's School at Waldbach is evidence of this. But it is true that the possibilities of parental supervision of children were greater prior to the large-scale employment of both men and women away from their homes, however inadequate this supervision may have been. More important, the concentration of people into small areas, as a result of urbanization, made obvious, even to those who wished to remain blind to it, the degrading conditions of the working population which earlier might have gone unnoticed. These constituted the disequilibrating conditions described by Smelser, which enhanced the dissatisfaction with the performance of familial roles, resulting from the industrial pressures.

The work of Oberlin also indicates that, although the prime aim of the nursery school in its pristine form may have been the protection of the children of working mothers, attempts to educate these children were not neglected. Oberlin did considerable work on the development of teaching methods with young children. He provided excursions, pictures and stories, and ensured that the children spent much time in play. His scheme attracted a great deal of attention, and his school many visitors. Amongst those who were influenced by Oberlin was Robert Owen, whose work will be considered later. He too was concerned with the education of the children in his care. It is possible that in attempting to delineate the presence of a bifurcation in the origins of pre-school education, the difference between the two prongs has been overstressed. If this is so, it should be emphasized that the working-class tradition was also affected by the work of Rousseau and Pestalozzi, and later by Dewey and Thorndike, and although their prime aim was custodial, it would be oversimplified to suggest that this was their only aim. This was also true of Cochin, a philosophical lawyer, who opened a model 'salle d'asile' in Paris in 1831. A number had been opened during the 1820s, but after 1831 they spread rapidly, so that by 1838 there were nineteen in Paris with an enrolment of 3,600 children. The aim of the 'salle d'asile' can best be described in Cochin's own words: 'It is to supply the needs, the instructions, the impressions, which every child should receive from the presence and example of his mother, that it is necessary to open rooms for the hospitality and education of these very young children' (Cochin, 1853, p. 17). It appears that although education was not entirely disregarded, activities of an educational kind were limited, for in the 1850s Madame Pâpe-Carpentier found it necessary to introduce reforms into the 'salle d'asile' in order to establish occupations for the children which were intended to educate them (see Hawtrey, 1936).

At the same time, similar efforts to provide care and protection for the children of working women were being established in Germany. 'Kleinkinderbewahranstalten' flourished during the first twenty years of the nineteenth century. They were founded and maintained by religious societies and private philanthropists. Women's societies, which were active in all spheres of German philanthropic life, played an important part in running them. There were also efforts by little known individuals such as Princess Pauline of Lippe, who wished to emulate the philanthropic works of the French '*salle d'asile*' and in the 1850s founded a school for the young children of the poor in Detmold (see Rusk, 1933).

In England, information about these Continental projects reached a few men with contacts abroad. One of these was Robert Owen, the socialist factory owner. In 1816 Owen opened his infant school at New Lanark. It is unnecessary here to document Owen's other activities at New Lanark, such as the humanity with which he treated his employees, his high standards of workers' accommodation, and his experiment in cooperative ownership and living. Of all the wonders of New Lanark, the infant school provoked the greatest interest, attracting many visitors from both home and abroad. 'The institution for the formation of character with the establishment of New Lanark generally, while it kept its immediate direction, was considered by the more advanced minds of the world one of the greatest modern wonders' (Robert Owen, 1858, p. 145). Owen was very aware of the role of the early years of life in the formation of personality and in this sense anticipated modern psychological theory. He was an ardent environmentalist. 'For it is through the education, or the influence of circumstances, or of the conditions in which he is placed, that man becomes good or bad, inferior or superior' (Owen, 1852, p. 202). Where he differed from the majority of today's psychologists was in the kind of environment he believed to be most suitable. Thus he advocated the attendance of very young children from the age of one year at his infant school. His belief that character is formed in infancy, and that the early years are the most impressionable led to the admittance of one-year-old children to the school, for he regarded the latter as an ideal educational institution. He did not, however, press for formal training for children under six; in fact he insisted on its exclusion.

The children were trained and educated without any punishment or any fear for it . . . the infants and young children, besides being instructed by sensible signs — the things themselves or models or paintings — and by familiar conversation, were from two to four years and upwards taught dancing and singing. . . . The children were not to be annoyed with books but were to be taught uses and nature or qualities of the common things around them, by familiar conversation when the child's curiosity was excited so as to induce them to ask questions respecting them . . . with these infants everything was to be amusement (R. Owen, 1858, p. 140).

His work stood out from the typical educational philosophy of his day. He was not concerned with breaking wills and creating individuals satisfied with their station. Nor was he concerned with saving souls, or even teaching the principles of Christianity. He wished with the aid of informal teaching and physical activity to create an individual who would be a useful citizen later. The success of Owen's infants' school owed much to James Buchanan, the man he employed to be the teacher, a description of whose work is given in a

Victorian journal a quarter of a century later. 'There was in the first instance no especial intention of forming an infant school, but the youngest child able to walk was to be admitted on the principle that education should begin from the cradle.' Buchanan 'found the act of winning infantile attention – amused while he instructed his little classes with pictures and objects, instead of books and made them happy. . . .' (*Westminster and Foreign Quarterly Review,* 1847). The principles on which Owen ran his school are very similar to those of the modern nursery school. 'Unceasing kindness in tone, look, word, and action, to all the children without exception, by every teacher employed, so as to create a real affection, and full confidence between the teachers and the taught.' 'Instruction by the inspection of realities and their qualities, and these explained by familiar conversations between the teachers and the taught, and the latter always allowed to ask their own questions for explanation or additional information. . . .' 'No regular in-door hours for school; but the teacher to discover when the minds of the taught or their own minds, commenced to be fatigued by the indoor lesson, and then to change it for out-of-door physical exercise in good weather; or in bad weather for physical exercise under cover, or exercises in music' (Owen, 1858, p. 232).

In a world hostile to the extension of education, either in its role of socialization or training, the experiment at New Lanark failed to spread. It was instead an object of curiosity for European royalty and aristocracy, ambassadors to the Court of St James and British clergy and administrators, rather than a feasible system to be copied extensively in other parts of the country.

Yet England was not devoid of institutions for the education of young children at this time, although Pollard has suggested that the late eighteenth and early nineteenth century may have been marked by a deteriorating rather than progressing educational system. In contrast to the Continent, there was little pedagogical experiment, and the high demands for child labour may have actually reduced the numbers of children in educational institutions. However, in spite of the stories of children who could scarcely walk picking up pieces in the mills, the employment opportunities for such young children must have been limited. On the other hand, their elder brothers and sisters, who earlier would have fulfilled an important role in caring for younger siblings, were no longer available as mother substitutes. Therefore it seems likely that there was a proportionate increase of children under 5 or 6 to older children in such institutions that existed, even if there was no real increase in their numbers. There were four major types of school: the charity schools, the schools of industry, the dame school and the common day school. It is perhaps misleading to speak of different types. All these organizations were similar in their structure and aims in the early part of the nineteenth century. The different nomenclature can be traced to divergent origins.

The original charity schools were started in 1678. They were religious foundations and at their peak provided a large number of children with basic education. By the early nineteenth century they had declined a great deal, particularly in the quality of their instruction. The schools of industry were originally set up in 1775 when the first spinning factory was founded. The children were employed from the age of 5 for long hours, but spent part of their day at the school learning to read. The dame's school took a small number of children for payment. They were not always run by women, as their name suggests, although this was more usual. They rarely took place in buildings specially assigned for the purpose. The children were housed in the cottages of the 'dames' who were frequently poor widows or spinsters, dependent for their livelihood on the pennies brought by their charges. The common day schools were run on similar principles and, like the dame schools, in appalling conditions. A man was usually in charge and they catered for larger numbers of children. All of these schools were attempting to meet the needs of the working-class mother by offering her child some protection while she was working and they do represent early attempts to produce more differentiated social units for the care and socialization of young children. Some of them were simply establishments where the children were minded, with little attempt to educate them; most of them, however, attempted to teach the children to read and write. They relied on formal methods, and in this sense belong to the elementary tradition and the history of infant schools in the nineteenth century.

It is not intended to describe the development of the latter, which has been well documented elsewhere (Adamson, 1964). It is necessary, however, to consider certain aspects of the growth of a national system of universal compulsory education, in particular the factors behind the choice of 5 as the compulsory starting age.* This decision has had important consequences for the development of pre-school education, which will be considered later, and the growth of the infant school was in part a response to the working-class need already described above. Both the infant school and the nursery school can be seen as a response to dissatisfaction with the operation of familial roles. The infant school was initially seen as one way of supporting the family, although not necessarily supplanting it, in occupying these roles. When the infant school was no longer recognized as adequate in the fulfilling of these roles, and was regarded as an unsuitable remedy for other reasons, the notion of the nursery school developed. It is for these reasons that certain aspects of its history are relevant.

The founding of Robert Owen's infant school was closely followed by the Factory Act of 1819, which prohibited the employment of children under 9 in the factories. Both this and later acts led to a greater awareness of the presence of young children and their needs, by showing up evils which had

* In only two other countries, who are members of UNESCO, is the age of 5 chosen. These are Ceylon and Paraguay. In all other countries compulsory education begins at a later age (Blyth, 1965, p. 42). Israel is an exception in the sense that one year of pre-school education from the age of 5 is compulsory.

never been revealed under the domestic system. More directly it presented the problem of what to do with children, who were neither at work nor under supervision at home. 'The exclusion of the youngest children [from the labour force] led philanthropists to look to the provision of schools and particularly infant schools as a means of reform' (Wood, 1934). Already in 1818 an asylum for infancy had been opened in London by a committee consisting of James Mill, Henry Brougham and Lord Lansdowne amongst others. In 1820 the third infant school was opened in Spitalfields, again by philanthropic interests, with Samuel Wilderspin as its master, and in 1824 Wilderspin became superintendent of the London Infant School Society. This was followed by the opening of more infant schools by Wilderspin and his colleagues, most of the schools taking children between the ages of 3 and 5, as well as older pupils. The young children were treated the same as the older ones. The philanthropists and political radicals like Lord Henry Brougham were convinced of the educability of children at an early age, by formal methods. Brougham, speaking in the House of Lords in 1835, stated that:

Schools in the country are only open to children too far advanced in years. . . . Whoever knows the habits of children at an earlier age than six or seven — the age which they generally attend the infant schools . . . is well aware of their capacity to receive instruction long before the age of six . . . the truth is that he [the child] can and does learn a great deal more before that age than all he ever learns or can learn in all his after life (House of Lords, 1835).

The content of this early education tended to be rigid and formal with emphasis on religious and moral instruction and repressive discipline. A quotation from the *Manchester Times* during this period illustrates the belief in the need for repression: 'We are strenuous advocates for the establishment of infant schools . . . even in the mother's arms the child may be tutored . . . its unruly passions may be repressed and its kindly affections cultivated.' Health received little attention, although there was some emphasis on the need for the child to have fresh air. Dr Kay, later Sir James Kay-Shuttleworth, was exceptional in seeing the infant school as a method of reducing infant mortality as early as the 1830s when he was working in Manchester. Pestalozzi's influence was felt in this direction, by people like Charles and Elizabeth Mayo, who started the Home and Colonial Infant School Society in 1836 and who were concerned with such problems as ventilation in schools. By this time the monitorial system was flourishing, but not without its critics. Leonard Horner, one of the four chief inspectors appointed after the Factories Regulation Act of 1833,* was one of these. In 1838 he translated Cousin's *On the state of education in Holland,* written in 1836. This was a Frenchman's study of what was probably the most advanced

---

* This Act reinforced the 1819 legislation which had proved ineffective. Children under 9 were not to be employed and those under 13 were to be employed for eight hours only, of which two hours was to be spent undergoing schooling.

system of education in Europe at the time. In his preface to this translation Horner set out his plans for education. His most important recommendation was the establishment of a state system of education, with 'well conducted schools . . . where all children of the working classes and the poor may receive an education suited to their circumstances and to their station in life, and calculated to improve their religious, moral and intellectual character' (Cousin, 1838, p. xxi). These schools he called primary schools. He believed that:

primary instruction must embrace Infant Schools, as well as schools for older children and should be provided for the poor and the working classes separately. . . . The improvement of the primary school must depend in a great degree upon the establishment of that initiatory branch of education; and it cannot be considered as complete without such a nursery for its future scholars (p. xiviii).

He does not specify the age of the children for which these nurseries are to be provided, nor the type of instruction. But he is adamant on the need for separation of the working-class child from his more favoured cousins, even at this young age, where the importance of preparing the child according to its supposed roles in later life would not have been so obvious. This belief that education should be suited to the circumstances and station in life of the pupils lay behind the distinctions made in the secondary system later in the nineteenth century (see Banks, 1955, p. 2). It is interesting to compare the beliefs behind the structure of secondary and primary education; they share a great deal in the early stages of their development. It is not till a more sophisticated approach to the role of the different stages of education develops that differentiation occurs. This is true of the education of both pre-primary and primary school children and pre-secondary and secondary school children.

Naturally there were objections to the education of young children, which were expressed with increasing force as the possibility of a state system of education became likely. Parliamentary debates reveal the attitude that it was dangerous to educate the poor since it would lead to dissatisfaction with their station. This belief was applied to all levels of education including the infant school. In 1833 the first step towards state education was taken when Parliament awarded a grant of £20,000 for the building of schools for the poor. In 1839 Lord Melbourne appointed a committee of the Privy Council to concern itself with education, with Dr Kay as its first secretary. The next twenty years marked a change in the attitude of those in power towards popular instruction. Up to this time all forms of education provided for the working class had been sponsored and financed largely by charity. This was true of special institutions such as Lady Noel Byron's agricultural school for poor boys at Ealing Grove in the 1830s. It was true of the pioneering work done in the field of technical education by Quintin Hogg at the Regent Street Polytechnic in the 1860s (see Cotgrove, 1958, p. 65). Many of these philanthropists, such as Hogg, were motivated by evangelical Christianity, which was of such power that it overrode the traditional views towards education held by the upper middle classes to which they belonged. Whatever their motives, the charity of these individuals and their organized counterparts the religious societies,* was considerable. In 1861 the Newcastle Commission published its findings. Seven thousand schools were assisted by state grants at the time, and 15,750 were unassisted voluntary schools.† Once again the origins of early education share vital characteristics with the origins of education of older children. This is caused in part by the lack of differentiation between the stages. The change away from philanthropy towards the notion that it was in the state's interest, if not its duty, to instruct its citizens, initially affected the education of young children as significantly as that of the older age groups. Subsequently the state relinquished much of its responsibility, and this will be discussed in detail later.

The objection that infant schools would lead to the insubordination of the working classes was overcome. The 1870 Education Act set up School Boards, which were to provide schools where they were needed; and in 1880 elementary education became compulsory for all children from the age of 5 while the schools also admitted large numbers under this age. The second objection to the education of children of 5 and under was that at this age they should remain at home in the care of their mothers. This objection was not overcome, and it probably increased rather than receded. It therefore requires some discussion in the context of the time. The attitudes of the Victorian middle class on this subject were neither uniform nor consistent. They varied from the belief that all children, rich and poor, should attend educational institutions outside their home at an early age, to the assertion that the home was the only place suitable for young children. Between these two poles lay a number of intermediate attitudes including one that recommended that educational provision should be made for the children of *working* mothers, or the children of the destitute. In a report in 1845, the Honourable Mr Fletcher, commenting on the benefit of infant schools for working mothers, said:

at the same time, they [the mothers] may render to themselves and their country incalculable benefits by placing their little ones under a teacher who knows how to inplant in the tender life of infancy those truthful habits of heart and mind, the value of which even for the temporal welfare of their offspring, the vexed and burdened spirits of the poor do not always comprehend (Committee of Council, 1845, p. 216).

His attitude has a patronizing tone, but his belief that the working woman 'very properly seeks a nursery' for her children, and that the more prosperous

* The National Society for Promoting the Education of the Poor in the Principles of the Established Church, and its rival supported by the Nonconformists: the British and Foreign Schools Society.

† Royal Commission on English Education. The validity of these figures is questionable. However, although they may not be perfectly accurate, it is unlikely that the distribution between voluntary and assisted schools is greatly distorted.

ought to supply her with one, is more realistic and humane than the alternative view which opposed provision. The inconsistency in attitudes of those who belonged to the latter group and yet employed numbers of domestic servants, from nursemaids and nannies to tutors and governesses, to look after their own children is striking. Their objections represented perhaps a more fundamental adherence to *laissez-faire* philosophy than simply the belief that children should remain at home with their mothers. There is no evidence that they advocated alternative measures to extra-familial institutions, such as aid and instruction to working-class mothers in their home, or the relief of these women from the need to work. It was those who proposed educational institutions for young children who advocated extra or alternative measures to help mothers fulfil their roles in the socialization of their children. Samuel Wilderspin, for example, saw schools for young children as a method of educating parents too.

Sretzer has documented the facts behind the decision to begin compulsory education at 5. One reason was that an early start would make possible an early finish and children would be able to enter the labour force at the age of 10 without any loss of their education. 'The circumstances of the time – as well as the general climate of opinion on socio-economic problems – made an early starting age of elementary education a desirable measure in the eyes of progressive men' (Sretzer, 1964, p. 21). There was a strong belief that an early start would prevent the exploitation of young children in the home and remove them from the unhealthy physical conditions of the slum house and the dangers of the street. The decision to admit children under 5, where their parents desired this, was motivated by the same beliefs. In 1871–2 there were 18,755 children under 3 and 268,879 children aged 3 to 5 in the elementary schools (Board of Education Statistics, 1908–9, p. 18). There was still no conception of a special education for these children. They sat in galleries and were drilled in numbers and letters. Thus in the same way that the grammar school is far older than the term, or the concept of secondary education, so the education of a considerable proportion of pre-compulsory school children is older than the concept of pre-school education. The development of this concept was hindered significantly by the notorious Revised Code of the Committee of Council on Education of 1862. This began the principle of payment by results in education. Grants were to be paid to the schools, on the basis of the results of examinations taken by the children from the age of 7 onwards. Standards were laid down for each age group, and a grant, which was paid per child, was not allocated for those children who failed to reach the required standard. Although in theory this strange system of incentives was not applied to the youngest children, in practice they were affected by it. If they were to reach Standard I by the age of 7 it was necessary for them to begin formal instruction before this age. On the principle that constant repetition eventually produces results, the earlier this was begun the better, and great strains were placed on the teacher who rejected this principle.

Payment by results was not abolished completely until 1890. After this date a relaxation in formal teaching became possible. In the years leading up to 1890 there had been glimmerings of the changes which were to come. The London School Board showed particular interest and went so far as to appoint an instructress on the kindergarten system as early as 1874. But there were difficulties in incorporating a system requiring small groups of children, and a considerable amount of space per child, into schools with big classes where children were crammed together in galleries or sat at fixed desks. In 1884, in conjunction with an International Health Exhibition held in London, a conference was held on the education and health of children. The following comment was made on attempts to use kindergarten methods in the infant school: 'the introduction of a box of cottons, sticks and blunted needles to be played with once or twice a week was a hollow sham' (Woodham-Smith in Lawrence, p. 58). The dissemination of Froebel's principles had been slowly taking place and, although frequently applied in a misguided and ham-handed fashion, they began to have an effect on the infant school curriculum. At this point it is necessary to return to the early education of the middle-class child, and trace the growth of kindergarten.

In 1851 the first English kindergarten was founded by two German immigrants, Johannes and Bertha Ronge, who had been influenced by Froebel. They were typical of wealthy German immigrants who arrived in England in the late 1840s and 1850s, chiefly as a result of the increase in trade between Britain and Germany but partly due to the reaction after the unsuccessful revolution of 1848. There were thus amongst them a number of the liberal-minded, who were more prone to accept, and even to initiate radical change than most of their contemporaries. Their significance for the establishment of the Froebel movement in England is obvious. The first kindergarten in both Britain and the United States were for German children only. It seems probable that they were established for more complex reasons than an interest in the new theory. In an alien country, the kindergarten was one way in which the children of these immigrants could maintain their identity with their own ancestry. It provided them with the opportunity of meeting others of their kind, and of undergoing instruction in their own language. However, it was not confined to German children for long. Those convinced of the value of Froebel's educational principles began to publicize them. One of his most devoted disciples, Baroness Marenholtz-Bülow, arrived in London from Germany in 1854 and delivered a number of lectures, which had some impact. In the same year, the Society of Arts promoted an educational exhibition in St Martin's Hall, Long Acre. Exhibit Number 182 was: 'English Kindergarten, 32 Tavistock Place, Bertha Ronge, Mistress'. Exhibits of the work of the children aged 3 to 7, and apparatus from the Froebel system, were on show, and this promoted further publicity. During the 1850s several articles on the kindergarten appeared, including one by Charles Dickens who praised the kindergarten highly in *Household Words. The Times* and the *Athenaeum* were also impressed. The movement was probably strongest in Manchester where there was a large German colony. Miss Biele, a young German pupil of Froebel, who went to practise his principles there, said that 'Madame Ronge had been invited to Manchester by some of the prominent families, in order to lecture on the New Education and to organise a kindergarten' (G. Wood, 1847). It affected a similar stratum of people in the English population.

There was a sprinkling of rich cultured upper middle class people, Manchester merchants and the like, who cared about education, both for their own children and those of the proletarian masses. . . . Some members of the wealthy Jewish Community encouraged the movement with the greatest generosity. Then the group of powerful pioneering women who were fighting for higher education for women and public school education for girls found the new doctrine to their taste (Woodham-Smith in Lawrence, p. 12).

The strength of their desire to found kindergarten for the children of the proletariat was limited. During the period from 1851 to the beginning of the twentieth century only a couple of free kindergarten in working-class areas were set up. The 1870s and 1880s saw the establishment of a number of kindergarten, but they did not cater for the children of the working classes. Even within the middle class they did not become widespread. They were confined to a small group of the middle-class urban population willing to push aside the traditions of the nursery and the nanny, in exchange for the experimental institution of the kindergarten and its supervisor. Initially the kindergarten were run by German women, mostly unmarried, and later by English spinsters of varying ages. Throughout the last quarter of the nineteenth century efforts were made to provide a systematic training for young women who wished to work in kindergarten. The Froebel Society began this work soon after it was founded in 1874.*

During the early years of the kindergarten, the social background of the young women entering this training was probably similar to that of the private governess. During the second half of the nineteenth century the public boarding schools for boys were extended and preparatory schools to prepare children for entry to the former began to flourish. Entry to the public schools was limited to a more precisely defined age level and entrance tests were imposed. Both the aristocracy and landed gentry, and the new rich of the

---

* In 1887 the National Froebel Union was founded to take over this part of the Society's work. It provided courses, examined candidates and awarded diplomas. In 1895 the Froebel Educational Institute was opened. This, unlike the Union, provided living and teaching accommodation for students, and became a college for the training of teachers in Froebel's methods. The provision of permanent full-time courses with examinations at the end of them became possible. Many years later, in the 1920s, the courses followed by these young women received Board of Education recognition. Colleges running them, such as the Froebel Institute, became training colleges attached to the University Institutes of Education.

industrial society, saw the advantage of specific schools set in the country-side, away from the grime of industry, for the preparation of their sons for the public school. The revival of the day grammar school and the first public schools for girls began to reduce the amount of education that took place in the home for their daughters, too. There was thus a decreasing demand for the services of the governess, without a decrease in their supply. Kindergarten teaching provided one of the first acceptable alternatives to taking a post in a family, in more favourable conditions than elementary school teaching, although the number of posts was limited. However, the Code of 1892, besides reforming the curriculum and methods of the infant school by moving away from formal teaching of the three Rs, gave recognition to the Froebel Certificate as a qualification for appointment as assistant mistress in an infant school. In view of the decrease in the demand for governesses and the large number of unmarried women in the less prosperous sections of the middle classes, it is surprising that some of the early kindergarten supervisors found difficulty in obtaining teachers and sent to Germany when they required staff. However, this can perhaps be explained by a lack of *trained kinder-gartnerin*. Once establishments like that of Frau Ronge in Manchester, which provided classes for 'teachers and ladies' in kindergarten methods, were flourishing, the problem of teacher supply probably became less acute.

The kindergarten appealed to the radical, intellectual sectors of the middle classes, partly because it attempted to produce a quasi-scientific formula for the teaching of young children, based on a knowledge, however incoherent, of the child's development. In 1855 the Ronges wrote:

Infant training has been, until now, less cultivated than school education; and the civilisation of our century so much praised, has not yet paid that attention to this subject which is needed, if we would fulfil sincerely our duty to our children and the rising generation. The more tender the age of the children the more important is their development, because impressions are the more deep and lasting. Mothers have been left without the assistance of science in their nurseries . . . (Ronge, 1855, p. iii).

The application of 'science' to the nursery appealed to groups, for whom the notion of science itself involved a high degree of approbation. The kindergarten also reduced the responsibility of the parent in terms of the amount of the child's time for which he had to provide beneficial activity, yet the theory flattered him in stressing his role in the process of educating the child. Thus the Ronges wrote, 'Millions of children are now deprived in large towns of the beneficial influence of nature, and it is high time that in education the necessary steps were taken to give children this influence. The kindergarten system is a medium between home and school, bringing both in co-operation' (p. v). Little is known of the amount parents were prepared to pay for this experimental education, or whether its expansion was limited because many parents were deterred by the payment of fees, which might have been higher than the wages of a nursemaid.*

Whatever the effect of fees on the enthusiasm of the middle classes may have been, it is clear that the working-class parents would have been unable to pay them. However, the presence of a free kindergarten financed by a William Mather is reported in the *Manchester Guardian* in 1872. He founded a second kindergarten a year after the first. These constituted the only exceptions to the rule that the kindergarten was an early form of pre-school education, confined to the middle-class child. Mather aimed to remove as many of the children of the poor from the streets as possible, and for this purpose set up the first kindergarten in 1871, accommodating 100–150 children from the age of 2 upwards and supervised by 'a committee of lady friends'. A German *kindergartnerin* was employed with a number of English assistants and Froebelian methods of play and rest were used. Special accommodation was built the following year, which could take up to 500 children, with two large rooms and kitchens, baths and resting rooms. It appears that standards were sacrificed in favour of numbers, if so many children were accommodated in two rooms. The second of the free kindergarten took place in the Working Men's Hall at Pendelton. Thirty years later Adelaide Wragge founded the first free kindergarten in London, at Woolwich.

By 1900, the date of the founding of Wragge's kindergarten, concern for the young working-class child was growing, and receiving attention from a larger number of people. This applied both to the child attending the infant school, and those not yet at school. The health of the population had become a national scandal at the outbreak of the Boer War which revealed that the poor physical condition of many of the men recruited made them unsuitable for enlistment. The high incidence of diseases such as tuberculosis, and deformities such as curvature of the spine, could be traced to early childhood and it was clear that many of the men's imperfections had been preventable but that insufficient care, knowledge and money had stopped their parents seeking medical advice. The war did not suddenly bring about a new revelation of the role of environment in disease, and the possibilities of preventive medicine. Pioneers had been campaigning for systematized preventive medicine, such as school medical inspections, for some years. The war was to persuade those who had previously demurred, or been unaware of the situation, of the need for reform; and much of the welfare legislation passed by the 1906 Liberal government owes its passage in part to the Boer War. Amongst this legislation was an Act passed in 1907 making the provision of regular school medical inspection by local authorities compulsory, although children under 5 would still receive no medical care. One of those involved in

---

* The first kindergarten in Manchester opened in 1857, was run by a Miss Barton, who had learned Froebel's methods under the Ronges. She advertised her kindergarten in the *Manchester Guardian* where the terms were stated as £1 7s. 6d. (probably per month) and £1 5s. when more than one child from the same family was attending.

the campaign for medical inspection in the schools was Margaret McMillan. She was also the founder of the first nursery school, which she set up in an effort to remedy this situation. Thus although the Boer War helped to high-light the extent of ill health amongst the working class, and pointed to its genesis in early childhood, action to redress the situation was left to volun-tary organizations and individual effort. It took another war to bring about the acceptance of public responsibility.

Meanwhile the fulfilment of the working-class need for the early education of young children was at its height, but there was dissatisfaction with the way this need was being fulfilled. It was seen that the public elementary school might not be the most suitable environment for the 3-year-old child. The numbers of children under three attending school had dropped from the 1875–6 figure of 19,303 to 3,228 for the year 1899–1900. The 2-year-olds disappeared altogether after the 1902 Education Act, when it was established that grants would be paid only for children over 3. However, the numbers in the 3-to-5 age category had almost doubled since the year 1875–6, when they amounted to 359,229. By 1900 there were 622,498 children of this age at school. This increase cannot be accounted for by increases in the child population as a whole. Table 2.1 for the census years indicates this.

Table 2.1. Number of children at school aged less than 5 years, 1870–1910

Date	Number of children on school registers aged 3–5	Total number of children aged 3–5	Percentage at school
1870–1	276,000	1,179,000	24·2
1880–1	393,000	1,340,000	29·3
1890–1	458,000	1,378,000	33·2
1900–1	616,000	1,429,000	43·1
1910–11	351,000	1,541,000	22·7

Source: Board of Education Statistics, 1912, Table 3(b).

The proportion of children involved by 1900 was thus very high. Under the existing regulations, children of 3 could not be refused admission, and in 1900 nearly a third of the children in infant schools were between the ages of 3 and 5. They were usually placed in what were known as baby classes consisting primarily of children under 5, but in spite of the liberalization of the code of 1892 the curriculum still gave cause for concern. Amongst those most concerned were some of His Majesty's Inspectors of Education, who were best placed to observe and record the way young children were treated in infant schools. One of them paints a horrific picture of the activities of the infants' department of the elementary school, and the conditions under which the children were working (Bathurst, 1905, pp. 818–27). In describing the pupil and his environment the writer states:

He is placed on a wooden seat (sometimes it is only the step of a gallery), with a desk in front of him and a window behind him. . . . He often cannot reach the floor with his feet, and in many cases he has no back to lean against. He is told to fold his arms and sit quiet.

He was then subjected to learning letters from the blackboard by monotonous repetition.

I have actually heard a baby class repeat one sound 120 times continuously, and from fourteen to twenty times is a matter of common occurrence. With the exception of a little drill or marching between the subjects, it is an incontrovertible fact that lessons unbroken by a single manual occupation are actually in progress the whole morning in many of our baby classes in the big infant schools.

Bathurst goes on to say, 'The discipline expected is military rather than maternal, and can only be maintained at the expense of much healthy, valuable and as far as the children are concerned necessary freedom'. With this in mind the author demands a revolution in the infant school, advocating a play-room atmosphere, informal methods and sleeping accommodation for children in the form of hammock beds, 'hammocks being less likely to harbour vermin than any other type of bed'.

This article was a prelude to 'the Report on Children under Five Years of Age in Public Elementary Schools' by the Women Inspectors of the Board of Education, published in 1905. The following quotations from the 'introductory Memorandum' by the chief inspector of elementary schools summarizes the recommendations of the report:

It will be seen that there is complete unanimity that the children between the ages of three and five get practically no intellectual advantage from school instruction.

The inspectors agree that the mechanical teaching in many infant schools seems to dull rather than awaken the little power of imagination and independent observation which these children possess.

'No formal instruction' is the burden of all the recommendations 'but more play, more sleep, more free conversation, story telling and observation'. The aim of the big town Infant School is too often to produce children who at the age of six and a half have mastered the mechanical difficulties of Standard I work. It should be to produce children well developed physically, full of interest and alertness mentally and ready to grapple with difficulties intelligently.

It would seem that a new form of school is necessary for poor children. The better parents should be discouraged from sending children before five, while the poorer who must do so, should send them to nursery schools rather than schools of instruction.

The most significant underlying belief to the new recommendation for nursery schools is that they should be confined to the working-class child. Thus the nineteenth-century philanthropic conception of education for young children as rescue work was carried over into the new conception of pre-school education. It was not conceived in terms of a pedagogical principle, which should be applied to all children, in spite of the undoubted influence of Froebel on those that devised it. Yet it would not be true to say that a concern with educational reform was totally lacking. It was, however, of a negative rather than a positive kind; that is, it arose from a distrust of the efficacy of the system. The mechanical teaching of young children was not effective, therefore there should be no formal instruction. This negative aspect to educational reform has also characterized changes in the system as it affects older children. The widespread introduction of a common school at the secondary level is only now becoming effective twenty years after the 1944 Education Act, which laid down secondary education for all children. Education authorities extended divisions which had existed before 1944, adhering to a traditional separatism in preference to an experiment on comprehensive lines. In twenty years the disadvantages of tripartism have been well documented, particularly with reference to the failure of the 11-plus examination as a method of selection, the difficulties of transferring pupils from one type of school to another and the wastage of talent which results. It appears that there is consensus on these fundamental disadvantages, which has helped to persuade politicians, administrators and teachers that reform is necessary. However powerful the arguments in favour of the common system may be, resistance to change is so strong that reform cannot come about on the basis of the merits of the system to be innovated alone. It is only when considerable dissatisfaction with the existing system is generated that change becomes possible.

Uneasiness over the suitability of the teaching methods employed in the infants school and the belief that the children under 5 'get practically no intellectual advantage from school instruction' led not only to the introduction of a different kind of instruction, but equally important to the belief that no school instruction at all was most appropriate for the majority of the child population. The children of 'the better parents' should remain at home. Thus the nursery school was devised in response to a social need, although the timing of its origin was caused by acceptance of the need to differentiate on educational grounds.

The Report of the Women Inspectors was followed by the Report of the Consultative Committee upon the school attendance of children below the age of 5. This Committee was set up by the Board of Education in 1907, as a response to concern generated by the earlier 'Inspectors'' Report. Its terms of reference were 'to consider the desirability on educational and other grounds, of discouraging the attendance at school of children under five years'. The possibility of a reduction of the numbers of pre-compulsory-school-age children receiving school education was thus written into the terms of reference. The Committee estimated that during the fifteen years previous to their inquiry at least one third of all children between the ages of 3 and 5 were on the registers of the public elementary school. This is borne out by an examination of the Board of Education figures (see Table 2.1, p. 28). As a result of their recommendations, there was a drastic fall in the number of these children at school. By 1910–11, two years after the publication of the report, the 1900 figure of 622,000 had been almost halved. The views of the Committee were similar to those of the inspectors; they believed that the best training for children, aged between 3 and 5, was at home with their mothers, provided that home conditions were satisfactory. The education of children outside the house was to be confined to those whose particular circumstances warranted it. The Committee recognized that home conditions were far from ideal in many families, and that the numbers needing special consideration were high. They therefore advocated the *public* provision of early education and training for all children whose home conditions and parental care were inadequate. This provision was to take the form of a nursery school, but with separate accommodation, equipment and curriculum, and a teacher trained in the care of young children. There were to be no more than thirty children per class. Any kind of formal lessons were to be excluded. Instead there was to be freedom of movement, fluidity of timetable, adequate play outside. The Committee believed that such an institution would have moral, physical and mental advantages. The child would be removed from the taint of the streets, it would have regular hours for sleep and meals, and an environment stimulating to intellectual growth. They cite similar objections to attendance of the under-5s in the infant school to those put forward by the Inspectors, and they also lay some stress on the poor physical conditions of the elementary school, pointing to the high risk of infection in badly ventilated, crowded class rooms for young children who are especially susceptible. The amount of accommodation necessary in each area will depend on 'the industrial and social conditions of the area, and the proportion of children under five years the conditions of whose homes are unsatisfactory' (Consultative Committee Report, p. 48). The suggestion that educational provision should be based on the needs of the area has been applied outside the field of pre-school education occasionally, for example at the secondary level (see Banks, 1955). It has dominated policy directives in the field of pre-school education from its initial introduction in 1908 to the 1950s, and has been an important factor in the patchy development of nursery schools, in that it allows those in power at the local level wide powers of interpretation as to what the needs of the area involve. The Consultative Committee stressed that in most urban areas the majority of children aged 3-to-5 should be regarded as eligible. The number of nursery school places provided would indicate that this has never been accepted by the local authorities. Throughout the history of nursery schools, arrangements have not been made in any area for the majority of children.

The direct result of the report, as already indicated, was a large fall in the number of children under 5 in attendance at school. Many of the local authorities took advantage of the change in the Board's regulations, which allowed them to refuse entry to the elementary schools to children under 5. Alternative provision was not made for those children excluded, since the Board did not act on the Committee's second major recommendation. It made no funds available for the public provision of nursery schools.

In terms of the extension of educational provision for the pre-school-age child, the immediate results of the report might be described as a step backward rather than forward. However, the report did mark a fundamental change in attitude towards the needs of the young child. Those who gave evidence represented a number of different groups: medical officers; His Majesty's Inspectors; head teachers; representatives of local education authorities and various interested individuals. All of these groups to a greater or lesser extent accepted that the requirements of the children must form the basis of provision for them. The report marked the first public statement of what Blyth has described as the developmental tradition in English primary education. He suggests that there are three separate traditions which he calls the elementary, the preparatory and the developmental. 'The first of these is associated with the limited utilitarian atmosphere of the Board School; the second, with the upward-looking socially exclusive orientation of the private or preparatory school; and the third with what is usually described as a child-centred conception of education' (Blyth, 1955, p. 55). The elementary tradition he suggests grew out of the necessity for preventive measures to deal with changes in the industrial system which resulted in unemployed children, the need for more skilled workers, juvenile crime, the demands of religion and the extension of the franchise. The working-class need for the socialization of pre-school-age children outside the home was solved in the context of the elementary tradition until 1908. The preparatory tradition involved the notion 'that the education of younger children is mainly to be conceived in terms of preparation for the later stages of education rather than as a stage in its own right' (p. 30). This conception has virtually no place in the history of pre-school education either for the working-class or the middle-class child. The exception to this is the belief that pre-school education will make the adjustment to full-time compulsory education easier for the child, and in this sense may be said to embody a preparatory function. The developmental tradition, on the other hand, 'is bound neither by the limitations of an education felt or intended to be cheap and inferior, nor by the demands imposed by its own sequel' (p. 35). It is based on the notion of child development. It is the child to be educated, and the child and his needs which must be considered. The reason that such a philosophy was applied first and has since been applied most successfully to the education of very young children is obvious. The further away the external demands of the labour force and their accompaniments, such as the wish to classify children according to their attainment and talent, and examinations which aid this process, are, the easier it is to reject such demands.

The emergence of this developmental tradition marks the first stage in a convergence between the methods of dealing with the middle-class and working-class needs for early education. In the nineteenth century this tradition applied to the kindergarten for the middle-class child only. The two separate strands in the origin of pre-school education have been traced here. These different strands have not been obliterated in the twentieth century. Differentiation is still made in terms of the sources of the necessity for pre-school education for children from different social classes. However, the institutional form in which the education is provided for children from various socio-economic backgrounds, and the content of this education are not rigidly separated. Indeed, children from very different social backgrounds may be found attending the same institutions. The convergence of the two strands, the growth of movements to foster the spread of pre-school education and the various ways in which it expanded in terms of the model of structural differentiation, the proliferation of ideas, the specification and outline of the new institutional forms, and their implementation will be described in the next two chapters.

3. The growth of pre-school education, 1908–39

The thirty-one years covered by this chapter incorporate the development of the notion of pre-school education and the spread of institutions undertaking it. The outbreak of the Second World War marked the start of a new phase. Growth did not take place at an even rate; there were periods of stagnation, followed by periods of activity with increases in the number of institutions. This chapter aims to trace this growth and to provide an explanation for its existence in terms of the changing role of the family as an agent of socialization. Second, it looks at the rate of growth in detail, and attempts to isolate some of the factors which have affected this – other than the more fundamental changes in the family which operated throughout the period.

Chapter 2 described the recommendations for nursery schools for children whose home environment warranted it, that is working-class children living in urban areas, in overcrowded conditions. The family system of socialization for young children was still felt to be the most satisfactory for the majority. For the minority no public provision was made, in spite of the recommendations, so a considerable number of children who had attended elementary schools were left with no provision at all. Once again the tradition of the middle-class philanthropist came to the fore in the provision of voluntary nursery schools. The most important members of the movement to set up such schools were Margaret McMillan and her sister Rachel. They were not typical of the early twentieth-century philanthropist in that they did not have resources of their own, but relied on financial help from others. They were orphaned at an early age and their first posts were as governesses.

While thus employed in London, Margaret attended socialist meetings, and supported the dockers from a platform in Hyde Park at the time of the Great Dock Strike in 1892. In conjunction with her support for the 'dockers' tanner' and her membership of the Fabian Society, she established herself in socialist circles, and in 1893 was invited by Fred Jowett to go to Bradford and work for the Independent Labour Party, founded there in January of that year. Thus socialism was a major influence on her later work with young children, rather than the Church and the apolitical humanitarianism of more typical philanthropists of her time. In Bradford she was elected to the school board, where she campaigned successfully for the appointment of a school medical officer who, in 1894, was the first to be appointed in Britain. She worked with him in a campaign to improve the health of school children in the first school clinic which was opened in 1895. Realizing that baths would reveal curved spines, crooked legs and other defects of malnutrition and inadequate physical care, as well as eliminate vermin, she and the medical officer demanded their provision and in 1897 the first school bath in the country was introduced in Bradford. Margaret McMillan then became a leading member of the campaign for school meals. In 1902 she returned to London and became a member of the National Administrative Council of the Independent Labour Party, and joined the council of the Froebel Society. In 1908, with the help of a wealthy American industrialist and the reluctant sanction of the London County Council, she opened, with her sister, the first school clinic in London, at Bow. In 1910, for financial reasons, the clinic moved to Deptford and in 1911 the London County Council became convinced of the value of its work and gave the clinic its first grant. At this time the sisters became aware that the work they were doing was only curative and not preventive; the children were returning a few weeks later reinfected as a result of poor home conditions. Believing in the efficacy of fresh air, they started their night camps in which children stayed in open-air shelters for the night. Out of these night camps developed the camp school and the open-air nursery school. The tradition of fresh air is still prominent in nursery schools and children sleep outside even in cold weather.

This school and those that followed it were founded in response to the need for better medical care and improved hygiene and diet. Doubts had arisen about the working-class family's ability to undertake the rearing of children to a physical standard that would be adequate for the tasks required of them later in life. These families were failing to respond to outside pressures generated by higher standards of medical care and the realization that the nation's security and prosperity depended in part on the physical fitness of its members. Thus it was with the custodial and care roles that dissatisfaction was first expressed. The system was failing to achieve the goal of healthy children. This failure was related to the inadequacies of the family economy in providing adequate resources. The boundary between the family economy and the family system of socialization is of significance and the organization of the family economy and its effect on the organization of socialization will be referred to again. Because of their interdependence it is sometimes difficult to separate them into two distinct social systems.

It is important to note that the dissatisfaction in this case is not directly expressed by the actors involved. This characterizes the sequence culminating in the provision of nursery schools. It is not until after 1945 that the parents of young children are predominant in expressing dissatisfaction. By then the pressures bringing about dissatisfaction had changed entirely, as had the source of the dissatisfaction and the social class of the family, about which dissatisfaction is expressed. From being predominantly working class it has generalized to cover the middle-class family. This partly explains the change in the characteristics of those who express dissatisfaction; the middle-class parent is more articulate, has readier access to the means of expressing dissatisfaction and is perhaps more consciously aware of the goals he wishes to attain. Thus he plays an active part in the campaign for change, rather than relying on others to bring it about. In the period which we are discussing, the symptoms of disturbance were mild and often non-existent. The violent reactions to dissatisfaction with the family economy, described by Smelser, which consisted of strikes, the breaking up of machines, food riots and attacks on the friendly societies do not take place in the sequence of structural differentiation described in this study. This is partly because violent reaction, such as the classic food riot of the eighteenth and early nineteenth century, has been replaced by new patterns of institutionalized agitation. It is partly because of the probably equally fundamental, but less dramatic, nature of the pressures on the family described here. Lack of food seems more likely to initiate uncontrolled outbursts than an inability to prevent children becoming sickly, a condition which had been accepted as inevitable by the families involved. The dissatisfaction in this earlier period is expressed by those outside the system.

There is a proliferation of new ideas to aid the family in its task of dealing with the physical care of young children. Amongst these was a suggestion in a Fabian Society Pamphlet of the early 1890s for 'Power to be given to school boards to provide a crèche for every infant school'. It was later discarded, and altered, in a reissue in 1894, to a clause suggesting regular visits to schools by trained nurses. Other ideas include the setting up of school clinics, lessons in child care and hygiene for mothers, which might be free, or subsidized, and, in 1905, the suggestion that nursery schools should be set up. The majority of these were specified in a particular institutional form and then set up in a few areas — for example the school clinic started at Bow, then Deptford by the McMillans. It was the inadequacy of this method to initiate any long-term improvement, which led to the setting up of the night camps, which were themselves short-lived, and then open-air nurseries. The sisters became convinced that they were not dealing with children early enough to act as a successful preventive force. In 1911 they started using the garden of their night camp which was vacant during the day, for children aged 2 to 5, six children attending initially. In March 1914 the London County Council offered the McMillans a large site to extend their facilities for young children, which they let to them for 1s. per year, stressing, however, that the offer was temporary and might be withdrawn at short notice; in 1915 they offered a grant of 9d. per day for the children of war workers; married women, some of whom had young children, were now needed in the munitions factories. Their employment outside the home brought further pressures on the family system of socialization. It would be wrong to imply that such employment was new, but during the war years it involved larger numbers of women, and was encouraged by the government and other agencies. However, the London County Council was the only public authority that accepted financial or other responsibility for the children of these workers. It was not till 1918

that the government passed legislation, making the possibility of such provision general. Meanwhile it was left to voluntary groups and organizations to
undertake the role.

In Manchester and Salford, for example, three nursery schools run on a
voluntary basis were in existence by the end of the war.* The history of these
schools (see Grace Wood, 1847, Chs. V–IX) illustrates the kind of organization involved and their aims in improving the health of the children and
caring for them while their mothers were working. The first of these was
founded in Salford by a Miss Hood, a kindergarten teacher. It was financed
by voluntary subscription and housed in the old schoolroom of a Wesleyan
mission. Children were initially recruited by going round the streets at
10 p.m. and picking them up, after which their parents were contacted.
However, once the school was established, the demand from parents for
places was high. Miss Hood wrote that 'The people in the district were
anxious to send their children; more than we could take. Sometimes children
were pushed through the door and left' (p. 39). By 1914 eighteen children
aged 2½ to 5, were attending for the whole day. There was a great deal of
emphasis on the health of the children.

The second nursery school was started in 1915, although its origins went
back to 1885 when the Collyhurst Guild for Social Service was founded,
involving various philanthropic schemes to help the sick and poor. In 1899 it
started a sand-garden for small children, run by a small committee and with a
matron to supervise. It was open daily during the summer, and was said to
have 5,000 attendances. Out of this the nursery school developed, taking
twelve children at the time of its founding, who attended from twelve o'clock
to two and paid 1d. for lunch. 'The children spent much time in the washing
of hands and faces and the cleaning of teeth. They were taught to sit quietly
at table, which they helped to set and decorate with flowers, and to eat
daintily. There were consequent improvements in cleanliness and manners.'

Teaching slum children from Manchester to decorate the dining table with
flowers seems an unrealistic preparation for their future life. In 1916 the
hours were extended from 9 a.m. to 5 p.m. and the committee decided to
maintain the school for delicate children. The numbers were increased to
thirty, and a trained nurse and a masseuse attended daily; the improvement of
the children's health thus became the sole aim of the institution.

The third school was also started in 1915 by a local church as part of its
social work. The premises were two cottages, with the back yards joined to
make a playground. It was situated in a run-down industrial area, dominated
by big iron and chemical works, and a large number of the local women were
employed at the munitions factories in the area. At first the school only took
nine children, hardly a significant contribution to the problem of caring for
the children of munitions workers. Like the other schools, it was financed by
voluntary contributions and had a long waiting list. It was staffed by a super-

* The first nursery class was also set up in Manchester in 1917.

intendent and two untrained helpers, 'either girls of good education or older persons ready to work at a nominal salary'. The majority of nursery schools at the time were staffed partly by untrained helpers, often middle-class girls for whom such part-time work was acceptable. The school maintained close contact with the parents, records being kept of such things as family wages and the incidence of disease.

An important characteristic of these schools is the small numbers for whom they catered. The McMillans' school in Deptford was an exception. Once they began receiving help from the London County Council they were able to build open-air shelters, each taking an average of thirty children, so that by the early 1920s over 200 children attended. They arrived at 8 a.m. and left at 5.30 p.m., which it was felt was necessary to make listless and undernourished children strong and healthy. In a broadcast speech in 1927 Margaret McMillan suggested that the nursery school was the fundamental remedy for disease in childhood. She maintained that the incidence of death from measles fell to 0·5 per cent whereas outside the school it was 7 per cent, and that on entry to the school 80 per cent of the children had rickets but that all cases were cured within a year. She argued that 'much of the money we spend on education is wasted because we have not made any real foundation for our educational system'. Children whose health was already blighted would find difficulty in learning. In her book, the nursery school is presented above all, as a 'healing agency' in a slum area, although she does also suggest that it should be open to children from all social backgrounds, 'the open-air nursery school is here for rich and poor' (McMillan, 1919, p. 113).

McMillan had been influenced by continental progressivism in education and the work of John Dewey and had published a book, *Education Through the Imagination,* in 1904, which argued that the children's timetable was to consist of 'above all free movement and experience'. She also campaigned for a school with buildings which would allow greater freedom. 'This new school should be a vivid contrast to those barrack-like piles we know today. Instead of heavy walls and barred gates, it should have low palings and open railings. . . . Instead of hard dark asphalt, one should look in here at an expanse of green, at flower beds. . . .' (McMillan in Haden Guest, 1920).

After the death of her sister in 1917, Margaret McMillan set up a centre in her memory to train women for work in nursery schools. By 1919 there were twenty students who spent part of their day in study, and part in practical work at the nursery school. In 1930 this training centre became the Rachel McMillan Training College. However, most of her time was spent in lecturing and propaganda to convince the public of the value of nursery schools. She' was an excellent speaker, with power to sway an audience by her oratory, her eloquence and her dedication to her cause. She succeeded in winning over many influential men of her generation, amongst whom were Sir Robert Morant, at the Board of Education, and Sir Victor Horsley, the eminent doctor, who took part in the campaign for better medical facilities for school children. Other admirers and helpers included Nancy Astor, Cyril Burt, Earl Russell, Arnold Gesell and Bernard Shaw. The latter described her as 'cantankerous', but admitted she was one of the best women of her time and owed much of her success to this quality (Lowndes, 1960, p. 35). She can perhaps be described as the outstanding individual in the early history of nursery schools, converting many to her concept of 'nurture', which formed the basis of the content of nursery school activities. Nurture consisted of nourishing food, therapeutic physical activity including music and movement, fresh air and sunshine. Her propaganda probably played a part in the inclusion of nursery schools in the Education Act of 1918.

This act made support for nursery schools out of public funds possible for the first time and Section 19 stated that:

(1) The powers of local education authorities for the purpose of Part III of the Education Act 1902, shall include power to make arrangements for –

(a) Supplying or aiding the supply of nursery schools (which expression shall include nursery classes) for children over two and under five years of age, or such later age, as may be approved by the Board of Education, whose attendance at such a school is necessary or desirable for their healthy physical and mental development, and

(b) Attending to the health, nourishment and physical welfare of children attending nursery schools.

(2) Notwithstanding any Act of Parliament the Board of Education may, out of moneys provided by Parliament, pay grants in aid of nursery schools, provided that such grants shall not be paid in respect of any such school unless it is open to inspection by the local education authority, and unless that authorities are enabled to appoint representatives on the body of managers to the extent of at least one third of the total body of managers, and before recognising any nursery school the Board shall consult the local education authority.

At the first reading of the bill, Herbert Fisher, the President of the Board of Education, proposed that local education authorities should be allowed to raise the age of entrance to elementary schools to 6 as soon as there was an adequate supply of nursery schools in the area. In the same speech he said that, where the home was satisfactory, children under 5 should be encouraged to stay with their mothers. He envisaged that the supply of schools, which he hoped would be open-air, would lead to a genuine improvement in the health of children.

The pressures on the family system of socialization and the dissatisfaction with its ability to cope on its own with the care of children under 5 had not changed fundamentally since 1908. There was still concern with the health of children which was the main factor affecting the decision to allocate public funds to nursery schools. This is illustrated in Fisher's statement. Perhaps he had been influenced by the annual report of the Chief Medical Officer of the

c

Board of Education on the care and training of children under 5, which had said that neither the physical nor mental well-being of children under 5 was provided for satisfactorily. Medical inspections of children aged 5, on entering the infant schools, showed that one third of them were suffering from preventable physical defect.

But it is necessary to ask why the Act was passed in 1918, rather than at some earlier or later date. The reason appears to be that the pressures were intensified by the First World War. As Titmuss stated, 'In no particular sphere of need is the imprint of war on social policy more vividly illustrated than in respect to dependant needs — the needs of wives, children and other relatives for income-maintenance allowances when husbands and fathers are serving in the Forces.' Here he refers to money payments, but he applies this to public expenditure on social provision in general. 'The more in fact that the waging of war has come to require a total effort by the nation, the more have the dependent needs of the family been recognised and accepted as a social responsibility' (Titmuss, 1958, p. 84). Conscription had revealed again the low standard of physical health of many recruits. The resources available to the family system of socialization were reduced by the absence of fathers abroad and, in industrial areas, of mothers in the factories. The role of war in increasing the recognition of the family's needs was also noticed by Margaret McMillan. In her 1927 broadcast speech she commented that 'women who had never thought of the masses' suddenly became concerned with the soldiers' children. Their attitude in McMillan's words was 'We'll not only have Homes for Heroes, we must have gardens for the Heroes' children'.

An article written in 1917, advocating nation-wide nursery schools, reveals some of the attitudes which influenced the framing of the 1918 Act (Bompas-Smith, 1917). It also voices a new dissatisfaction with the working-class family's system of socialization, which some years later became of much significance, although at this time it was not widely felt. The author shares the official attitude that the nursery school is an institution to make up for bad housing, low wages, defective sanitation and parental ignorance, that 'the right place for the education of children below the age of six is a healthy and happy home of which the mother is the providing genius'. But because of the deficiencies of the vast majority of homes, alternatives must be provided. He went on to make the following points:

(1) There was a need for working-class mothers to have adequate means for placing their children when working. The dangers and abuses of the child-minder were outlined.

(2) There was a need for a system of co-ordinated institutions with responsibility for young children, such as infant welfare centres and day nurseries for children under two and a half, and nursery schools for children aged two and a half to 6.

(3) The high death rate amongst children under 5 from the working class should be reduced.

(4) 'It is no more unreasonable for such mothers to send their children to a nursery school than it is for more wealthy parents to employ a nurse or governess.'

(5) Young children might suffer intellectual retardation as a result of poor environmental conditions. 'Recent investigations into intellectual and social status appear to warrant the belief that the intellectual development of children from poor homes is much retarded.'

(6) Education was an instrument for creating a more appropriate environment for children.

The last two points are an early expression of a new dissatisfaction with the intellectual stimuli for young children in many homes. This is reiterated in another article written two years later (Drummond, 1919). The author points out that many children are mentally starved in the most important years of their life, and stresses the role of the nursery school as a means of widening the child's experience, and diverting it from an unfavourable environment. The proliferation of such discussion and the innovations of the Act were limited in their extent and consequence by post-war conditions. The act allowed a 50 per cent grant from the Board of Education for nursery schools. Provision by Local Education Authorities was not mandatory. 'We do not desire to compel the provision of nursery schools, but we propose to enable such schools, attendance at which must be voluntary, to be aided from the rates. . .' (Fisher, 1918).

The permissive nature of the act is of great importance to later developments. It left the choice to set up nursery schools to the local authorities. As their development meant extra rates, the incentives to create them were negative, particularly as many regarded them as unnecessary or even undesirable. This was the first obvious manifestation of resistance at the stages of specification and implementation of the new structural unit. However, it is difficult to imagine that Fisher could have done otherwise. The 1902 Act, which had laid down the responsibilities of the local authorities for education, embodied the principle of local autonomy. Attempts by the Board to impose standards in the areas as happened in 1905 in secondary education met with hostility and resentment. 'Is this policy of interference not directly opposed to the spirit and intention of the Act, which was to allow local authorities to develop secondary education as they considered best for their own districts?' asked Mr Wilkinson in his Presidential Address to the Annual Meeting of the Association of Directors and Secretaries for Education in 1905 (Banks, 1955, p. 62).

The prohibitive costs of building in the post-war years also had an effect. In 1918—19 only thirteen nursery schools received recognition for grant, of which only one was a new local authority school, the rest being voluntary schools already in existence. The total number of children accommodated was 288. Thus the clause in the 1918 Education Act which recommended raising the age of entrance to 6 when sufficient nursery schools were available was never implemented. By 1920–21 the number of maintained schools had risen to eight and the number of voluntary schools eligible for grant to twelve. These accommodated 744 children.

Then in 1922 the Geddes axe fell. In an atmosphere of economic crisis, the Select Committee on National Expenditure had attacked 'the atmosphere of financial laxity in which questions regarding education are apt to be considered'. In 1921 a circular was sent out by the Board of Education asking local education authorities not to incur any new expenditure (Board of Education Circular 1190/1921). The nursery school was one of the first institutions to be axed, but many more fundamental aspects of educational expenditure were affected (see Tropp, who recounts how the Burnham Committee nearly vanished from the scene, as a result of demands for economy in education). In February 1922, the first Interim Report of the Committee on National Expenditure, that is the Geddes Committee, was issued. It contained a virulent attack on 'overspending' in education including recommendations for cuts in teachers' salaries, transference of their pensions to a contributory scheme, the closing of small schools, the limiting of expenditure on secondary and higher education, an increase in the size of classes and the raising of the school starting age to 6 (Geddes Report, 1922, p. 109). The government rejected most of these, including the last; but educational progression was halted even if the reaction was less severe than it might have been. As a result of the report a second circular was sent out in 1922 placing restrictions on the development of nursery schools, and by 1923 only eleven 'exceptionally important' applications had been conceded by the Board of Education since the original thirteen.

Dissatisfaction with the system still remained and was accompanied by an increasing 'sense of opportunity for changes in the terms of potential availability of facilities', as a result of the 1918 Act, which made the *possibility* of extensive provision of nursery schools a reality. The frustration for those who felt strongly about the problem was increased and a pressure group was formed. At a conference to discuss the possibility of founding an association, the following resolution was passed unanimously:

The members of this conference on nursery school education, being workers in and for nursery schools, deplore the slowness of growth of the nursery school movement, and wish to see the public recognition and establishment in our own generation of nursery school education for all children under school age.
    They therefore resolve to form a Nursery School Association to undertake a campaign of propaganda and to work for the general advancement of nursery school education.

The Association was founded in 1923.
    The primary aim of the founders was propaganda to arouse public opinion and extend provision, with the subordinate aims of intercourse and discussion

amongst those already working in the field.* The first President was Margaret McMillan, and the honorary secretary, Grace Owen, a Training College principal. Thirty-five members were enrolled initially and by the end of 1924 this had increased to 226 with eight associate groups giving an estimated total membership of 500. No information exists on the characteristics of these early members, but those on the committee were all women, a large proportion of whom were teachers, sometimes in infant or nursery schools, but more often involved in the training of teachers, particularly for nursery schools. It has an impressive list of Vice-Presidents, including Lady Astor and Mrs Wintringham, Sir Michael Sadler and Ramsay MacDonald, and in 1926 Bertrand Russell joined them. The initial proposals of the Association were modest: to hold two conferences a year, one in London and one in the provinces, and 'to watch events and take such practical steps as may seem advisable to forward the objects of the Association'. They also decided to hold open meetings with eminent speakers from the field of nursery education. It seems that these and the conferences especially may have been 'preaching to the converted'. However, they were valuable for the subsidiary objects to exchange views between experts and to keep workers in the field up to date. Their other activities, which had a more obvious function of propaganda, were to be the publication of pamphlets, deputations to public bodies and informal consultations with other organizations.

The occupational characteristics of the Association's officers appear to have affected the channelling of some of the aims and activities of the Association. Much of their work was concerned with the technicalities of the operation of the new unit rather than with its extension to supplement the old unit, which had become inadequate. Many of them were professionally involved in the new system of pre-school education, and it was in their interest to ensure that this system should be protected and should grow, whatever their personal convictions about the family's needs. They were not directly involved in the demand for other agencies, such as infant welfare clinics, free school meals, family allowances, child guidance clinics and day nurseries. They were concerned particularly with the position of teachers in nursery schools. One of their first moves was the demand in 1924 for the recognition for superannuation of teachers' service in nursery schools. During their first deputation to the Board of Education, they proposed not only 'that large Nursery School Centres should be established in congested districts' and 'that smaller Nursery Schools should be opened wherever they are needed', but also 'that Nursery School Staffs should include a reasonable

* At the first committee meeting the objects of the Association were drawn up in the following clauses:

(1) To secure the effective working of clause 19 of the Education Act of 1918 for England and Wales and of clause 8 of Education (Scotland) Act 1918.
(2) To furnish opportunity for discussion.
(3) To help to form and focus public opinion on all matters relating to the Nursery School movement.

proportion — not less than one to every forty children — of trained and specially qualified teachers as well as other helpers' (Nursery School Association, 1924). This has remained a central policy of the Association, and it has spent much time on the formation of schemes for the training of nursery school teachers and superintendents. The first of such schemes was devised in 1924 and submitted to Local Education Authorities, the Board of Education and the Training College Association. It has also held many conferences on administrative problems connected with nursery schools, such as buildings, equipment, organization and staffing.

It is worth describing some of the work done by the Association during its first ten years. In 1924 it sent the first of many circular letters to local education authorities either pressing them to action, or obtaining information on the extent of their provision, their plans and their standards. The response indicated that only four authorities had plans for new nursery schools. The reasons given by other authorities for their lack of plans varied from the more pressing needs of later education to a lack of need for nursery schools. In 1927 they followed up this disappointing response by passing a resolution at their Annual Meeting: 'That this Association desires to see the Nursery School Clause in the Education Acts of 1918 and 1921 so amended as to make it incumbent on the local education authorities to re-establish Nursery Schools within their areas.' An appeal for support was sent to all M.P.s and to a number of other organizations.* As a result three M.P.s, one Labour, one Liberal and one Conservative, made a strong appeal for more nursery schools in the debate on the Education Estimates in 1927. However, this was unsuccessful and there were no prospects that local authorities would open more. Nevertheless the following year the Association again circulated letters to M.P.s at the time of the Education Estimates on the need for more nursery schools. Whenever local or national elections took place, letters were sent to candidates asking them to support the demand for more nursery schools, and they attempted to put pressure on the government by letters and deputations to the responsible minister. Deputations to the Board of Education and later to the Ministry of Education have been a significant form of protest by the Association. They also gave evidence to such bodies as the Consultative Committee of the Board of Education, who in 1928 were about to start an inquiry into the curriculum of the primary school. The Association urged that the nursery and infant school period should be included, and there was eventually a separate inquiry on this stage. It is difficult to comment on its success or lack of success over particular issues. How far was the withdrawal of restrictive circulars due to the Association's efforts, and how far to other pressures? In terms of its aim to provide nursery schools for all children, it

* Amongst those that responded favourably were the Child Study Society, the Froebel Society, the Sunlight League, the TUC, the Standing Joint Committee of Industrial Women's Organisations, The Women's Co-operative Guild, the WEA, six Women's Labour Advisory Councils, ninety-seven Women's Sections of the Labour Party and four branches of the Labour Party.

has been unsuccessful since after forty-three years this aim is far from achievement; but to discount its influence would be unfair. It was first consulted and asked to submit evidence by a government committee for the Hadow Report in 1928, and since this date has been consulted by such committees on many occasions.

In 1930 the Association held a conference to discuss the administration of nursery schools and to secure support for recent circulars encouraging expansion. All local education authorities were invited to send delegates, as were a large number of other organizations including the National Union of Teachers, the Association of Education Committees and the National Council for Maternal and Child Welfare. They cooperated and conferred with these bodies, and others concerned with the family system of socialization such as the National Society of Day Nurseries. In the same year the Association was granted £500 for three years by the United Kingdom Carnegie Trust in order that it might 'further establish its work of educating public opinion'.

Its chief method in the attempt to reach the public was the publication of pamphlets stressing the value of nursery schools. By 1939 it had issued forty-seven publications. During 1929 it issued 200,000 pamphlets and in later years this figure increased. But how widely these were read by the public is not known. Interest in some of the publications may have been confined to members.

During its first ten years the Association increased its membership considerably; by 1934 there were 1,040 individual members, with forty-one associate groups and six branches. The policy of forming branches, each with its own officers and headquarters, was started in 1926 and by 1939 there were twenty-six of them. They enabled propaganda to be carried out and contact to be established with the general public at the local level and a number of branches ran exhibitions during the pre-war period, some of which attracted large numbers of visitors. Whatever its success in generating interest and action amongst the public, it did have an important role to play in conveying dissatisfaction directly to the authorities.

The restrictive circulars sent out as a result of the Geddes axe were withdrawn by the first Labour government in 1924. At the Nursery School Association's summer conference in Bradford, Mr Charles Trevelyan, the new President of the Board of Education, sent 'a message of whole-hearted approval and encouragement'. However, his office was short-lived, and any extra expansion that might have been hoped for as the result of a Labour government did not materialize. A few new nursery schools were recognized between 1925—9, but expansion was slow, and was partly counteracted by the Circular sent out by Lord Percy, President of the Board of Education, reducing the grant for children under 5 in elementary schools and thus discouraging the development of nursery classes.* In 1925—6 there were

* Circular 1371/1926. Nursery classes were attached to the elementary schools (later primary schools) rather than existing independently, as in the case of nursery schools.

thirteen local education authority nursery schools, and fifteen recognized voluntary schools. These catered for 1,391 children. By 1929 there were still only twenty-eight schools altogether, although more of these were local education authority schools than in 1925, providing accommodation for a total of 1,564 children.

At the 1929 election Labour was returned. In the pre-election campaign it had included the wide provision of nursery schools in its policy outline. However, the Nursery School Association reported on its contacts with the political parties, saying 'all in varying degrees expressed willingness to include Nursery Schools in their programmes and distribute our literature' (Nursery School Association, 1929). Nevertheless the commitment of the Labour Party appears to have been greater than that of the other parties. During 1929 the new government sent out a circular to local authorities giving them strong encouragement to open nursery schools.

As Minister of Health and President of the Board of Education we make a strong appeal to local authorities to use the powers which all possess but only some exercise. Now that all Local Education Authorities are framing pro-grammes for the next three years we would ask them earnestly to consider provision of Nursery Schools for children between three and five years old. . . . Open air Nursery Schools where infants are tended, washed, fed and taught have passed the stage of experiment. They are a comparatively in-expensive and entirely efficient means of securing a fair start in life even for infants whose home life is most depressed.

It went on to advocate the different ways in which provision might be made for children between 2 and 5, stressing that the nursery school was only one of a number of alternatives: nursery classes, day nurseries or infant schools could all be developed. With regard to the latter it urged that, 'In planning new infant schools the desirability of including provision for children be-tween three and five should be carefully considered'. It offered assistance to all local authorities who undertake 'a new effort to deal with the problem of the start of child life' (Circular 1054 (Health), 1405 (Education), 1929).

As a result, nine new nursery schools were opened in 1930, plans for twelve more were approved and plans for an additional fifteen were put before the Board. In 1929 several local authorities had appointed sub-committees to investigate the need for nursery schools within their areas. The resulting three-year programmes included preliminary proposals for forty-four new nursery schools, other than those already mentioned. Thus in one year nine local authority nursery schools were established with plans for many more, compared with nine in the previous nine years.

The ideology of the Labour Party was associated with this expansion. Its concern with the underprivileged members of the community is reflected in its encouragement of nursery schools. Its members were aware that many working-class families were unable to take complete responsibility for the socialization of their children, without their health and their mental develop-ment suffering. In 1926 the Labour Party and the Trades Union Congress published a joint statement on education: *From Nursery School to University. A Labour Policy*. This stated:

We are in favour of the most rapid possible increase of nursery schools and baby classes consistent with efficiency. . . . Our object is not to put these schools in place of the home, but to add to the latter something which the children of the rich have always had, and those of the poor always lacked, namely a nursery or play-room, a place that is where children can be, under responsible supervision, with other children in surroundings suited to their needs and interests. . . . While we do not think it desirable that parents should be compelled to send little children under five to school, we take the view that mothers who wish to do so should be given the opportunity.

The Party therefore advocated the mandatory provision of nursery schools by local education authorities, where notice was given by a sufficient number of parents that their children would attend. This demand for nursery schools represented the attempt to equalize the environment of children and hence further the pursuit of equality, which cannot be achieved while the family alone takes total responsibility for the socialization of young children.

A more extreme version of this belief was expressed by the Bradford Independent Labour Party in a pamphlet on nursery schools also published in 1926, recommending the setting up of nursery schools for all children aged 2 to 7, and the abolition of infant departments. It argued, 'we cannot exaggerate the importance we attach to this programme. We feel that all other educational reform is secondary, is a superstructure to be built on the foundation of mental and bodily health and all-round growth in the earliest years.' Such extreme views were not shared by the Labour Party itself. The pamphlet indulged in eulogistic and almost metaphysical interpretations of the role and value of the nursery school, and stated for example, 'that it allows the full realisation of the essential human unity in which mind and body cohere', and that 'a working class trained in the Nursery School spirit would not tolerate existing conditions, economic or social; and such intolerance is a necessary condition of permanent advance'. This view, which sees the nursery school as the panacea of working-class life, comes close to the unrealistic aspirations described by Smelser as phantasy behaviour and has been called, with anxiety and aggression, one of the three classic symptoms of disturbance (Parsons and Bales, 1954, pp. 205–6). Smelser says 'Phantasy goes beyond the cultural definitions of the "given data" of the empirical world in so far as there is a denial of certain elements, such as a belief in the impossible "if only" someone would do something' (Smelser, 1959, p. 38). Some symptoms are often characterized by pessimism about the present, and the promise of paradise in the near future. On the few occasions where symptoms of disturbance* occur in this example of structural differentiation, they take the form of phantasy behaviour.

* 'The criteria for defining a symptom of disturbance, therefore, are that it be sufficiently undirected or misdirected to be considered unrealistic; that its occurrence can be correlated with conditions that give rise to it; and that it bear a plausible symbolic relationship to these conditions.' (*Ibid.*, p. 39.)

C*

All those who saw the nursery school as the answer to the family's in-sufficiencies were careful to argue that it should not replace the home, but supplement it in order to ensure better standards of health and care. This is stated by the Trades Union Congress—Labour Party pamphlet. Emphasis was frequently laid by the Nursery School Association, and others involved in the movement for nursery schools, on the need to maintain close contact with parents, particularly mothers.

In the early stages of its existence, as in the USSR,* the nursery school was seen as a method for educating mothers in the needs of the young child. The literature on the subject in the 1920s and 1930s abounds with statements attempting to protect the nursery school from criticisms that it was destroy-ing the vital roles of the family. Margaret McMillan stated, 'No one has a right to ask that she [the mother] part from her little one, and we shall not part them if this thing is well done' (M. McMillan, 1930, p. 29). She suggested that 'there is no reason why the nursery school should not one day be presided over by the mothers themselves' (p. 23). Another writer states, 'it is not our intention to take away the responsibility of the mother. Our aim is rather to awaken her to a sense of her own great responsibility. We try to educate the mother with the child. . .' (Stevinson, 1923, p. 8). Such constant reassurances were necessary, and still are, in a situation where the prevailing values uphold the sanctity of the family's roles in the sphere of early socialization. The following quotation illustrates this attitude. 'The great problem is to assist the home and the parents, not to replace them. The natural and basic agency for the education of the pre-school child is in his own home — with his own father, mother, brothers, sisters, even with his own grandparents. . . . To make the home most effective in rearing the child for which it was really created is a durable social problem' (Gesell, 1925, pp. 148—50). This is a mild expression of this value, by someone who favoured the development of agencies of pre-school education outside the home. To many, such an insti-tution has been regarded as a threat to the survival of the family as a social organization, and any such aid to the family is bound to result in a growing disregard of parental responsibility. This attitude has played an important part in the slowness of the growth of pre-school education.

This slow growth was affected by events. The expansion, sanctioned and encouraged by the Labour government in 1929 and 1930, was cut off abruptly by the financial crisis of the following year. However, although a number of local education authorities withdrew their plans for nursery schools, the government began by renewing its support for them and urging that the need in 1931 was greater than ever and that it was essential to proceed with plans for their establishment and maintenance. But by 1932 it had changed its mind. In answer to a question in the House of Commons on 16 July the Parliamentary Secretary of the Board of Education stated that,

* Here it was recognized that it offered potent opportunities for parental education, which were immediately seized.

'The number of nursery schools at present recognised by the Board is 56. No new provision of Nursery Schools has been approved since October 1st last, but there are 15 cases in which the provision of the schools had been approved before that date and in which formal recognition has been given or will shortly be given. In existing circumstances it is improbable that more will be sanctioned.'

In 1933 the Nursery School Association reported:

The reactionary policy of the government with regard to the opening of new nursery schools has continued throughout 1933. There has been no encouragement to Local Education Authorities to proceed with new schemes, in spite of the obvious need occasioned by the overwhelming number of parents unemployed and the consequent insufficient food available for the healthy rearing of young children. Only one municipal nursery school has been completed and opened during the year. . . (Nursery School Association, 1933, p. 10).

There is an interesting difference in the effect of the slump in the United States and the United Kingdom; in the former it resulted in a great increase in nursery schools. However in Britain, voluntary effort increased and partly counteracted the government's decision. The Save the Children Fund had opened eight Emergency Open Air Nursery Schools in 'distressed areas' by the end of 1933. They were built by unemployed men working voluntarily and financed by the National Council of Social Service, the Pilgrim Trust, individual donations and the Save the Children Fund itself. In 1932 a nursery school was set up in Lincoln in connexion with Occupational Centres for the unemployed, and a number of others were planned and sponsored by individuals.

In 1934 three of the Emergency Nursery Schools were recognized for grant. By 1934 there were sixty-two recognized nursery schools of which thirty-four were maintained and twenty-eight voluntary, and they contained 4,933 children. Some relaxations were made by the government during this year; two new nursery schools were sanctioned, and places for others were considered. The London County Council undertook a programme for the development of nursery schools and other local education authorities reconsidered pre-1931 plans which had been dropped. In 1935 the expansion of provision was able to continue. Large-scale unemployment had resulted in increased sensitivity towards the possibilities and dangers of malnutrition amongst children. This resulted in a forceful campaign for nursery schools by organizations such as the Association of Education Committees. In 1934 they sent a deputation to the Board of Education pressing for the establishment of nursery schools, 'in all poor and overcrowded areas in order that children of pre-school age might have suitable medical attention, nurture and nourishment'.

From 1933 to 1935 the Nursery School Association ran a campaign for the reservation of sites for nursery schools in connexion with slum clearance and rehousing schemes. The campaign began with a letter to *The Times* in 1933. The following year candidates at local elections were asked to support the reservation of sites for this purpose, and in 1935 a deputation went to the Board of Education. 'It drew attention to the opportunity which existed for comprehensive planning of new estates in order to secure the amenities necessary to supplement the home in respect to the health and all-round growth of young children' (Nursery School Association, 1935, pp. 12—13). This was received sympathetically, the Board offering to consider any plans for new nursery schools from local education authorities, although permission to go ahead would depend on the limited funds available. The Nursery School Association also organized propaganda in the provinces. With the Workers' Educational Association they ran an exhibition on town planning, housing and the nursery school which toured a number of large towns. This campaign illustrates the four major methods employed by the Association in their efforts to extend pre-school education. They also enlisted the active support of the Church. In February 1935, the Church Assembly passed a resolution urging Christians to use their influence in obtaining sites for nursery schools, particularly in congested areas and those in the process of being rebuilt. Finally at the 1935 election all three parties included the nursery school as part of their electoral programme, and the demand for nursery education was not without support from the Establishment.

During this period there were significant developments in the dominant conception of the role and function of the nursery school. As early as 1926 Bertrand Russell said 'I think the arguments in favour of nursery schools are quite overwhelming — not only for children whose parents are poor, ignorant and overworked, but for all children, or, at the very least for all children who live in towns' (Russell, 1926, p. 224).

In 1930 at a conference of Education Associations, Susan Isaacs argued that the greatest achievement could take place only if 'the primary intention of the school is to give its children the positive conditions which they need as developing human beings of those particular ages irrespective of social conditions'. In her book *The Nursery Years*, she stressed one of the reasons for this — that children need other children, 'with other children they can work out their fantasies more easily ... and can get real concrete experience of social relations, on their own level of desire and control'. She maintained that the corrective function of the nursery school should be incidental to the above, rather than central. This new emphasis reflected a growing interest in the emotional needs of young children, and the way these affect mental and physical growth.

In the United States the growth in the study of child development led directly to the establishment of nursery schools, as they were used as laboratories for the study of child behaviour. The growth of interest in the mental testing of young children was important as were increasingly numerous attempts at empirical studies by the various psycho-analytic schools.

In Britain, intellectual developments of this kind had less direct effect, but they were one of the factors in the move towards regarding the nursery school as a primarily educational institution, which should be available to all children. Typical of the conception of the nursery school that was developing during the 1930s amongst those with a knowledge of the field, is the following statement:

The nursery school is first and foremost an educational institution, which takes the whole child for its province. . . . It is equally concerned with the physical, mental and emotional phases of child development and is specifically designed to provide conditions which will contribute to the natural and progressive growth of the child's faculties, the development of robust physique, the formation of desirable habits, the stimulation of healthy mental and spiritual reactions to social environment (Cusden, 1938, p. 51).

The Nursery School Association noted in its Annual Report of 1930 that, 'This year has also seen a notable increase in small private Nursery Schools, staffed by trained Nursery School teachers and charging fees for attendance. Some of these are carried on in private houses. These vary considerably in size and character but serve to demonstrate clearly that the nursery school meets a need that is urgently felt in families of all types and circumstances.' No figures are available giving the actual number of private nursery schools in existence, so it is impossible to ascertain the dimensions of the growth. However, if we can accept the Association's statement, it is apparent that the change in conception is reflected in the institutional structure, with the growth of agencies catering for a different sector of the child population which, unlike that of the lower working class, were not attending nursery schools because of the family's inability to ensure adequate physical development.

This change was not a sudden innovation. The Nursery School Association had always expressed the belief that the nursery school was a desirable adjunct to the home for every child, although up to the middle-1930s it had concentrated most of its energies on procuring facilities for children who would benefit from their corrective function. There had been kindergarten whose purpose was primarily educational since the middle of the nineteenth century. Many continued to cling to the old conception long after its abandonment. The public authorities themselves were slow to recognize that new dissatisfactions with the family's system of socialization were changing the role allocated to the nursery school.

In 1933 Part III of the Hadow Report* was published. The terms of reference of the Consultative Committee of the Board of Education were, 'To

---

* A committee to study secondary education was set up under the chairmanship of Sir W. H. Hadow, publishing its report in 1926; Part II was on primary education, and was published in 1931.

consider and report on the training and teaching of children attending nursery schools, infants' departments of public elementary schools, and the further development of such educational provision for children up to the age of seven plus'. The major recommendations of the report were:

(1) The compulsory starting age to remain at 5.

(2) Children to continue to be admitted between 3 and 5 where this is demanded.

(3) Separate departments for children under 7 to be established.

(4) 'The fundamental purpose of the nursery school or class is to reproduce the healthy conditions of a good nursery in a well-managed home, and thus to provide an environment in which the health of the young child — physical, mental and moral — can be safeguarded.'

(5) The home is regarded as the best place for children under 5, but the fact that the home conditions of many make it an unsatisfactory environment is recognized. Children from such homes would benefit by attendance at a nursery class or school. 'We are of the opinion that the nursery school is a desirable adjunct to the national system of education; and that in districts where the housing and general economic conditions are seriously below the average, a nursery school should, if possible be provided. The nursery school should be designed primarily for those children who by reason of unsuitable environment require careful attention to their physical welfare and need to spend longer hours at school and to be provided with meals.'

The report does not show any acceptance of a universal system of nursery schools on educational grounds. The Committee had been influenced by reports to the Chief Medical Officer of the Board of Education, who had strongly advocated the provision of nursery schools in order to improve the health of the children. In 1930 he wrote, 'The experience of the past twelve years shows that the nursery school child is less susceptible than others to the ordinary ailments of childhood' (Newman, 1930). His reports at this time revealed that a large number of 5-year-olds, being inspected for the first time, were still suffering from preventable disease, including decayed teeth, rickets, bronchitis, anaemia and with tonsils and adenoids requiring operation. In 1925, 23 per cent of children aged 5 were found to require treatment other than dental. By 1935 this figure remained high at 17 per cent. Official opinion, expressed by Newman in particular, that the child's health was not being cared for effectively, was backed up by the experience of school medical officers in various parts of the country. The Assistant School Medical Officer for Derby did some research which compared 100 children aged 5 and 6, who had attended nursery schools previously, with 100 children from the same district who had gone direct to infant schools. He found that nursery school children were on average 2·04 lb heavier; that 2 per cent suffered from malnutrition compared to 15 per cent amongst the non-nursery school group; that the dental figures were very favourable for nursery school children.*

Three years after the Hadow report was published, the Board of Education brought out a new pamphlet on *Nursery Schools and Nursery Classes*. This still held the view that, 'Nursery Schools have as their primary object the physical and medical nurture of the debilitated child' (Board of Education, 1936A). As a result of this, the Nursery School Association submitted a memorandum, 'The Educational needs of children under 7', to the Board deprecating this policy of confining nursery schools to remedial work in slum areas. According to the Association 'the document received wide publicity and much favourable comment' (Nursery School Association, 1945). This greater stress on the role of education in the nursery school by non-government organizations interested in the field was stimulated further by the flourishing of the progressive movement in Britain during the late 1920s and 1930s. The influence of the ideas of Froebel and Dewey became more pronounced. The idea of a child-centred education, in which education is based on the pupil as he is, and his present interests in life, rather than on the attempt to mould the child into our mental image of the ideal adult, grew in status as did the belief that the child's social environment should be fully utilized, and that deeper educational formation comes *unconsciously* as the child indulges in different activities in various groups to which he belongs. The 'activity' method, the notion of learning by doing, was advocated with increased force. All these principles had been accepted implicitly by those responsible for the day-to-day organization of the nursery school, with the exclusion of formal instruction and the attempt to give the child a large variety of experience and increase the scope of his environment, with conditions of freedom and spontaneity. The increased publicity generated by the progressive movement for the incorporation of this kind of curriculum at all stages in education appears to have encouraged the greater interest in the *educational* role of the Nursery School.

The progressive movement welcomed the nursery school movement, and close links were established between the two; *New Era,* the journal of the former, regularly gave space to the Nursery School Association during the 1930s. The hope was expressed by the progressivists that the nursery school would help to initiate reforms further up the educational system. In an editorial on the nursery school, *New Era* stated that 'children who have begun

* In the United States at the same period, 'it was observed that a by no means negligible proportion of entrants into the first grade were hampered by physical defects which had fastened upon them during pre-school years. In the light of this discovery rather than in any other way, the pre-school child began to secure the attention of his community.' (See Hughes and Roberts, 1922.) Official reports of the Children's Bureau found that in very low-income groups 92 per cent of 7-year-olds had never been to the dentist and that in slightly higher income groups 78 per cent had never been. More than 60 per cent of the very low groups drank no milk at all. Studies done in New York City found that over 1,000 children examined on entrance to school only 33·3 per cent were without some kind of physical defect. Many of the latter could have been prevented.

their education in a certain way will require – and demand – the same kind
of treatment in the school to which they proceed on leaving the nursery'
(*New Era*, 1930). In 1938 a whole issue was devoted to the pre-school child.
The following claims were made for the nursery school in the editorial:

> The difficult child and perhaps even more obviously the difficult adolescent,
> is the one who has been mishandled in his pre-school years, and who, there-
> fore, grows up suspicious or aggressive, grudging of praise to others because
> uncertain of his own deserts, over anxious to please the authorities or hard-
> ened against all praise and blame. The good nursery school can undoubtedly
> mediate the emotional difficulties that are bound to beset the small child, as
> well as fostering his intellectual and aesthetic strivings for mastery and growth
> and weaning him from early dependencies and attachments. . . . Our adult
> problems of citizenship are difficult and inescapable, but even if we could
> resolve them here and now in a just and creative social system, we should still
> leave unresolved the timeless flowering of individual human spirit. It is that
> growing point that the nursery school must foster, for it is through it, not
> through any political perfections that good itself evolves (*New Era*, 1938, p.
> 295).

This is a further example of phantasy behaviour by certain groups.

Meanwhile this growing interest in the education of young children combined with a fundamental demographic change, the decline of the birth-rate
and the growth of one- and two-child families to generate new dissatisfactions
with the family system of socialization. This change reached its peak during
the 1930s when the Net Reproduction Rate fell to below unity. Unfortunately little information has been collected on the experiences of families of
different size. What is the typical life of the five-child family as against the
two-child family? It seems likely that families of different size do have differential needs of societal support and supplementation. James Bossard is one of
the few sociologists who has been concerned with the relationship between
the size of the family group and the nature of the interactive process within
it. In formulating his pretentiously named 'law of family interaction', he
mentions the 'significance of the mere size of the household for the young
child' (Bossard, 1945). The law simply enables the exact number of interactive relationships to be counted. Thus in a family of four there are six sets
of relationships. In a family of twelve there are sixty-six sets of relationships.
'Such a comparison reveals the precise nature of the revolutionary change in
the intimate response pattern of the average family member, which has come
about as the result of the small family system.'* The magnitude of the change
becomes more obvious when seen in these terms. The range and complexity
of the interactive process is reduced greatly by the removal of one member
from the group. The resulting belief has grown that the child must spend

---

* 'With the addition of each person to a family or primary group, the number of
persons increases in the simplest arithmetic progression in whole numbers, while the
number of personal relationships within the group increases in the order of triangular
numbers.'

some time outside the family during his pre-school years for his adequate socialization and preparation for future relationships.

Bossard also attempts to isolate some of the distinctive features of large families and show how they affect the process of child-rearing. He found that in eighty-two families out of his sample of 100 the role of siblings in the general management of children and the child-rearing process, including discipline, was extremely important. Older children were encouraged to assume responsibility for their younger brothers and sisters. He found that children from large families, as would be expected, customarily play together when younger. One informant stated that 'there were playgroups within the family based mostly on close age'. It appeared that children learn a great deal in sibling interaction, and that consensus with and consideration of others had to be learned in the large family. At least this is what the informants believed, even if it did not happen. Such propositions are difficult to test, and may be as much myth as the common supposition that younger siblings learn to speak more quickly because of interaction with their elders. But these ideas have some bearing on the demand for pre-school education. The notion that sibling interaction aids the learning process is accompanied by the notion that sibling rivalry and conflict is a useful preparation for later life, and an aid to personality development in general. This leads to the belief that children from one- or two-child families who were denied this opportunity would require some alternative experience with other children outside the home. There are many examples of this belief amongst both English and American writers.

The nursery school provides the only child with the opportunity of associating with children of his own age. It has long been recognised by sensible parents and others intelligently interested in the welfare of children that it was highly desirable to provide such association whenever possible in the case of only children. Of late many people have come to think it desirable for all little children to have the experience of playing with others of their own age, with whom they may compete on a fairer basis than that upon which they play with older or younger brothers and sisters (Forest, 1927, p. 344).

The writer continues that to keep a small child happily and profitably occupied all day, to amuse, entertain and teach him is a task at which few mothers, alone, at home, can have total success. The nursery school could provide conditions which few parents can provide for their own children, and save the child from boredom.

The decline in the child population made possible an increase in the supply of pre-school education, involving less capital expenditure than would have occurred had the population remained stable. In 1936 the Board of Education issued Circular 1444, which suggested that local education authorities should decide, in the light of a survey, on the needs of the area for nursery schools. A large number undertook such a survey, and of those who took action the majority decided to develop nursery classes rather than nursery

schools. The main reason for this was that the decline in the school population had resulted in empty classrooms. Provision could be made more quickly
and more cheaply by the adaptation of existing accommodation. Willesden
was an example of a local education authority which did this extensively. Its
Director of Education wrote in 1936 that,

with the exception of three new schools on a large housing estate, all Willesden schools were built for the pre-1915 population, with the inevitable result
that there were thousands of empty places in 1930. The empty places in what
were once termed the senior departments were utilised when schools were
reorganised on Hadow lines, and though suggestions that empty classrooms in
infant departments were to be appropriated for a similar purpose, the authority resolutely set its face against the suggestion. They adopted the principle
that our infant schools were for infants only, and that empty places should be
utilised for the admission of children under five.
    Thus began the process of establishing nursery classes, which has now
extended to the majority of council schools within the borough (Davies,
1936).

However, the nursery class was criticized by a number of advocates of the
nursery school on the grounds that the standards of the infant school would
be forced on the nursery class, and that the child would be subjected to too
formal a classroom situation. Various technical aspects of the organization of
pre-school education such as this, were subjects of controversy at this time.
Another area of contention was the age group for which nursery schools
should make provision. There was a strong movement to establish nursery
schools with informal methods for children between 2 and 7. It was argued
that this age group should be regarded as one unit in relation to mental
growth and physical nurture (Cusden, 1938). Two experimental schools for
children of these ages were set up, one in Bradford, the other in South Wales.
They received Board of Education recognition and apparently operated
successfully, but this experiment was never implemented on a large scale.
    The nursery class, however, expanded rapidly during the late 1930s.
Manchester, in particular, fostered them, having begun a policy of including a
nursery section in their plans for all new infant schools as early as 1927. By
1933 there were sixty nursery classes in Manchester providing for 2,000
children. Leicester decided to try to provide nursery class facilities for all
children in the area, and by the late 1930s, 27 per cent of the 3 to 5
population in Leicester were so provided for. Today this authority still has
the highest proportion of children receiving pre-school education in England
and Wales. The number of nursery schools also increased during the years
before the war, although still at a slow rate.
    Table 3.1 shows that whilst the number of places in nursery schools was
slowly expanding during the inter-war years, particularly during the later part
of the period, the number of places for children under 5 in the elementary
schools was declining, except during a few years in the mid-1930s, when the
decline in the birth-rate made possible the establishment of nursery classes.

Table 3.1. **Provision for children under 5, 1919—36**

Date	Number of nursery schools LEA	voluntary aided	Accommodation	Number of children under 5 on the registers of the public elementary schools	Percentage of all children under 5 at school
1919—20	3	17	—	199,094	17·4
1927—8	12	15	1,367	164,855	—
1930	14	16	1,894	159,335	13·1
1933	32	26	4,765	156,164	13·1
1936	36	43	6,040	159,642	14·0

Source: Annual Reports of the Board of Education.

By 1937 there were forty nursery schools maintained by local education authorities and forty-five voluntary schools receiving grants from the Board of Education. In addition, there were two recognized schools, not eligible for grant. These catered for 6,735 children of whom 1,422 were in London nursery schools. By the same date the Board had approved proposals for another thirty-four nursery schools, and by 1939 there were 111 schools altogether. Cusden estimates that, for the year 1936—7, less than one tenth of a total estimated population of 1,671,100 children between 2 and 5 were accommodated in grant-aided schools. There were 159,615 children on the registers of elementary schools of whom 78 per cent were over 4. It appears therefore that only a small proportion of this 10 per cent were in institutions specifically for pre-school education, that is nursery schools or nursery classes. By the same year only twenty-six local education authorities out of 316 had established or assumed responsibility for nursery schools. Most of these only had one, Bradford being the outstanding exception with eight. It was one of the first local education authorities to stress the educational significance of the nursery school, maintaining that it should be a universal experience. In London too there were educational facilities for a larger proportion of young children than elsewhere. However, most nursery schools were situated in large industrial towns in the North and Midlands. This would be expected in the light of the prevailing official belief that nursery schools should be sited in areas with poor housing and a poor health record. It was true of voluntary nursery schools provided by charitable organizations* as well as local education authority schools.

No information is available on the number or distribution of private nursery schools. Cusden suggests that at the time of writing (1938) there was an increasing demand for nursery schools by parents who could not be

* E.g. the Save the Children Fund, the Society of Friends, the St Pancras House Improvement Society and the National Council of Women.

described as necessitous, and therefore would not obtain places for their children in voluntary or indeed most local education authority nursery schools. There were throughout the period a number of Montessori and Kindergarten schools in existence, for those who could afford the fees and some private schools had a special department for children under 5. In addition there were a few private nursery schools and occasional cooperative efforts by groups of parents, but Cusden maintained that 'the number of these falls far short of the demand' (Cusden, 1938, p. 194). With the growing stress on the need for nursery schools on educational rather than health grounds, the distinction between the middle-class and working-class institution became less obvious, in spite of such private schools.

It appears that a considerable number of parents were frustrated in their ambition to obtain pre-school education for their children during this period. Demand exceeded supply in the maintained and grant-aided sector. In 1923 a Joint Parliamentary Advisory Council on the Nursery School indicated that the majority of nursery schools then in existence had long waiting lists, an example being given of a school in Birmingham with three times as many children on the waiting list as in the school.

Various pressures appeared to operate as barriers to the extension of provision to meet the need. The high cost of the nursery school in a period marked by two major recessions was one of them. In 1935—6 the average cost of the nursery school per head per annum was £17 7s. compared with £14 7s. 3d. for the elementary school, and criticisms were made of their expensive nature.

Another argument levelled against the nursery school was that it exposed the child to infection at an unnecessarily early age, when the child is particularly susceptible. This was one of the reasons for the advocacy of the small school, which further increased costs per head.

However, more fundamental than such criticisms was concern over the morality of removing the child at an early age from its home. Strongly held values about the traditional roles of the family and its members conflicted, and continue to conflict with new values about the needs of children, which have grown as the result of structural changes, such as the demographic change, described earlier. Thus fears were expressed, and are sometimes still heard today, that facilities for pre-school education would encourage more married women to seek employment outside the home, thus threatening the stability of the family, when they *ought* to be fulfilling their duties as wives and mothers. Powerful counter-arguments were put forward by those who advocated pre-school education, that the presence of a nursery school in the neighbourhood is of little significance in a mother's decision to go to work and that other factors such as the family's financial situation and economic needs and the mother's own personality needs and career ambitions all surmount it. The role of the employment of women, and the extent to which traditional values deprecating this have fallen behind the realities of the situation, and acted as barriers to the extension of pre-school education, will be described in the next chapter. During the period from the Second World War to the present day the increasing demand for women in the labour force has become one of the major pressures on the family system of socialization, which has in turn increased the demand for pre-school education.

4. Pre-school education, 1939–65

The administrative history

The Second World War may be regarded as a watershed in the history of pre-school education. It gave rise to a greater extension in provision than has taken place in any five-year period, either before or since.

Table 4.1. Provision of nursery schools in 1938 and 1946

Date	Schools (LEA and direct grant)	Accommodation	Schools voluntary	Accommodation
1938	46	4,881	57	2,884
1946*	370	19,048	4†	134

Source: Ministry of Education Annual Reports.

* No figures were published during the war years. Thus no records exist for 1939/40 and 1945/6.

† These figures refer to schools recognized as efficient by the Ministry of Education. A large number of those schools which before the war had been voluntary, receiving a grant from the Board of Education, were taken over by the local authorities or became direct grant schools, which explains the fall in numbers in this column.

Comparable figures do not exist for nursery classes, nor for independent nursery schools or classes. It is not, therefore, possible to indicate the degree of expansion in these categories. There were, however, 166,405 children aged 2 to 5 on the registers of the public elementary schools in 1938. By 1946 this figure for 2 to 5s has risen to 184,700. It should be noted that the total child population had also increased. Before examining the reasons for the increases, it is necessary to document the administrative changes that took place in pre-school education which amounted to total reorganization. At the outset of war, facilities for this age group suffered as much from the chaos and dislocation brought about by evacuation as did those for older children. In spite of this upheaval, or perhaps because of it, the period is marked by extensive change in the structure of British education. Dent suggests that it was being transformed 'by the force of circumstance rather than by conscious endeavour, being transformed into "something new and strange" the shape of which we have not known before' (Dent, 1944). Many of the changes grew out of emergency measures which eventually became permanent, for example the extension of school meals. Although school meals had been established as early as 1906, they had never catered for more than a small minority of the school population; in the years immediately preceding the war this amounted to no more than 3 per cent. With the war they became an integral part of the school day, and this continued afterwards. However, changes in the structure of nursery school education did not become permanent and in 1945 it reverted to its pre-war form, although the increase in the numbers of children concerned, remained.

At the outbreak of the war all nursery schools, nursery classes and day nurseries were closed down in the neutral and reception areas until air-raid shelters could be provided. In most of the evacuation areas they were closed and not re-opened, or transferred to the country where they became residential nurseries. Thus no provision was made for the children remaining in evacuation areas, while in the reception areas the number of evacuated children under 5 far exceeded the number of places in evacuated nurseries. These children were billeted in private houses, and this gave rise to various problems. There were often large discrepancies between the standards of living of the evacuees and their hosts, and the latter were not always prepared for the 'disruption' accompanying small children. As a result, plans were made for the provision of nursery centres in these areas which children could attend daily. In 1940 the Ministry of Health and the Board of Education issued a joint circular urging local authorities to set up nursery centres in reception areas. The centres were:

To be established by joint action by the Local Education, Welfare and Reception Authority.

To be financed by the Local Reception Authority in conjunction with the Ministry of Health, who will regard it as part of the evacuation account. To be run as economically as possible, employing voluntary workers where possible.

To be confined to evacuated children: 'It should be emphasised that Nursery Classes are intended primarily for evacuated children. In some cases it may be possible for local children to be admitted if there is room for them after the evacuated children have been provided for or if withdrawals of evacuated children create vacancies.'

The setting up of Centres is justified and recommended (a) to relieve households where young children are billeted; (b) to free their mothers 'to occupy their day profitably' and (c) to cater for the needs of the young children themselves.

There were many obstacles to the implementation of this circular, and by the end of 1940 only six centres had been established. Premises were difficult to obtain, householders refusing to allow spare accommodation to be used for housing nursery centres, and dual control at the centre involved elaborate administrative arrangements. Also, under the terms of the circular, centres could not be established where they were needed most, that is in the evacuation areas, to which many children were returning, and in industrial regions, which were classified as neither evacuation nor reception areas. So in 1941 a new joint circular (Board of Education 1533, M.O.H. 2388, 1941) was sent out which swept some of these obstacles away, by advocating special War Nurseries which might be established in any area where they were wanted. They were to be financed by one central body, the Ministry of Health, and one local body, the Maternity and Child Welfare Departments. They were to meet the needs of all children in wartime, regardless of whether their mothers were local or evacuated and regardless of the nature of their employment. This was followed by a memorandum encouraging local authorities to co-operate with voluntary organizations in the development of wartime nurseries. The greatest share of responsibility for running the wartime nurseries, which can be regarded as a combination of the day nursery and the nursery school, fell on the Ministry of Health. The district inspectors of the Board of Education were responsible for advising the local health departments on all matters concerning the child aged 2 to 5, which was intended to ensure that the educational aspects were not neglected. The Ministry of Labour was also responsible for certain aspects of the provision. It undertook the siting of nurseries, assessing the industrial needs of the area concerned, the urgency of the demand for women's labour, the potential supply of the latter and how far a war nursery would help in securing more married women.

The need for married women in the labour force was important in bringing about further action. The full-time nurseries, which in some cases were open for twelve to fifteen hours per day, were open only to the children of mothers working full time, and this rule was adhered to carefully. A charge of 1s. per day was made, in exchange for which the child obtained free medical attention, meals and overalls. The full-time nursery can therefore, in many senses, be regarded as an agency of care rather than education. The part-time war nurseries which were open for school hours were available for a less limited sector of the child population, but gave priority to evacuated children, and those of mothers at work, including those working part-time.

Although the extension in provision as the result of the pressures of war on the family was considerable compared with earlier years, it could not be regarded as spectacular. The following quotation refers to the situation in 1943: 'the war-time growth of nursery facilities has still only scratched the surface of the problem to be solved' (Planning, 1943). The following table indicates the rate of expansion.

These figures refer to war-time nurseries. In addition to this there were in 1943 seventy nursery schools running on the old basis and 570 nursery classes catering together for approximately 28,000 children. Still a very small proportion of the total child population in the age group were receiving some kind of nursery education.

Table 4.2. Wartime development of nursery facilities

Date	Number of nurseries			Accommodation		
	part-time	full-time	total	part-time	full-time	total
July 1941	82	36	118	–	–	–
July 1942	144	500	644	–	–	–
Dec. 1942	154	975	1,129	5,117	42,468	47,585
July 1943	127	1,218	1,345	4,103	54,613	58,716
July 1944	112	1,446	1,558	3,710	67,546	71,256
Sept. 1944	109	1,450	1,559	3,625	68,181	71,806
Jan. 1945	104	1,431	1,535	3,501	67,749	71,250

Source: Ministry of Health Annual Reports.

However, contemporary commentators felt that the extension of female employment and the war nursery were affecting both public opinion and that of policy-makers. 'These good war-time nurseries are doing much to popularise the idea of a nursery stage in education and are opening the eyes of numerous parents to the high quality of the nursery school' (Dent, 1944, p. 81). The belief that parental responsibility would be weakened with the establishment of more facilities for the education of the young child lost its force in the emergency situation. It was now felt that married women ought to work.

There are various facts that support Dent's statement. The Nursery School Association increased its membership from 3,489 to 9,000 and its branches from twenty-six in 1938 to eighty-five. Schemes for educational reform provided by such bodies as the Council for Educational Advance,* placed the adequate provision of nursery schools and classes high up in their programmes for reform. The ideal of equality of opportunity in education was receiving considerable support at this time, and many saw the extension of pre-school education as one embodiment of this ideal. There was also a general movement for the extension of education in all directions. A leading article in The Times stated 'Nothing less than a service which provides for all ages which is given full responsibility for, and control over the entire period of childhood and youth up to the age of citizenship . . . could possibly hope to succeed' (The Times, 12 July 1942). In a later leader The Times went on to advocate 'full and proper provision for the pre-school child' (19 July 1942).

These sentiments were expressed in the formulation of new government policy. The White Paper on educational reconstruction advocated

Improvement of the facilities for the training of children below compulsory school age by the provision of nursery schools wherever they are needed. The duty to be laid on local authorities of making such provision as the Board of

* Chaired by R. H. Tawney and representing the TUC, the NUT, and the WEA and Co-operative Union Education Committee.

Education judge necessary.... Such schools are needed in all districts, as even when children come from good homes they can derive much benefit, both educational and physical, from attendance at nursery school (Board of Education, 1943).

This was the first time official recognition had been given to the notion of pre-school education for all rather than a special class of needy children. These proposals became part of the legislature with the passing of the 1944 Education Act, which stated that:

a local education authority shall, in particular, have regard . . . to the need for securing that provision is made for pupils who have not attained the age of five years by the provision of nursery schools or, where the authority consider the provision of such schools to be inexpedient by the provision of nursery classes in other schools (Section 8(2) G).

This is the statutory position today. The new Act led contemporary commentators to believe that a nursery stage in education would become a universal and accepted institution. It seemed as though the sequence of differentiation ending in the routinization of nursery education would soon be complete. A brief review of post-war developments will reveal that their optimism was unfounded.

In October 1945 Aneurin Bevan said in the House of Commons:

The existing financial arrangements will continue until 31st March 1946. I shall shortly be asking Welfare Authorities to work out before that date, in conjunction with the local education authorities, how a comprehensive nursery service consisting of nursery schools, nursery classes, day nurseries and other measures, can best be organised, using existing services as a basis, to meet the needs of their areas.

The government then sent out a circular asking the local authorities to review the current arrangement of wartime nurseries. A decision was to be made in accordance with the needs of local areas, as to which of these were to be converted into day nurseries and which into nursery schools or nursery classes, which to be closed, and which to be replaced by a system of registered and supervised daily guardians. The assessment of local needs was to take into account the requirements of industry in the area, and to consider the educational, social and health factors, relating to density of population, the 'character of the area' and 'local custom'. The meaning of the last two criteria is unclear. This circular was followed by two memoranda on the staffing and structure of facilities, and the training of staff. The first advocated small self-contained nursery schools with approximately forty children. The second laid out the details of a new scheme* to train nurses and assistants to work with teachers in the considerable expansion that was envisaged,

* Circular 59 Education, 126 Health advocates the setting up of the Nursery Nurses Examination Board, and the award of a Nursery Nurses' certificate after a two-year course.

and suggested that the 150,000 or so children under 5 in the ordinary classes of the infant school should be accommodated in properly constituted nursery classes.

Local authorities were asked to submit their schemes for approval. The return to the pre-war structure, with various different kinds of institutions, the continuation of dual control and the arrangement whereby local authorities might decide the form and extent of provision to be made, on the basis of vague concepts, such as 'the needs of the area', did not seem likely to produce the comprehensive nursery service of which Bevan had spoken. The need for mandatory rather than permissive legislation was expressed in a Fabian Society Pamphlet: 'permissive powers are not enough. Experience shows that they are usually operated only by the progressive public-spirited authorities' (Jones, 1945, p. 16).

However, during the years since the war various restrictions have arisen which have prevented even the most progressive authorities from achieving any substantial expansion. Those that made plans for expansion, such as the London County Council, were unable to carry them through. In the London School Plan published in 1947 ambitious schemes for nursery education were presented. It states that:

in 1939 about half the children in London aged three to five attended school, where they were mainly accommodated in 'babies' classes in infant schools. . . . A small number of children under five years of age including some two year olds, were attending nursery schools and classes where conditions were distinctly better than in the 'babies' classes. It will be necessary in the new act to follow up the magnificent pioneer work which has been done by nursery schools and nursery classes in much larger numbers for all children under five attending school.

They hoped to accommodate most children in new nursery schools on new sites, or in blocks of flats on housing estates, estimating that 1,350 units of forty pupils would be required to satisfy the demand for these schools. The remaining children would be accommodated in nursery classes, and their numbers might have to be higher than anticipated because of the greater costs per place in nursery schools.

Such expansion was not allowed to proceed, in London or elsewhere, for three reasons: the shortage of teachers in infant and primary schools; the dramatic rise in the birth-rate in 1946; and national economic difficulties which led to cuts being made in expenditure on the social services. In June 1948 the Ministry of Education sent out the first post-war circular dealing with the problem of teacher supply (Circular 175, 1948). It pointed out the difficulty in providing an adequate number of trained teachers for nursery schools and classes because of the demand for them in the infant schools. At the same time it suggested that the need for women workers in industry made it imperative to increase provision for the children of working women, particularly in the textile areas. For these reasons it recommended the employment of women who had received short emergency training courses in child care, to be approved as temporary teachers in nursery schools and nursery classes, stressing that these arrangements were temporary, and hoping that they would be changed as soon as an adequate supply of fully trained teachers was available. This circular is interesting in its departure from previous peacetime policy, as it recommended that provision should be extended because of the needs of industry and working mothers, and it accepted staff with more limited qualifications than those of teachers and nursery nurses. During the 1950s and 1960s the Ministry retreated from both of these policies, although shortages in the labour force in general and of teachers continued.

A year later the following request was made by the Ministry. 'Local education authorities will be aware that the economic difficulties of the country have called for a close review of Government expenditure' (Circular 210, 1949). They were told that no major change of policy would be made, but they were asked to exercise the strictest economy in the administration of education. Although this makes no specific reference to nursery education, it made the possibilities of expansion negligible, and may have encouraged some authorities to reduce expenditure on it. A further circular in 1951 on educational expenditure resulted in four county councils deciding to end their nursery education as a measure of economy* and other local education authorities making proposals to contract nursery school education (Circular 242, 1951). 1952 marked the end of a period of expansion in the provision of nursery *schools* which has not been repeated since. In 1946 there were 374 maintained schools (including direct grant schools); by 1952 there were 480; in 1965 there were only 477. However, from 1948—52 the number of nursery *classes* declined from 2,457 to 1,965. This was due to the need for extra accommodation in the infant schools for children of compulsory school age during the 'bulge' years.

By the middle-1950s the problem of over-large classes began to affect policy towards pre-school education. Two circulars were sent out on the admission of children under 5 to maintained primary schools (280, 1954 and 313, 1956). The first asked local education authorities only to admit children under 5 if their admission did not impede reduction in the size of classes in the compulsory sector, and if the conditions for the under-5s were of a suitable standard. The second maintained that there was then an even stronger case for limiting the entry of children under 5, in the interests of older children. Local education authorities were therefore asked to review their admission policies and to ensure that by January 1957 'the numbers of children under five then attending school does not exceed the number in attendance in January 1956'. This meant that no more new nursery classes could be set up, beyond the transference of places used by children under 5 in the infant schools in 1956 into nursery class places.

* However, at the Annual Conference of Education Associations in 1953 a proposal put forward by one chief education officer, that local education authorities should charge for nursery education, was heavily defeated.

Why was this restriction introduced when the peak of the 'bulge' had passed through the infant schools? During 1955 the numbers of children attending infant schools decreased by approximately 120,000, and it was estimated that there would be a further decrease in the number of infants during 1956 and 1957. Apparently the restriction was made to reduce the size of classes in the infant and junior schools, and to free more teachers for the secondary schools which would soon have to bear the brunt of the high post-war birth-rate. It was felt that an increase in the number of under-5s would prevent the transfer of teachers into secondary schools and make it harder to reduce the sizes of classes in primary schools. It was said that, even if some areas had no difficulty recruiting teachers at the primary or secondary stage, they should remember the needs of those that did, and should not be exempt from controlling the admission of children under 5. This policy seems to involve many untested assumptions about the transferability and mobility of teachers, both between age groups and different areas.

A further circular in 1958 told authorities, 'it is imperative in the present economic situation of the country, that the utmost economy should be observed' (Ministry of Education Circular 334, 1958). Six areas were marked out in which economies might be made, one of these being the admission of children under 5 to the infant schools. This was followed by Circular 8 of May 1960 which, with the addition of two addenda, remains government policy to the present day. The circular forbade any expansion of the number of places in either nursery schools or nursery classes.

No resources can at present be spared for the expansion of nursery education and in particular no teachers can be spared who might otherwise work with children of compulsory school age.

At the same time the Minister values the excellent work being done in nursery schools and classes, and is anxious to ensure its continuance, both for its own sake and as a base for expansion in the future when the time comes for a full application of the principles set out in the 1944 Act.

Authorities were recommended to maintain existing schools and classes at their current level. In addition a recommendation was made that some of the existing full-time provision might become part-time, which would allow a greater number of children some pre-school education. This was based on the view that:

During and immediately after the war one of the main purposes served by nursery schools and classes was to release mothers of young children for work of national importance. To serve this purpose it was necessary for nursery education to be full-time. The Minister believes that it is now widely understood that nursery education, in common with all primary and secondary education of which it forms a part is provided in the interests of the children. The aim is always to meet the needs of the particular child.

Once again the educational needs of the child were used as the rationale behind policy decisions. Thus it was argued that 'normal children' from 'normal homes' may well need part-time rather than full-time education, and change towards the former would give 'a better introduction to school life to twice the number of children'. At the same time the proviso was made that certain children would continue to need a full day at school, and certain mothers would be 'forced by circumstances' to work. The use of this phrase seems misleading in the light of current trends in the employment of married women including the mothers of young children. In 1962 it was estimated that half a million married women working had children under 5 (see Hansard, 21 February 1966, col. 24).

The first addendum was sent out in July 1964. This relaxed the restrictions on the expansion of nursery classes, where new provision would enable married women to return to teaching, who would otherwise be prevented from doing so through lack of provision for their own pre-school-age children. Addendum No. 2, in December 1965, reported that only a few authorities had made use of the above concession, although more planned to do so. It pointed out 'that the existing system of nursery schools and classes already produces more teachers than it consumes, i.e. that the number of qualified women teachers whose service in maintained schools is facilitated by their children's attendance at maintained nursery schools or classes, exceeds the number of teachers who are employed in the maintained nursery system'. For this reason the addendum introduced more flexible arrangements and more exact guidance whereby authorities might expand their nursery class provision as long as they provided a certain proportion of teachers, giving priority to the children of returning teachers. Thus there was some return to the notion of pre-school education as a method of freeing women for employment, although the Minister took pains 'to reaffirm that nursery education is primarily designed for the benefit of children, and is only secondarily of value in helping to promote the return to service of married women teachers'.*

This completes the description of the government policy towards maintained pre-school education since the war. The following table shows the growth of maintained provision, which since 1956 has been negligible.

These figures show that only a small proportion of the age group has been catered for by maintained provision. Does this indicate that dissatisfaction with the family's ability to undertake the socialization of the young child discussed in the previous chapter is limited to a small proportion of the population whose needs are satisfied by this provision? Does it mean that general dissatisfaction does exist amongst a larger proportion of the population, but that it is an underlying dissatisfaction with few outward expressions which somehow fails to be communicated to politicians and administrators, who are responsible for making provision? Does it mean that obvious and manifest dissatisfaction does exist, but that it is not solved by the provision of pre-school education by the state, because of conflict with

* It should be noted that the addendum stresses the cost of any building work must be part of the minor works programme, which limits the expansion possible.

Table 4.3.   **Provision for children under 5 in nursery and primary schools, 1947–65**

| | Numbers of maintained nursery schools and children in them | | | |
| | Schools | | Accommodation | |
Year	LEA	direct grant	LEA	direct grant
1947	353	17	18,173	875
1955	464	20	23,127	817
1965	461	16	23,649	1,303

| | Numbers of children under 5 in primary schools | | | | |
Year	Under 3	3–4	4–5	Total	Estimated population aged 2–4	Per cent
1947	953	32,437	151,310	184,700	1,964,000	9·4
1955	76	13,226	139,488	152,790	1,973,000	7·7
1965	208	9,967	187,301	197,476	2,337,800	8·4

Source: Ministry of Education Annual Reports; Department of Education and Science, Statistics of Education.

other aims, or because of lack of resources? The evidence seems to point to the third of these possibilities.

The pressure to expand

Taking the length of waiting lists and a few surveys which consider this question as an indication, there has been a high demand, which by far outweighs the supply, for places in maintained nursery schools and classes, and there has been a great increase in pre-school education provided from sources other than the state. This growth appears to have been particularly rapid since 1960, when Circular 8 was published, destroying hopes of expansion in the maintained sector. The question must be considered as to why the demand for this facility has been so powerful that it has induced people who have failed to obtain a place in the state system to buy it privately* or to set up cooperative agencies of their own?

The answer seems to lie in various demographic, economic and social changes, which have put pressure on the structure of the family and the roles of its various members, in particular the wife and mother. Some of these changes had started in the pre-war period and have been referred to already.

* There is, of course, a small section of parents who will prefer private education for their children whatever alternatives are available.

Since the war they have been accelerated,* with the exception of the trend towards smaller families. However, the post-war increase in family size has by no means meant a return to the large family of the mid-Victorian era and it does not affect the validity of the statements made earlier (see pp. 54—5, Ch. 3) with reference to the belief that children need the companionship of others of a similar age, which has led to demands for pre-school education. Even in the three- or four-child family, the spacing of children is likely to limit the degree of companionship a child of pre-school age may obtain from its siblings.

The second important demographic change is the consistent trend towards earlier marriage. This has meant that the family responsibilities of women are over at an earlier stage in their lives than in the past. It is not yet clear whether this has any effect on the demand for nursery education. Are younger mothers more dissatisfied in a domestic role than older mothers? Do they feel less willing or able to care for their children throughout the day until they are 5? There is no evidence to indicate this, although there may be indirect effects. Smaller families, an earlier age of marriage and longer life have freed many women for outside employment (see Stewart, 1963). This is likely to enhance the isolation felt by the mother of young children, who is not free. She may have fewer neighbours at home during the day on whom she can rely for adult company. Feelings of deprivation, frustration and lack of status are likely to increase when others are seen to have achieved the goal (that is a job) desired by those who are deprived of it. The lack of status involved in the full-time care of young children at home is a frequent complaint of mothers. 'Being at home all day is terribly boring, frustrating and to my mind *inferior*' (Gavron, 1966).

Changes in patterns of employment are also beginning to have a direct effect on mothers' desire and ability to take full responsibility for the care of their children, in that numbers of women with children of pre-school age are themselves working. No national statistics are available which would indicate the exact size of this trend. Douglas found in his national sample that 15 per cent of mothers were working by the time their children were 4 years old (Douglas and Blomfield, 1958), but this figure is now sixteen years out of date. Somewhat later Jephcott found in a sample of women in Bermondsey that 20 per cent of mothers of children under 5 were working (Jephcott, 1962), and later still a study carried out in Aberdeen (Thompson and Finlayson, 1963) found that from a sample of predominantly working-class women 35 per cent had worked at some time during the four years since the birth of their first child. Gavron found that 37 per cent of her sample of

* It is not intended to discuss the nature of these changes in detail but rather to list them, then indicate their relevance to the growth of pre-school education. For a more detailed discussion, see H. Gavron, *The Captive Wife* (1966), Part I; A. Myrdal and V. Klein, *Women's Two Roles* (1956); V. Klein, *Britain's Married Women Workers* (1965); R. Fletcher, *Family and Marriage* (1962); C. Rosser and C. Harris, *The Family and Social Change. A Study of Family and Kinship in a South Wales Town* (1965).

middle-class mothers continued working after the birth of their first child and 29 per cent of working-class mothers did so.* It is dangerous to generalize from small samples of women from particular areas but it would appear from these that there is a growing trend towards employment.†

Various changes in the role of married women have occurred as a result of the demand for them in the labour market. The proportion of women who give up work at marriage is now small. It is not until the first child is born that a substantial proportion opt out of employment. The independence gained through working outside the home has been a major factor in the decline of the authoritarian husband and the growth of a more equal share in decision-making by husbands and wives (Blood and Wolfe, 1960). The division of labour in the undertaking of household chores and the care of children has become less clear-cut. The only piece of English evidence on the participation of husbands in the latter is the work of the Newsons in Nottingham (J. and E. Newson, 1963). This finds that husbands play a considerable part in the care of their children when the latter are under 1 year old and applies to all social classes, although less to the unskilled manual worker. From further work by the same authors it is apparent that this continues during the child's pre-school years, 51 per cent of fathers taking a 'highly participant' role and a further 40 per cent taking a 'fairly participant' role (J. and E. Newson, 1968).

It might be argued that these changes in the roles of husband and wife would allow the mother greater freedom, and make her task in the social-ization and care of the young less irksome. However, partly because of her earlier independence, this does not seem to be the case. She appears to suffer from role conflict in her position as a mother and her desire for status in the external world. This seems particularly true of the educated, middle-class mother. Her schooling and later training have prepared her for a career which is destined to be relinquished after a short period for the very different experience of child-rearing.

The belief that it is motherhood rather than marriage which gives rise to such conflicts of role is reinforced by evidence from Gavron's sample of women. She writes 'it is children not marriage that present problems of role and expectation to the women of this survey' (Gavron, 1966, p. 58). She found that the difficulties of adjustment experienced by working-class mothers were greater than those felt by their middle-class counterparts, and the great majority in both groups reported boredom and loneliness. Mirra

* Since these studies a National Survey found that 14 per cent of mothers with children aged 0–2 were working, and 19 per cent of mothers with children aged 3–4 were working. See Audrey Hunt, *A Survey of Women's Employment* (1968).

† This has also been noted in the U.S.A. where more adequate statistics are available. In 1954 one in seven women with pre-school-age children were working. See M. F. Nimkoff, 'The Increase in Married Women in the Labour Force', *Transactions of the Third World Congress of Sociology*. By 1960 this proportion had reached one in five. See F. Ivan Nye and Lois W. Hoffman (eds.), *The Employed Mother in the United States* (1963).

D

Komarovsky, working in the United States, has found considerable empirical evidence of this kind of role conflict. She states that 'profound changes in the roles of women during the last century have been accompanied by innumerable contradictions and inconsistencies ... cultural norms are often functionally unsuited to the social situations to which they apply ... sometimes culturally defined roles are adhered to in the face of new conditions without a conscious realisation of the discrepancies involved' (Komarovsky, 1946), and in a later article 'behaviour patterns at some stage become dysfunctional at another' (Komarovsky, 1950).

It is not only the woman's role before motherhood which puts pressure on her ability to socialize and care for her child. The role of the child, as a precious individual to be carefully nourished and protected, creates heavy demands on its parents, particularly its mother. A mass of literature on the physical and psychological needs of young children has permeated the popular press and women's magazines. The following quotation indicates the kind of effect this readily available advice may have: 'I used to think that I would go on working, but I then read articles and books about leaving little children and, well, I decided I would not' (Gavron, 1966, p. 68). Most parents appear to take their responsibilities seriously. A second quotation from a working-class mother illustrates the child-centred attitudes of today. 'People nowadays think more about what's good for the children from the children's point of view. Everything I do with him I try to do the best thing *for him*, I'm *thinking about* that all the time...' (J. and E. Newson, 1968, p. 258). The role of the child in the family has changed. Large numbers are no longer necessary as an insurance against the death of some of them. It has been argued that there has been a movement away from quantity towards quality (Musgrove, 1961), and that increases in real incomes have 'intensified rather than satisfied the desire to give each child more' (Blood and Wolfe, 1960, p. 121). The growth of knowledge on the physical and educational needs of the young child has been described in the previous chapter. The belief that the child needs adequate facilities for play and contact with other children has become widespread, and is confirmed by the few empirical studies of parental attitudes towards children of this age group.

Further, in spite of better standards of living, the ability of parents to cope with the demands of higher standards in the care of young children has been reduced in some ways. The growth of 'high-flat living' has meant that many young children spend large parts of their day cooped up in small flats with their mothers. In the past they would at least have had the freedom offered by the street. An inquiry into the play provision of children living in high flats in London was carried out in 1960. None of the estates in the survey provided facilities for supervised play. Most of the children 'are rarely or never away from mother and play mainly in the flat with their siblings or by themselves.... The chief preoccupation of the mothers was with safety and the lack of socialising and educational opportunities for their young children. . . . Altogether 80% expressed the wish to have the use of a playroom (as distinct from playground) and 75% a nursery school' (Maizels, 1961, p. 34).

Lastly, the decline of the extended family has probably contributed to the isolation felt by the young mother and the extent to which she alone must take responsibility for her children. This process of decline is not complete; a number of studies have shown this, particularly in the older working-class areas of large towns (Young and Willmott, 1957). There is still a considerable amount of contact between generations, but it would seem that the economic and demographic changes already described must change the nature of this contact. Since women are marrying and having children at a younger age, they will become grandmothers earlier. Because of the tendency to return to work, they will not be available to spend part of the day with their married daughters and relieve them of some of their child-minding duties. Increasingly contacts are likely to be reduced to week-end visiting and, where possible, telephone conversations. Occupational and geographical mobility further accentuate this trend, a factor of particular importance for the middle-class family. Jane Hubert found a high degree of mobility amongst a small sample of middle-class families in North London. Relationships between kin, although based on strong ties of affection, tended to be infrequent, and did not involve 'intense interchange of contact and services or mutual dependence' (Hubert, 1965). Help was given at times of crisis, particularly by mothers during their daughters' confinements, but in normal circumstances it was not expected.

This has been confirmed by other studies carried out in the United States. Ruth Albrecht found that only 5 per cent of grandparents regularly took care of their grandchildren, and that 19 per cent of grandparents took on child-supervision jobs occasionally. The predominant value system appeared to be that parents should be responsible for their children and that grandparents should only intervene in special circumstances such as the birth of a child, illness or bereavement (Albrecht, 1954).

It remains to discuss the evidence that such pressures, which lead to dissatisfactions with the family's ability to socialize the young child, generate in turn a demand for nursery education. What kind of symptoms of disturbance have appeared during the post-war period? Who has been responsible for voicing dissatisfaction and who has taken practical steps towards solving the problem? There have been two major symptoms: the growth of pressure groups, attempting to persuade the government to change their policy towards pre-school education; and the frequent appearance of letters in the press from women complaining of their lot at home with small children and asking for better nursery school facilities.

The number of the pressure groups involved has grown since before the war, when the Nursery School Association was the only body solely concerned to promote the growth of pre-school education and a few other organizations took some interest in encouraging its promotion. Since 1960 a small-scale social movement has grown up. A social movement has been defined as 'a joint endeavour of a considerable group of persons to alter or change the course of events by their joint activities' (Burgess, 1943—4, pp. 269—75). It does not necessarily imply revolutionary activity or co-ordination of the various groups. The movement for pre-school education has been reformative rather than revolutionary and the various pressure groups have cooperated rather than co-ordinated.

The Nursery School Association has continued its work on the same lines as before the war, with few changes in its objectives, organization and technique of spreading the movement. Yet there have been some adjustments to the content of its work. For example, in the second decade since the war it has been increasingly involved in advisory work on the setting up of nursery schools. It receives many requests for information on all aspects of nursery education including administration, plans for new schools, equipment, teaching techniques and the training of nursery assistants and teachers. With this increase of work of an advisory kind there appears to have been a reduction in its propaganda activities, and more emphasis on the working out of standards for nursery schools and the consideration of the content of pre-school education. Their publicity campaigns seem to have lacked their pre-war and wartime intensity and this is perhaps reflected in their reduction in membership from 9,000 in 1945 to approximately 5,000 in 1965.*

Its most important contribution in the years after the war was the fostering of international contacts by its Chairman, Lady Allen of Hurtwood, which led to the formation of an international federation of associations concerned with nursery education. This association which became known as the Organisation Mondiale pour l'Éducation Préscolaire was founded in Paris in 1946, Alva Myrdal being elected the first Chairman and Lady Allen Vice-Chairman. In 1948 the first of its biannual conferences was held, and extracts from the resolutions illustrate the philosophy of the movement. Having expressed concern with the social conditions in which children were living in many countries, they continue:

In addition to such betterment of material circumstances during early childhood, the educational care of young children must be improved as far as present day knowledge and resources permit. The greater understanding of cause and effect in the forming of personality, which has been won through advance in the science of education, must be spread much more efficiently to all countries and to all groups within the countries. . . . This conference believes that in good nursery schools and kindergartens, harmonious living with other people can best be learned. A good nursery education supplements but does not attempt to supersede the home where the basic needs of all

* In 1950 Lillian de Lissa, who had been a prominent member for many years, wrote: 'Has the time not come to revive the crusading spirit of the early days and to give it precedence over all else we are doing? Inspiration is infectious and would attract more of the members we want.' Neither inspiration nor a crusading spirit has characterized the Association recently.

children should be met. . . . We want to work for a wider understanding of early childhood education and to further the right kind of nursery education. To achieve this we must be able to appeal effectively to local and national authorities and to co-operate with UNESCO, WHO and non-governmental international organisations on all matters concerned with early childhood education. We must share all knowledge and mobilise all forces for progress.

The Utopian element noted in Chapter 3 is apparent here in the belief that pre-school education will promote harmonious living, as is the desire to adhere to existing norms and values in the stress on the home as the prime socializing agent. It is difficult to assess how effective such international organizations are in promoting the goals they set out to achieve. The major contribution of the Organisation Mondiale pour l'Éducation Préscolaire has been the holding of international conferences on various aspects of early childhood education. These must serve to 'share all knowledge' and act as an important means of communications between interested groups in different countries, but that they or any of the organization's other activities 'mobilise all forces for progress' is unlikely.

In Britain the Nursery School Association continued to hold conferences on the content of nursery school education, to write to the press and to initiate questions in Parliament. The Nursery School Association's annual reports and news-sheets also note the increase in private and independent nursery schools. This is first recorded in 1948 when a resolution was passed demanding the registration and inspection of all privately administered nurseries and schools for young children. The Nurseries and Child Minders Act aiming to ensure this was passed later in 1948. In 1961 the extension of such schools was noted and two motions were passed, the first advocating that advice and information should be made available by the Association to those wishing to set up nursery schools, and the second advocating representations to the Ministry of Education to safeguard standards. Much of the work of the Association is now taken up with the first of these tasks.

Its major rival is the Pre-school Playgroups Association. This organization was founded in 1961 in direct response to the frustration felt by a group of mothers, with the continued existence of Circular 8/60, with little hope of it being rescinded.* A number of interesting differences exist between this organization and the Nursery School Association. The first of these is in the membership of the two organizations. From a subjective impression and a study of the officers of the Pre-school Playgroups Association it would appear that the majority of its members are the mothers of young children themselves or of slightly older children, women whose experience with pre-school-age children is sufficiently close to motivate membership. Many of these

* A nursery school campaign was started by Mrs Belle Tutaev during 1961. It began with 200 members, apparently all of them mothers of children under 5. 3,000 signatures were collected for a petition asking for the withdrawal of Circular 8/60 which was presented at the Ministry of Education in January 1961. Most of the signatures were those of mothers with small children who would like but were unable to attend nursery schools.

women are actively involved in the running of what have come to be known as pre-school playgroups. Their motives can be described as 'goal-orientated'. That is, they subscribe to an ideology and set of goals, but at the same time they are motivated by the belief that they will benefit from the social changes to be effected if the movement is successful.

If the officers of the Nursery School Association are representative of its members, a far smaller proportion of them are mothers of young children and a larger proportion have 'altruistic'* motives, that is they are guided by ideals which they believe will lead to a more efficient or more just society and are not motivated by benefits they might themselves obtain. But a considerable proportion of the executive are still nursery school teachers, who perhaps have vested interests in the growth of nursery education, and therefore belong to the 'goal-orientated' group. The aims of the two organizations are broadly similar but there are differences in the stress each one puts on particular aims.

The Pre-school Playgroups Association is concerned primarily with encouraging the growth of playgroups set up by voluntary and cooperative effort, rather than with the provision of maintained nursery schools by the state, which has been the major target of the Nursery School Association.† A playgroup is defined by the Pre-school Playgroups Association as 'a group of from six to thirty children aged two and a half to five years who play together regularly daily or several sessions weekly'. The difference between a playgroup and a non-maintained nursery school is negligible. The latter is sometimes run on a full-time basis, whereas playgroups are almost always run on the basis of attendance at a morning or afternoon session. Secondly, a larger proportion of private nursery schools are run on a profit-making basis, playgroups usually making small charges to cover or contribute to costs only. The Minister's refusal to promise any changes with regard to Circular 8/60 led the Nursery Schools Campaign, which preceded the formation of the Pre-school Playgroups Association, to concentrate on an alternative form of provision, rather than continuing to expend all their energies in fighting for more state nursery schools. The New Zealand Federation of Nursery Play Centres Associations provided a precedent. Playgroups for pre-school-age children, run on a cooperative basis by parents, frequently at community centres, and receiving state aid, were well established there. The Pre-school Playgroups Association has emulated this system, with the exception of

* See C. Wendell King, *Social Movements in the United States* (1956), for a typology of the motives of members of social movements.

† For the formal aims of the Nursery School Association see Chapter 3, pp. 42—4. Pre-school Playgroups Association states that it has three objects:

'1. To encourage and promote the formation of local playgroups for children between the ages of two and a half to five years.

2. To encourage the study of the needs and problems of such children and to promote public interest in and recognition of their educational needs and in particular that of education by means of organised recreation.

3. To hold lectures, discussions, conferences and meetings and publish magazines, books, pamphlets and papers dealing with the above mentioned objects.'

financial help from the state which has not been forthcoming. The growth of playgroups since 1961 has been rapid and is an indication of the success of the Association. In September 1965 there were approximately 600 groups affiliated to the Association, and 950 members. Since then the growth of playgroups has been such that the number of affiliated groups has more than doubled.

The early work of the Pre-school Playgroups Association in considering ways in which dissatisfactions with the lack of state provision might be ameliorated represented the stages of proliferation of ideas and then specification. As a result of the failure to implement earlier ideas a new formula for aiding the family in early socialization has been worked out, with the conception of the playgroup and this is now being implemented on a fairly large scale. The major problem which faces both the central organization and local branches and individual groups is their lack of financial resources. Only a few local authorities have given grants to playgroups: routinization has not yet been reached. The degree of consensus on the value of pre-school education is not yet great enough to give rise to regular financial help being made from public funds to agencies carrying it out. There is no statutory means whereby playgroups may receive help, and grants are given by the use of various loopholes, usually the 1937 Physical Training and Recreation Act, Section 4 of which gives local authorities the power to help voluntary organizations. The Pre-school Playgroups Association has been active in trying to obtain more support of this kind and to change the statutory system by direct contact with local authorities, the press and the lobbying of Members of Parliament.* The rest of its work has been largely concerned with the laying down of standards for playgroups, and with efforts to obtain training by correspondence courses or at evening classes for women running groups.†

In 1965 a new organization calling itself the National Campaign for Nursery Education was set up. It is run by a small working committee and a National Council, which consists of representatives of a large number of different organizations, interested in the extension of nursery education. It aims to 'press for increased provision of educational and play facilities for children under five, with special emphasis on nursery schools and classes, as promised by the 1944 Education Act'. It is also interested in improving our knowledge of the need and demand for pre-school education by further research.

---

* The Department of Education and Science has given PPA an annual grant of £3,000 for three years from 1966 to help it continue its work.

† This issue has given rise to friction between PPA and the NSA, the latter deploring the use of untrained women to staff agencies caring for young children, the former arguing that they are mothers with considerable experience in handling children, who can be further helped by part-time courses. In fact a survey carried out by PPA revealed that a surprisingly high proportion of groups (53·5 per cent) were run by a qualified supervisor and 81 per cent of the groups had either a qualified supervisor, or assistant, or contact with a qualified person, who acted in an advisory capacity. See PPA, October 1965.

None of the other organizations at present promoting facilities for pre-school education has nursery education as its sole aim. It is a new interest for most of them, usually developing since 1960. Instead of detailed accounts of all these organizations, a few examples will be given of some of them, and the roles they play, which vary from the actual provision of pre-school education to occasional demands for it. The most important member of the first category is the Save the Children Fund. Its work began in this field during the depression, when it set up and financed emergency nursery schools in areas of high unemployment, and this work continued during the war. Since 1945 the Fund has set up and administered playgroups in urban areas of high density population. As would be expected from their location in run-down working-class areas, they cater for the under-privileged child and in this sense belong to the tradition of the early nursery schools. Many of the children attending have been recommended by Health Visitors, usually because of the inadequacies of their home environment. The groups are financed by subscriptions to the Fund, although in some cases accommodation or grants have been provided by local authorities. The Save the Children Fund runs twenty-five groups in large industrial towns in the provinces and thirty-six groups in London. The founding of new groups in recent years has been motivated in part by the conviction that free play is important for the full mental and physical development of the child.* This was recognized over a century ago by Robert Owen and Froebel but it is only in the years since the Second World War that the idea has become widespread enough to give rise to considerable provision for education through play.

The Adventure Playground has been one method by which this has been achieved and play parks another (see Benjamin, 1966 and Turner, 1962). Originally they were devised for older children and, with a few exceptions, are confined to London. It was found that resources could be utilized to their fullest by using buildings, equipment and outdoor space empty during school hours, for children under 5. At the Adventure Playgrounds morning and afternoon sessions are run on a similar basis to a playgroup, and a midday meal is provided by the mothers. Attendance is more informal than that of most playgroups and it is therefore difficult to obtain an accurate figure of the number of children involved. This is even more true of the 'under-5' provision at play parks. In that attendance is informal, and therefore often irregular, and that mothers must stay in the vicinity of the play park, the original definition of pre-school education does not apply. Nevertheless for many of the children the experience obtained is not dissimilar to that at a part-time nursery school. Since 1960 the National Playing Fields Association has also become concerned with facilities for children under 5. It has encouraged the use of football pavilions during the week, and has offered grants to members of the Pre-school Playgroups Association to start groups. It has

---

* In 1955 there were only five SCF playgroups. Thus fifty-six have been established between 1955 and 1965.

put pressure on local authority housing departments to provide staff. The other important groups demanding more pre-school education are the women's organizations.*

The work of most of these organizations can be equated with steps four, five and six (proliferation of ideas, their specification and implementation) of the model of structural differentiation, although not all of them actually reach the sixth stage of the implementation of new agencies. The work of some of them was preceded by letters to the press† representing step two of the model (symptoms of disturbance) in a mild form. The letters have usually arisen from articles on either the higher education of women or on the problems of housewives.‡

One of the standard arguments put forward during the 1950s in favour of higher education for women, which was under criticism owing to the wastage through early marriage, was that highly educated women would make better mothers. In the past five years a number of commentators have challenged this, suggesting that women may be dissatisfied with their role as mothers because an academic education has ill-prepared them for this role. This sometimes leads on to the suggestion that the content of women's education should be changed, and that university education is undesirable for them. Whatever the merits of this argument, it has usually given rise to outraged letters, mostly from women, by no means all of them with experience of higher education. Many of these letters indicate the feelings of frustration of women who give up employment to look after their children, or alternatively feelings of guilt if they continue to work. 'While housekeeping and looking after children use up a great deal of what an intellectual woman has to give to others, there is still enough capacity for service left over to make her feel that her life is not being used to the utmost, and like anyone else who sees life slipping away only partly used and partly enjoyed she is frustrated' (*Guardian,* 22 January 1960).

Increased provision of pre-school education is one of the solutions advocated in this correspondence. For example, one woman wrote, 'The wife with young children most needs some relief from family pressures and routine, yet is least likely to achieve it. The children need a change from mother too; all

---

* For example, in 1945 the London Women's Parliament sent a deputation to the Minister of Health with representatives from local authorities, nursery school teachers and mothers, demanding improvements in provision and since this date similar groups have supported similar demands.

† For example the origins of PPA can be traced to a letter to the *Guardian* in 1961, which led to the formation of the Nursery School Campaign and later the founding of the Association.

‡ For example the *Guardian*, January 1960, correspondence arising out of an article by Lois Mitchison on 'The Price of Educating Women', the *Observer*, September 1964, after an article by Sir John Newsom on the education of women. The *Guardian*, February 1960, article by Betty Jerman on 'Living in Suburbia', The *Observer*, May 1961, three articles by Elaine Grande on 'Miserable Married Women', The *Sunday Times*, July 1963, two articles by Elizabeth Gundrey entitled 'Breaking Out of Purdah' and 'The Way Back to Work'.

the affection in the world does not prevent mutual boredom at times. This is a national problem. Can't we have a really energetic policy of home helps and nursery school organisation to give mothers at least part time relief and the chance to exercise talent and training?' (*Sunday Times*, 28 July 1963). Other solutions were also suggested, such as better facilities to enable mothers to take their children with them to clubs or on shopping expeditions. A 'National Register of Liberal Minded Housebound Wives' was set up as a result of one aggrieved correspondence. In a short time this had fifty regional organizers and 3,000 members.*

The work of Hannah Gavron dispels the notion that education is the prime factor causing dissatisfaction amongst the mothers of young children; it is by no means confined to the graduate wife or even the middle-class wife. One of the solutions put forward, that is nursery schools, also appears to be advocated by other socio-economic groups. The majority of both middle- and working-class women in Gavron's sample wanted their children to attend nursery schools, and there were many complaints about the lack of provision. Eighty-eight per cent of the middle-class mothers either sent or said they would send their children if a good school were available. This compares with 79 per cent of the working-class sample. None of the latter group had children attending nursery schools, whereas 33 per cent of the middle-class sample had one or more children attending. Whether this difference can be explained entirely by the use of private pre-school education, which would not be attainable because of cost for the working-class group, or whether the middle-class group were having greater success in obtaining scarce places in maintained schools, is not known. A survey in Cambridge taking a random sample of mothers of children aged between 2½ and 4½ found that 27 per cent of the respondents had children undergoing some kind of pre-school education;† 40 per cent intended sending their children later, and the remaining 33 per cent would not send their children. However, over 50 per cent of this group would have liked to send their children had they been able to obtain a place at a nearby school or afford the fees of a private establishment. Once again the professional-managerial group were more successful in obtaining places for their children than lower social classes (Cambridge Association for the Advancement of State Education 1965). Another survey carried out in Derby in 1964 found 82 per cent of a sample of parents were in favour of nursery education (Derby Association for the Development of State Education, 1964).

A further indication of the high demand for pre-school education, which has given rise to the increase of private provision, is the length of waiting lists.

* The spread of the Women's Liberation Movement in Britain may lead to more militant demands for better facilities to care for children, including more nursery education.

† This figure is surprisingly high. One of the reasons is that Cambridgeshire has more maintained places per 1,000 population than any other county in England and Wales and most of these places are concentrated in Cambridge itself.

The Save the Children Fund has reported lists with up to 250 names for groups with places for twenty-five children. The National Union of Teachers carried out a survey of maintained nursery education in 1962. In a sample of 267 nursery schools and 405 nursery classes, almost all the latter had a waiting list and there was often a considerable time lag between application and obtaining a place. This was even greater for nursery schools for which:

nearly two-thirds of the lists contain more than 75 names, i.e. a list that is longer than the size of the average school of 61 pupils. Almost half the schools have lists of 100 or more names. The average waiting list has 108 names, which is one and three-quarter times the size of the average school's roll. In other words, the total demand for places (i.e. including those who have obtained entry) exceeds the supply on a ratio of eleven to four. More than half the schools have a higher number of names on their waiting lists than they have pupils in their schools (National Union of Teachers, 1964).

The above ratio is an underestimate of demand in that it does not take into account areas where there were no maintained nursery schools, nor is it able to estimate the extra numbers that would have applied, had waiting lists not been closed. In one third of the nursery schools the average time lag between applying for and receiving admission was over two years.

In the preceding pages it has been suggested that the growth of pre-school education during the post-war years can be explained by wider social changes, in particular changes affecting the structure and functions of the family and the role of women. At the same time, resistance to these changes has limited the growth of educational facilities for young children. The argument that pre-school education on a large scale will encourage more married women to work outside the home has been invoked more frequently than any other by the opponents of nursery education. It rests on the assumption that this is undesirable and that the family as a social institution will be undermined as a result. Those who disagree either árgue that nursery education does not encourage mothers to work, or alternatively that there is no reason why they should not work as long as they are sure their children are being well cared for at a nursery school of some kind. The lack of consensus is thus not directed at the educational advantages or disadvantages of pre-school education itself but at the indirect effects which it may have on the family.

Who holds these conflicting views? What are the attitudes of the producer? The producers of state-maintained pre-school education, that is those who make decisions about its scale, are politicians and civil servants at the centre, and council members and local government officers at the local level. Those at the centre have asserted their belief in the value of pre-school education and their hope to see the clauses of the 1944 Education Act implemented as soon as possible, ever since the passing of that Act. They stress that the restrictions are a matter of temporary expediency and not based on any issue of principle. This has been expressed in circulars sent to local authorities, in answers to various deputations and in replies by the Ministers concerned in the House of Commons. At the local level it is impossible to generalize about the attitude of different power groups and the form conflict has taken if any. The professed attitude of the Department of Education fits in with a general trend towards the extension of education, in all directions, and with a trend towards greater specialization of function within the system, thus the encouragement to remove children under 5 from the infants' classes in primary schools to special nursery classes of their own.

Vaizey reports that 'private education as a whole has declined relative to public education since 1920' (Vaizey, 1958, p. 151), and there has been a growth of state intervention in education as in other fields such as health and social security. There has, however, been opposition towards this increasing intervention by various groups in power who may be regarded as the producers of these services, or as having influence on the producers. The extremist members of this group have regarded such intervention as either redundant, a sign of weakness on the part of the British people, or even communistic and anti-individualistic. Although such extreme views do not seem to have been expressed by those who wish to restrict the growth of pre-school education, it is possible that such beliefs may colour their dislike of this institution.

In a later chapter it is intended to examine the processes by which decisions are made by local education authorities, with reference to pre-school education. In doing this the identification of some of those who hold negative attitudes should be possible. Light will be thrown on the question of how far conflict over the supply of pre-school education is part of the classical conflict between those who wish to extend the social services and those who advocate a *laissez-faire* approach. The relationship between consumer and producer should become clearer. How far has pressure by the consumer been successful in particular areas? The question is complicated by the fact that the consumer, in this case the parent of the pre-school child, has, by setting up the desired service, taken on a dual role of both producer and consumer. The suggestion that the producer is more likely to respond to the need for innovation does not seem to hold in this case. The supply of this service by public authorities has been somewhat insensitive to demands for places in pre-school education.

This chapter has suggested that there are various social causes for the growth of demand. However, policy itself may influence demand, thus the establishment of a new agency for pre-school education may generate extra demand. Parents who might not otherwise have been aware of the existence of nursery education become interested in it.* It is to the current supply of nursery education that the study now turns.

---

* Lambert found that the majority of parents did not know that they could have help with boarding education, if their children needed it. Those authorities giving most information received the most applications. (See Royston Lambert, *The State and Boarding Education* (1966), p. 38.)

5. The extent of pre-school education today

So far this thesis has been concerned with changes in nursery education over the period 1900–1965. This chapter and the one that follows discuss the extent and nature of pre-school education at one point of time. It would have been interesting to make a cross-sectional study for several different years; but this was ruled out by lack of data. Therefore it has been confined to 1965. This chapter describes the extent of provision for the education of children before compulsory schooling starts. The following chapter is concerned with the variation in provision from area to area, and with possible explanations for this variation. The units of analysis selected for study are the local education authorities. This is the obvious choice, since most policy decisions and the administration concerning early education are carried out by the local authorities. Moreover, the only available figures, apart from those describing the national situation, refer to local authority areas. These can of course be combined into larger regional areas (see Table 6.1, p. 96), though this measure hides some important variations within the regions; a breakdown into smaller units, such as urban and rural districts, is ruled out by absence of data.

The three major sources of the statistics presented below are data collected by the Department of Education and Science, the Ministry of Health and the local health authorities, none of it published other than in the form of national aggregates. The detailed sources are:

Department of Education and Science
1. Maintained Nursery Schools.
2. Maintained Nursery Classes attached to primary schools.
3. Independent Nursery Schools:
   (a) recognized as efficient;
   (b) other.

Ministry of Health
1. Day Nurseries.

Local Health Authorities
1. Registered premises for the day care of children, i.e. independent nurseries and playgroups not designated as schools.
2. Registered child-minders caring for eight or more children, i.e. independent nurseries and playgroups not designated as schools, and not coming into the 'registered premises' classification.

Further discussion of the sources and limitations of the statistics appears in Appendix 1.

The most meaningful statistics are those on the number of nursery *places*, rather than on the number of schools or institutions, since the latter vary greatly in size (see Appendix 1, Table A.1). Therefore most of the tables will give places rather than schools. They will show what share of the provision is maintained and what is independent, and the contribution of the categories within these two sectors to the total. Also they will present differences in the type of provision made by four different groups of local authorities. All the tables are for England and Wales. The following aspects will be discussed in turn: the distribution between public and private provision; between nursery classes and nursery schools; between independent provision under the auspices of health and education departments; between part-time and full-time; between day nurseries and nursery education. Up to this point the figures are based on absolute numbers. This is followed by figures discounting variation due to size of child population, which show the number of places in each type of local authority and the range of provision within each of those categories.

Maintained and independent provision

Table 5.1.   **Total number of places in pre-school education, 1965**

	Number of places	Per cent of all maintained places	Per cent of all places
Maintained			
nursery schools	28,504	33	19
nursery classes	58,784	67	39
total	87,288	100	58
	Number of places	Per cent of all independent places	Per cent of all places
Independent			
nursery schools	6,311	10	4
registered premises	41,130	65	27
registered persons	16,082	25	11
total	63,523	100	42
Total (maintained and independent)	150,811		100

Table 5.1 shows that the majority of places (58 per cent) are maintained. Most state provision is not, as is commonly supposed, in nursery schools, but in nursery classes, attached to primary schools. Two out of three maintained places are in such classes, compared with one out of three in nursery schools. This is surprising, since, as shown in earlier chapters, the central government has usually favoured nursery schools, suggesting that classes should be established as an alternative where expedient. Although the proportion of independent places is lower than the proportion of maintained places, the contribution of this sector is extremely high by comparison with other parts of the educational system. Many parents obtaining nursery education for their children in independent institutions later rely on the maintained schools to educate them.

Most independent provision of pre-school education comes under the auspices of the Ministry of Health and the local health authorities, who are responsible for registration and inspection. Only 10 per cent of independent nursery places come under the jurisdiction of the Department of Education and Science, these being the institutions with five or more children over 5

Table 5.2. **Number of nurseries, 1962–5**

Date	Independent registered premises	Maintained day nurseries	Maintained nursery schools
1962	932	462	475
1963	1,245	459	478
1964	1,585	455	480
1965	2,245	448	477

Sources: Annual reports of the Ministry of Health 1964, 1965 (Table 44),
         Statistics of Education, Part I, 1962, 1963, 1964, 1965 (Table 4).

Table 5.3. **Number of schools and classes under the DES, 1965**

	Maintained nursery schools	Maintained nursery classes	Independent nursery schools (recognized)	Independent nursery schools (other)
Administrative counties	207	433	5	141
County boroughs	180	920	2	31
Metropolis	49	285	2	22
Wales	41	284	—	2
Total	477	1,922	9	196

which are classified as schools. The rest have to register with the health authority, often reluctantly, as their organizers feel that they require advice on educational matters, rather than inspection to ensure that they are conforming to health and hygiene regulations. The proportion of independent places is increasing. Although no precise statistical evidence can be given, there is a great deal of circumstantial evidence, already considered in the preceding chapter, indicating that a rapid expansion of independent provision for pre-school education is under way. Table 5.2 confirms this impression.

The table shows the marked increase in the number of registered premises. Since these constitute by far the largest group in the independent sector, it would be reasonable to conclude that the sector as a whole is growing. This contrasts with the maintained sector, where the number of day nurseries has been declining and the number of nursery schools has not changed, although there may have been a small increase in the number of nursery classes, particularly since 1965. Nevertheless the maintained sector remains relatively static. It can be inferred from this that the middle-class demand for nursery education, described in the previous chapter, is manifesting itself in concrete forms in the private sector. Table 5.3 shows the number of schools and classes (rather than places) under the auspices of the Department of Education and Science.

It illustrates the very small number of independent nursery schools registered with the education authorities, 205 out of some three or four thousand.* Only nine of these schools are recognized as efficient, but this does not necessarily reflect low standards in the other schools. More probably their proprietors feel that seeking 'recognition' is not worth the trouble for schools which cater only for such young children. Should the Department of Education and Science decide on a new policy – as has sometimes been proposed – to eliminate all schools not recognized as efficient by refusing them recognition, a considerable number of independent nursery schools would be affected.

The distribution of nursery schools and nursery classes is analysed in greater detail in Table 5.4. This shows that most authorities opt for a mixture of nursery schools and nursery classes rather than allocating resources to one or the other.

However, in both the counties and the boroughs, and in Wales, the majority of authorities provide a higher proportion of places in nursery classes than in nursery schools. But the administrative counties in England have tended to rely more heavily on nursery schools than the other authorities.

Table 5.5 summarizes the picture presented so far. Clearly, there are considerable differences in the nature of pre-school education between types of authority. The proportion of maintained provision to total varies consider-

---

* It is impossible to give an exact figure because the number of so-called child-minders, who are running small independent nursery schools rather than 'child minding', cannot be ascertained.

ably. In Wales it is 82 per cent, whereas in the administrative counties it is only 37 per cent, the average for the whole country being 58 per cent. Differences in the extent of nursery school as against nursery class provision have been commented on already. Within the independent sector there is little difference between the groups of authorities in the proportion of places in independent nursery schools, registered premises or with registered persons.

Part-time provision and day nurseries

An important distinction needs to be made between part-time and full-time maintained provision, and this is brought out in Table 5.6. The majority of authorities clearly favour the latter. Nearly half of them provide no part-time places at all in either nursery schools or classes. The vast majority of the rest have mostly full-time places. There is a larger number of authorities where

Table 5.4.   **Breakdown of nursery school and nursery class places* by type of local authority,† 1965**

Number of authorities having:	Administrative counties		County boroughs		Wales		Total	
	number	*per cent*	*number*	*per cent*	*number*	*per cent*	*number*	*per cent*
Nursery school places only	2	4	4	5	1	6	7	5
Majority of its places in nursery schools†	16	33	17	21	3	18	37	25
Nursery class places only	8	17	24	30	7	41	39	27
Majority of its places in nursery classes‡	18	36	33	40	5	29	54	37
Those with no maintained provision	4	10	3	4	1	6	9	6
Total	48	100	81	100	17	100	146	100

* Part-time places treated as half the full-time equivalent.

† The number of places rather than the number of institutions has been used as a measure of provision. The picture would have been different had the number of institutions been taken, since the number of nursery classes is considerably in excess of the number of nursery schools in most areas (see Table 5.3). This over-emphasizes the contribution of nursery classes, since the number of children in each nursery class is usually much less than in each maintained nursery school.

‡ Excluding those authorities with nursery schools, or nursery classes only.

Table 5.5. Number of places in pre-school education by type of local authority and type of nursery place, 1965

	Administrative counties	Per cent	County boroughs	Per cent	Metropolitan area	Per cent	Wales	Per cent	Total	Per cent
Maintained										
nursery schools	10,986	18	11,331	23	4,047	14	2,140	19	28,504	19
nursery classes	12,176	19	24,806	51	14,700	52	7,102	63	58,784	39
Total maintained	23,162	37	36,137	74	18,747	66	9,242	82	87,288	58
Independent										
independent nursery schools	3,781	6	1,378	3	1,104	4	48	1	6,311	4
registered premises	25,270	41	8,176	17	6,189	22	1,495	13	41,130	27
registered persons	9,904	16	3,424	7	2,331	8	423	4	16,082	11
Total independent	38,955	63	12,978	26	9,624	34	1,966	18	63,523	42
Total	62,117	100	49,115	100	28,371	100	11,208	100	150,811	100

Table 5.6. **Part-time and full-time provision, 1965**

	Number of authorities*			
	Administrative counties	County boroughs	Wales	Total
Nursery schools				
No part-time places	14	25	5	44
Majority of places full-time	19	17	4	40
Majority of places part-time	3	13	–	16
No full-time places	–	–	–	–
				100
Nursery classes				
No part-time places	10	42	10	62
Majority of places full-time	30	29	4	63
Majority of places part-time	1	3	1	5
No full-time places	–	–	–	–
				130

* Excluding authorities with no places at all.

most places in nursery schools are part-time than there are authorities where most places in nursery classes are part-time. This indicates that local authorities and teachers regard nursery schools as more appropriate than nursery classes for part-time schooling, perhaps because it is administratively easier to organize in institutions entirely devoted to young children. Additionally, the administrative counties have more often opted for part-time places than the county boroughs or Wales. However, should the government adopt the Plowden recommendations, which advocate only 15 per cent full-time provision, a great deal of reorganization will be necessary.* The following table shows the percentage of part-time to full-time places.

The picture presented by Table 5.7 looks more favourable to part-time places than that of Table 5.6. The reason is the heavy commitment to part-time pre-school education of a single very large authority, namely, London.

There are no data on the proportion of part-time places in independent nurseries, but the indications are that there are more part-time than full-time places. The position in the maintained schools, where only one fifth of the places are part-time, may well be reversed in the private sector.

Finally, mention should be made of the provision of local authority day nurseries, because of a possible relationship between the provision of day nurseries and of maintained nursery schools and classes. In fact, the figures do

* There are in fact signs of an increasing trend towards part-time places.

not suggest that day nurseries are regarded as a substitute for nursery classes and nursery schools, or vice versa. However, there may be a few authorities where this is the case. The number of day nurseries has been on the decrease since the war, and few authorities have plans for expansion.* Table 5.8 illustrates the large number of authorities with no day nurseries.

Where they exist, day nurseries play a less important role in the provision of places than classes and schools. Only ten authorities have more places in the former than in the latter. The majority of authorities have only one or two day nurseries, although there are a few exceptional areas with large numbers. For example, Lancashire has fifty-three, Manchester twenty-four, Birmingham and Essex twenty, and Liverpool and Surrey thirteen. However, in the ten cases where day nursery places exceed the places provided by the education department, it is usually a result of negligible provision by the latter rather than generous provision by the health authority.

Places per 1,000 child population

All the data so far refer to absolute numbers and it is more informative to relate these to the size of the population, or preferably to the child population in the relevant age group. For reasons explained in Appendix 2, the age group 2 to 4 was used. It would in fact have been more realistic to use the age group 3 to 4, since the number of 2-year-olds receiving pre-school education is small; both maintained and independent agencies have tended to exclude them, because of the pressure for places from 3- and 4-year-olds. Table 5.9 shows the small proportion of 2-year-olds at school in institutions under the education authorities. In 1965 there were 242,055 children aged 2 to 4 in maintained schools, independent nursery and other schools, and special schools, out of a total population of 2,337,800, in the age group (i.e. 10 per cent).

Because of the small numbers of 2-year-olds in the schools, Table 5.10 is confined to children aged 3 to 4 but for the rest of the analysis relates the number of places to the number of children aged 2 to 4.

Thus, Table 5.10 shows that 9·9 per cent of children aged 3 to 4 receive pre-school education, 5·7 per cent in maintained schools and 4·2 per cent in independent schools. However, there are dangers in equating the number of children involved with the number of places available, since this certainly underestimates the former. The percentage of children obtaining pre-school education at one time or other during the period in which they are aged 3 to 5 is higher than the figures given here for two reasons. First, many children do not start attending until they are 3½ or 4 years old; second, some children

* In ten-year development plans submitted to the Ministry in 1962 only five local health authorities intended to increase the number of day nurseries. See Ministry of Health, *Health and Welfare*, Cmnd. 1973.

Table 5.7.   **Total number of part-time and full-time places, 1965**

	Nursery schools	Per cent of total	Nursery classes	Per cent of total	Total	Per cent
Part-time	8,292	29	10,420	18	18,712	21
Full-time	20,212	71	48,364	82	68,576	79
Total	28,504	100	58,784	100	87,288	100

Table 5.8.   **The relationship between the number of places in day nurseries, and nursery classes and schools by local authorities, 1965**

	Administrative counties	County boroughs	Wales	Total
Number of authorities with no day nurseries	20	23	17	60
Number of authorities with more places in nursery classes and schools	23	51	—	74
Number of authorities with more places in day nurseries	3	7	—	10

Table 5.9.   **Number of children under 5 in maintained schools, 1965**

	Aged 2	Aged 3	Aged 4	Total (aged 2—4)
All schools	2,793*	24,306	214,951	242,050
As per cent of the age-group	0·3	3	28	10

Source: Statistics of Education 1965, Pt. II, Table II.
* 1,109 of these are children in special schools.

Table 5.10.   **Number of nursery places per 1,000 child population aged 3—4, 1965**

	Maintained	Independent	Total
Administrative counties	47	48	95
County boroughs	88	32	120
Total	57	42	99

Table 5.11.   **Number of nursery school places per 1,000 child population aged 2—4, 1965**

	Maintained	Independent	Total
Administrative counties	29	30	59
County boroughs	57	21	78
Total, England and Wales	37	27	64

Table 5.12.   **Range of provision per 1,000 child population aged 2—4, 1965**

	Number of places		
	Maintained	Independent	Total
Administrative counties	0— 71	0—68	0—126
County boroughs	0—199	0—92	12—237
Metropolitan area	23— 67	0—48	57—102
Wales	0—153	0—41	0—153

drop out and are replaced by others. It is impossible to estimate how great an effect this has, or how much the effect will vary from one area to the next. But only under a perfectly ordered system, where all children start pre-school education at 3 and remain till they are 5, would the number of children be the same as the number of places available.

Table 5.11 indicates that between six and seven children in every hundred aged between 2 and 4 are obtaining pre-school education.* Slightly less than 4 per cent of the age group obtain this in state-maintained schools or classes. This is an under-estimate for the reasons given above.

The number of places in the independent sector is not the same in the Administrative Counties as in the County Boroughs. In the former there are slightly more independent than maintained places, whereas in the latter there are less than half as many independent as maintained places. The boroughs also have a higher total number of places than the counties. These differences become more marked when the Welsh counties and the Metropolitan area are analysed separately. They both have a far higher number of maintained places than the rest of the administrative counties, Wales having even more provision

* There is a discrepancy between the figure of 6·5 per cent for the percentage of the age group obtaining pre-school education, derived from Table 5.11, and the figure of 10·2 reproduced from the Department of Education and Science Statistics in Table 5.9. This is due to differences in definition and sources. There are a large number of possible definitions of what constitutes pre-school education, and each different combination will produce slightly different results. The Department's figures are higher because they include a large number of 4-year-olds, who are early entrants to the infant schools, not in pre-school education. Therefore this is not a valid measure of the numbers involved in pre-school education.

of this kind than the English County Boroughs. The chances of a child obtaining some kind of pre-school education are lowest in the English counties and highest in the Metropolitan area.

However, the range of provision within each type of authority is high and varies somewhat from one type to another. This is illustrated by Table 5.12.

The range is greatest in the county boroughs, where the total number of places is as low as twelve per 1,000 child population in one authority, and as high as 237 per 1,000 child population in another. The nature of this variation will be examined in the next chapter.

Limitations and conclusions

None of the figures above gives a completely accurate measure of the extent of pre-school education. They must be accepted as estimates only, since there are imperfections in the definitions and omissions in the data (see Appendix 1).

The weakest figures are those for nursery classes. It is important to distinguish between facilities which are specifically provided for the education of children of pre-school age and those which, though catering for such children, are not primarily aimed at nursery education. The Department of Education and Science's definition of a nursery class is not altogether satisfactory from this point of view. It defines a nursery class as any class attached to a primary school, having 90 per cent or more of its pupils under 5 years of age. There are many classes in this category which are not regarded as nursery classes by the local education authorities responsible for them. These are reception classes which accept a high proportion of children earlier than is usual elsewhere. Sometimes this is due to a long tradition of allowing children to enter the infant schools at an early age, as in parts of Wales. Sometimes it is due to policies of expediency in using available resources; for example, there may be a reduction in the number of 5-year-olds in the catchment area of a particular school, which results in the admission of 4-year-olds as an alternative to leaving places empty. This policy is immediately reversed when the pressure on places for 5-year-olds increases again. Thus a number of classes may be classified as nursery classes one year, only to be eliminated from this category the following year.

The number of nursery classes in England and Wales declined between 1964 and 1966. This seems hard to believe at first sight since the limit on the expansion of nursery classes was relaxed during this period for the first time for some years. However unresponsive local authorities might be to central government circulars, it seems unlikely that they would cut back on nursery classes just when the Department allows them to expand for the first time for some years. The probable explanation for the decline in the number of classes, as defined by the Department of Education and Science, is an increase in the birth-rate which has reduced the number of children local authorities can allow in to the infant schools at the age of 4. The discrepancy between figures based on the Department's definition of a nursery class and the figures given by individual local authorities is sometimes considerable. Overall the Department's figures are probably an over-estimate of the number of places specifically provided by local authorities for the purpose of nursery education.* That is, the number of reception classes, with 90 per cent of their children aged under 5, is higher than the number of nursery classes with more than 10 per cent of their children aged over 5. In spite of the serious consequences of this from the point of view of the validity of the data, one would not be justified to exclude maintained nursery classes from the analysis since they constitute the largest category in the provision of pre-school education.

There are also problems concerning the data on nursery education outside the state sector. Information on the number of children in registered premises and cared for by registered child-minders is subject to the deficiency that it omits the unregistered groups, which in some areas may constitute a large proportion of the total. However, it is impossible to 'track down' and count these. Even those authorities which are conscientious about registration, may have unregistered premises and minders operating in their areas unknown to them.†

A second problem is the need to distinguish those situations where the child is being minded from those where it is receiving education, however informal and limited. A large number of the registrations concern cases where two or three children are being cared for by a housewife while the mothers of the children are at work. The mothers are not removing them from their homes with the purpose of providing them with an educational experience and nor are those caring for the children aiming to offer them such an experience. These registrations are classified in terms of the accommodation the children occupy. If they are accommodated in the home of whoever is responsible for them, the woman is registered as a child-minder. If some other form of accommodation, such as a church or village hall or welfare clinic, is used, the premises, rather than the person responsible, are registered. This form of classification makes no distinction in terms of the degree to which educational aims and activities are involved. A method was devised for separating educational places from the rest. This is described in detail in the appendix, along with the implications for measuring the extent of independent provision. But it is necessary to note here that inaccuracies occur in this process.

* The evidence for this is given in the results of an inquiry by the Department of Education and Science into the number of nursery classes set up by local authorities under the Addenda to Circular 8/60 which also obtained information from the local education authorities on other nursery classes.

† However, in spite of this fault it seemed worth writing to local health authorities to try and obtain the nearest estimate of the information required.

In spite of all the faults in the data, it is possible to draw some broad conclusions about the provision of pre-school education in England and Wales in 1965. Although the contribution of the maintained sector is higher than that of the independent sector, the role of the latter is far higher than in the rest of the educational system. This is most true of the administrative counties, and least true of Wales. Within the maintained sector the majority of the places are in nursery classes, not nursery schools, but the degree to which this is true varies according to the type of authority. Within the independent sector most places are in nurseries registered as 'premises' under the local health authorities. Most maintained places are full-time, but circumstantial evidence suggests that most independent places are part-time. Finally the proportion of the child population receiving pre-school education is small. The percentage of 3- to 4-year-olds involved at any one time in either the maintained or the independent sector is approximately 10 per cent. Thus the implementation of extra-familial agencies to aid the family processes of socialization, discussed in earlier chapters, has not yet materialized on a large scale. The discrepancy between the numbers of parents obtaining nursery education for their children at one point in time (10 per cent), and the numbers who would like to obtain it (78 per cent) according to Gavron's sample, is even higher than anticipated when this study was begun (see Gavron, 1966).

6. The variation in provision between local education authorities

The standards of the social services, and the degree to which they are available to those who either need or want them varies considerably from one area to another (see Davies, 1968). This applies to various aspects of education as well as to such services as health, housing and welfare. The Robbins Report described the high variation in the proportion of children still at school, aged 17, and the proportion entering full-time higher education (Robbins, 1963, Appendix 1, pp. 64–7). Others have indicated the variation in the number of selective school places available (Douglas, 1964, pp. 23–30), and other aspects of secondary education (Sheridan, thesis). The provision of nursery education is no exception to the rule. As Table 5.12 (p. 92) showed, this varies from 0 to 20 per cent of children receiving maintained places, from 0 to 9 per cent receiving independent places and 0 to 24 per cent when maintained and independent places are considered together. The range is greater in the County Boroughs than in the Administrative Counties, which is because of a greater spread at the top end of the scale, a small number of Boroughs having

Table 6.1 **Nursery provision by region, 1965***

| Region† | Number of places per 1,000 child population | | |
	maintained	independent	Total
1 Yorkshire (East and West Ridings)	69 (0–158)	13 (0–38)	83 (19–163)
2 North-west	59 (0–157)	11 (0–39)	70 (11–128)
3 Wales	58 (0–153)	10 (0–40)	69 (0–153)
4 Metropolitan	51 (22– 68)	28 (0–47)	79 (57–102)
5 Midlands	41 (1–161)	12 (0–34)	54 (12–168)
6 West Midlands	38 (0–199)	14 (0–48)	52 (0–236)
7 South	33 (0–124)	47 (17–89)	81 (17–145)
8 North	26 (0– 53)	14 (3–32)	41 (17–152)
9 East	24 (1– 70)	30 (4–58)	55 (19–126)
10 South-east	21 (4– 78)	61 (31–73)	83 (58–109)
11 South-west	20 (2– 82)	26 (5–47)	46 (16– 61)

* The authorities making up each region and the figures for nursery education for each of them are given in Appendix 5.

† Standard regions used by the Department of Education and Science, with the exception of the Metropolitan area, which in the above table includes the County Boroughs of West Ham, East Ham and Croydon.

exceptionally high provision. Before listing the local authorities at the extremes and considering any common characteristics they might have, the differences between regions in the extent of nursery education will be considered. This is followed by an assessment of possible explanatory variables of a quantifiable nature, which might indicate the kind of characteristics of local authority areas associated with high or low nursery provision. Throughout, the variation referred to is quantitative rather than qualitative; it has not been possible to measure standards, as opposed to extent, of provision. The search for the characteristics of areas related to provision is carried out in the following sequence. Those authorities at each extreme, either with very high or very low provision, are listed. The study of the extremes provides a basis for going on to look at all authorities including those with average levels of provision, in terms of the way they are distributed on six variables and how this relates to their position with reference to nursery provision. This is followed by correlation coefficients, which can provide a more precise measure of the association between such variables and the provision of nursery education than distribution tables. Finally, the multiple effect of these independent variables is investigated by doing a step-wise multiple regression.

The data on which this analysis is based are presented in Appendices 3 and 4, and Appendices 1 and 2 discuss their sources and limitations.*

Nursery provision in the regions

The distribution of nursery education between the regions is shown in Table 6.1 in terms of the average number of places provided by the local authorities in each region. The table also gives the ranges of provision found within each region (bracketed). This provides a more detailed picture of the range of variation than that given in the previous chapter, which distinguishes only between types of authority.

Those regions with high maintained provision tend to have low independent provision, and vice versa, which might indicate that independent provision is a substitute for maintained provision. There are exceptions to this: the metropolitan area has high numbers of places in both sectors; the north has few places in both sectors; the south-west has very low provision by

* There are important differences between the figures given there and those used in this chapter, concerning part-time places. In Chapter 5 the aim was to obtain as accurate a picture as possible of the number of children receiving pre-school education. For this reason each part-time place was treated in the same way as a full-time place in compiling totals. This chapter is concerned with the variation in provision from area to area. Consequently each part-time place is treated as half the full-time equivalent. To do otherwise would give a false picture of the extent of provision made by those authorities which have adopted the part-time principle compared to those which have remained committed to full-time nursery education. It would exaggerate the resources devoted to nursery education in the former, in that, although the actual number of places they provided might be higher than in the latter, their expenditure on building, staffing and other current costs would not. It is not possible to apply this procedure to independent places, under the auspices of the Ministry of Health, since full-time and part-time places are not differentiated.

the local authorities, and does not make up for this with correspondingly high provision in the independent sector, as in the south-east. When the two sectors are combined (see Total column) the range of provision between the regions is lower than when the two sectors are considered separately, which is further evidence for the theory that they are substitutes. However, there is still a difference of forty places between the region with the highest number of places (Yorkshire, 83·6) and the one with the lowest (the North 41·4). The extent to which low provision in one sector is made up by high provision in the other is therefore limited, and any suggestion that they are substitutes must be treated with caution. Over half the regions have as few as ten to fifteen independent places per 1,000 child population, and the exceptions with higher independent provision are all in the southern half of the country. This can probably be explained by a higher proportion of individuals with professional and managerial occupations in the south of England, and its greater affluence. But there may be a North/South difference, unrelated to social class, in the extent to which parents are prepared to buy nursery education for their children.

At first sight it might seem surprising that the South of England, with the exception of London, is also less well provided with maintained nursery education. There are two possible explanations. The first relates to the way the figures have been calculated. By taking a mean figure for the authorities in each region (see Appendix 5), rather than calculating the total number of nursery school places in the region, and then correcting this for population, the large authorities receive no more weight than the small authorities. Regions such as Yorkshire and the north-west, where a high proportion of the authorities are County Boroughs, which tend to have higher provision than Administrative Counties, may therefore appear to have more extensive provision than is the case. On the other hand, areas such as the south-west and the east, which have proportionately fewer County Boroughs, may appear to have less provision than is the case. The second explanation derives from the history of nursery education. The earlier chapters of this study have described the motives of those responsible for setting up nursery schools before the Second World War. The prime aim was to alleviate the undesirable physical conditions in which many children in the working-class areas of large industrial towns were spending their days. The legacy of this is reflected in the distribution of maintained nursery education between the regions: the more rural, less industrialized areas in the south are still less well served than the more industrial regions in the north of England.

Local authorities with the highest and lowest provision

The high range in provision within each region, particularly for the maintained sector, where in the North Midlands, for example, it varies from 0–237 places, indicates the need to consider the individual authorities which make up the regions. The Administrative Counties with high provision will be considered first, followed by the Administrative Counties with low provision. The County Boroughs and Wales will be discussed after this. The purpose of this section is to discover whether these areas with high or low provision might share certain common characteristics.

On the whole, the results shown in Table 6.2 confirm the expected patterns indicated by Table 6.1 on the regions, although there are some exceptions which are difficult to explain. The authorities with the most maintained provision include London* and Middlesex and other highly urbanized or industrialized counties such as the West Riding of Yorkshire, Staffordshire and Lancashire. The two outstanding deviants in this list are Cambridgeshire and Westmorland. It is surprising that the former should top the table both for maintained and total provision, since such extensive provision by the authority is unexpected in a predominantly rural area of this kind. It seemed likely that a high proportion of the available places would be in Cambridge itself, the only large town in the county. The distribution of places within the authority was investigated and this assumption proved to be correct,† which indicates the need for intra-authority as well as inter-authority analyses. Because a predominantly rural authority has high provision for pre-school education it does not imply that places are available in rural areas. The high figure for maintained nursery education in Westmorland is also surprising for similar reasons. Most of the provision in this county dates from the war and unlike that of many other areas has survived attempts to economize since. It should be added that the child population aged 2 to 4 of Westmorland is smaller (2,790) than that of any other Administrative County with the exception of Rutland, therefore one or two nursery classes more or less would have a considerable statistical effect.

Those authorities with most independent places in their areas represent the predicted association between a high proportion of the population of high social class and high independent provision. The tendency for middle-class parents to seek places for their children in private nursery schools, and to set up such institutions where they do not exist has already been discussed in Chapter 4. Thus the Home Counties occupy nine of the top ten places, the remaining one being Devonshire. The list for total provision given in Table 6.2 is very similar and reflects the large contribution the independent sector makes to the provision of nursery education in the Administrative Counties.

The Administrative Counties with the lowest number of maintained places are mostly sparsely populated, rural areas in the south-west and eastern England. This provides further empirical support for the suggestion in the

* Although London was included with the counties because of its administrative status, it would have been more realistic in other respects to classify it as a county borough. Had this been the case it would not have appeared in this list. By comparison with many other authorities in this category it does not have high provision of nursery education.

† Less than one sixth of the total number of places in the county were provided outside the city of Cambridge.

Table 6.2. Administrative counties: ten authorities with highest provision

Maintained	Places per 1,000 child population aged 2–4	Independent	Places per 1,000 child population aged 2–4	Total	Places per 1,000 child population aged 2–4
Cambridgeshire	70	Surrey	68	Cambridgeshire	126
London	68	Sussex East	65	London	102
Westmorland	53	Hertfordshire	58	Middlesex	97
Middlesex	49	Cambridgeshire	55	Buckinghamshire	89
Yorkshire (West Riding)	36	Buckinghamshire	54	Surrey	86
Buckinghamshire	34	Kent	53	Hertfordshire	80
Warwickshire	33	Sussex West	52	Westmorland	71
Co. Durham	31	Hampshire	49	Sussex East	70
Staffordshire	30	Middlesex	47	Warwickshire	68
Lancashire	27	Devonshire	47	Sussex West	63

Table 6.3. **Administrative counties: ten authorities with lowest provision**

Maintained	Places per 1,000 child population aged 2–4	Independent	Places per 1,000 child population aged 2–4	Total	Places per 1,000 child population aged 2–4
Rutland	–	Rutland	–	Rutland	–
Isle of Wight	–	Huntingdonshire	0·9	Lincolnshire (Holland)	5
Lincolnshire (Holland)	–	Derbyshire	2	Lincolnshire (Lindsey)	10
Lincolnshire (Kesteven)	–	Yorkshire (West Riding)	2	Northamptonshire	12
Leicestershire	0·7	Co. Durham	3	Leicestershire	15
Hampshire	0·8	Herefordshire	5	Gloucestershire	16
Shropshire	1	Lincolnshire (Holland)	5	Shropshire	16
Suffolk East	1	Lincolnshire (Lindsey)	5	Isle of Wight	17
Devonshire	2	Northamptonshire	6	Lincolnshire (Kesteven)	18
Dorset	3	Gloucestershire	10	Cumberland	18

discussion on the regions that, as expected, the basis on which decisions were made in the past determines the distribution of provision at present. Three of these authorities reappear in the list of those with the lowest number of independent places plus two or three others of a similar kind, such as Huntingdonshire, Herefordshire and Gloucestershire. Amongst these agricultural areas, there are several counties which are characterized by mining and heavy industry, and a large working-class population which precludes the development of extensive independent provision.

On the question of complementarity between maintained and independent provision, three authorities appear in both the ten highest 'maintained' group and the ten highest 'independent' group (see Table 6.2). Similarly, two authorities appear both amongst those with the fewest maintained places and amongst those with the fewest independent places (see Table 6.3).* This provides evidence that the two forms of provision may be complementary. However, there are also a few authorities which appear in the 'high' list for maintained provision and the 'low' list for independent provision or vice versa,† which shows substitution. This indicates the difficulty of making generalizations about the relationship between public and private provision.

Turning to the County Boroughs, those with high maintained provision are all industrial towns in the Midlands and the North, with the exception of Oxford. Although they vary considerably in size, ranging from Manchester with a population of over 750,000 to Dewsbury with a population of less than 60,000 they do share some common characteristics. Their populations are similar in terms of social class composition, each having a fairly high proportion in Social Class IV and V, with one exception – Leicester – and each having a relatively small population in Social Class I and II with the exception of Oxford. Seven of the ten towns listed have high proportions of women in the labour force, the exceptions being Wakefield, Rotherham and Darlington. All these towns, except Oxford, have a high proportion of the labour force working in manufacture as opposed to service trades, but the type of industry which predominates varies considerably.

The list of authorities with the highest number of independent places provides a considerable contrast to the above group. All of these authorities have a high proportion of their populations in administrative and managerial occupations, a low level of industrialization and are situated in southern England. The only exception is Northampton.

The authorities with the lowest maintained provision defy generalization. They include resorts in the north and south, small administrative centres such as Carlisle and large industrial towns such as Huddersfield and South Shields. However, they do share the common characteristic of low proportions of

* They are Middlesex, Buckinghamshire and Cambridgeshire for the high group, and Rutland and Lincolnshire (Holland) for the low group.

† They are Hampshire (low maintained and high independent) and Yorkshire West and Durham (high maintained and low independent).

women in the labour force, in direct contrast to those boroughs with high provision; but there are three exceptions to this, Blackpool, Huddersfield and Eastbourne.

Like the administrative counties, the county boroughs do not follow a pattern of independent provision acting as either a substitute for maintained provision, or as a complement to it. For example, Oxford has a large number of nursery places in both sectors. On the other hand, Eastbourne and Ipswich are amongst the highest authorities for independent and amongst the lowest for maintained provision, whereas Burnley and Dewsbury have very high maintained provision, and no independent places at all. Those boroughs which have the highest total number of places consist of a similar group to those with the highest maintained provision, and this relationship is also true of authorities with low provision.* On the other hand, in the counties the opposite situation prevails with a large number of authorities with high independent provision appearing again in the total group.† This reflects the difference between the counties and the boroughs, already described in Chapter 4, in the proportion of places provided by the independent sector.

There is no definable pattern of nursery provision in Wales. In the maintained sector, areas as diverse as rural Breconshire and industrialized Glamorgan have the highest amount of provision, and equally diverse areas such as the mining area of Merthyr Tydfil and the sparsely populated county of Radnor have the lowest amount of provision. In the independent sector the total number of places provided is so small that generalization is difficult; nearly half the authorities have no independent places at all and the three authorities with the highest number of independent places have considerably fewer places than the equivalent English counties and boroughs. Nor is it easy to assess the degree to which independent places act as a substitute in this situation. Of the three authorities with the lowest maintained provision, Radnor and Merthyr Tydfil have no independent places, while Anglesey has a relatively high number of such places.

From this consideration of the authorities at the extremes a picture, admittedly hazy, emerges of the kind of authority in England, but not in Wales, that tends to have either a large or small supply of nursery education of one kind or another. The administrative counties with high maintained provision tend to be urbanized, industrialized areas where those with low maintained provision are sparsely populated agricultural areas predominantly in East Anglia, and sometimes in the South-west. Those with high independent provision are all home counties with large middle-class populations, whilst the group with low provision is a mixture of rural agricultural counties

* Seven boroughs from the high maintained list appear in the high total list. Five boroughs from the low maintained list appear in the low total list.

† Seven counties from the high independent list appear in the high total list. Five counties from the low independent list appear in the low total list. Several of these authorities also appear in the highest/lowest maintained groups reflecting somewhat more 'complementarity' in the administrative counties.

Table 6.4. **County boroughs: ten authorities with highest provision**

Maintained	Places per 1,000 child population aged 2—4	Independent	Places per 1,000 child population aged 2—4	Total	Places per 1,000 child population aged 2—4
Leicester	199	Eastbourne	92	Leicester	236
Stoke on Trent	161	Oxford	89	Oxford	213
Wakefield	158	Ipswich	88	Stoke on Trent	168
Burnley	157	Portsmouth	87	Wakefield	163
Dewsbury	125	Hastings	73	Burnley	157
Oxford	124	Reading	63	Reading	145
Bolton	120	Canterbury	55	Darlington	132
Rotherham	118	Southend	49	Manchester	128
Manchester	117	Northampton	48	Bristol	126
Darlington	116	Croydon	47	Southport	123

Table 6.5. County boroughs: ten authorities with lowest provision

Maintained	Places per 1,000 child population aged 2–4	Independent	Places per 1,000 child population aged 2–4	Total	Places per 1,000 child population aged 2–4
Blackpool	—	Barnsley	—	Blackpool	11
Carlisle	—	Blackburn	—	Burton	12
Huddersfield	—	Burnley	—	Wallasey	15
Wallasey	7	Burton	—	Bury	16
Solihull	8	Bury	—	South Shields	17
South Shields	10	Dewsbury	—	Huddersfield	19
Ipswich	11	Dudley	—	Sunderland	20
Plymouth	12	Halifax	—	West Hartlepool	23
Burton on Trent	12	Rochdale	—	Wigan	26
Eastbourne	12	Warrington	—	Bootle	26
		West Bromwich	—		
		West Ham	—		

Table 6.6. **Wales:** **(a) three authorities with highest provision**

Maintained	Places per 1,000 child population aged 2–4	Independent	Places per 1,000 child population aged 2–4	Total	Places per 1,000 child population aged 2–4
Brecon	153	Cardiff	40	Brecon	153
Glamorgan	100	Caernarvon	34	Caernarvon	127
Caernarvon	93	Anglesey	24	Glamorgan	117

(b) three authorities with lowest provision

Maintained	Places per 1,000 child population aged 2–4	Independent	Places per 1,000 child population aged 2–4	Total	Places per 1,000 child population aged 2–4
Radnor	—	Radnor	—	Radnor	—
Anglesey	7	Brecon	—	Anglesey	32
Merthyr Tydfil	9	Cardigan	—	Pembroke	27
		Carmarthen	—		
		Merioneth	—		
		Montgomery	—		
		Merthyr Tydfil	—		

and mining or heavy industrial areas with a larger than average working-class population. The county boroughs with high maintained provision are mainly industrial towns in the North and Midlands with large numbers of working women. Those with high independent provision are towns with a low level of industrialization; a large proportion of the population is middle class, and they are situated in the South of England. The county boroughs with low provision are a very diverse group about which generalizations cannot be made.

Frequency distributions

The following section moves on from a description of the extremes, by constructing frequency distributions for the provision of nursery education against various quantifiable characteristics of all local authorities in England and Wales. The point of these analyses is to investigate any possible associations between characteristics of areas, such as the extent of female employment and the provision of nursery education, on the basis of which it can be decided whether a more complex analysis should be undertaken. The total number of nursery places (independent and maintained) has been used as the measure of nursery provision. Separate distributions have been presented for the administrative counties and for the county boroughs. The county authorities are divided into four groups according to the extent of their provision for pre-school education. In the boroughs the division is into five groups.* The authorities were then grouped according to their characteristics on the following six variables:

1. Size of the child population aged 2 to 4 (see Chapter 5 for source).

2. Economically active females as a proportion of economically active males (1961 Census).

3. Males in semi- and unskilled occupations as a proportion of economically active males (1961 Census).

4. (a) Administrative Counties: per cent of population living in Urban
       District and Metropolitan Borough areas (1961 Census);
   (b) County Boroughs: population per acre (1961 Census).

5. Number of places in day nurseries per 1,000 child population (Ministry of Health Statistics [unpublished] 1965).

6. Oversize classes in junior schools: per cent over 30 (Department of Education and Science statistics).

* Administrative Counties		County Boroughs	
Nursery places	Number of authorities	Nursery places	Number of authorities
61 and over	17	121 and over	14
41–60	12	91–120	13
21–40	19	61–90	17
Under 21	12	31–60	27
		Under 31	12

In the counties it is apparent from the tables (see Appendix 3), that most of the variables under scrutiny are not strongly associated with the provision of pre-school education. However, in one or two cases some conclusions suggesting association emerge, especially if one excludes Wales which often presents a very distinct picture. For example, Table A.2 showing the size of the child population against nursery provision would look different if Wales were excluded, since most of the principality's counties are small yet have high provision. However, in England there appears to be a pattern whereby the large authorities have high and the small authorities low nursery provision, with the exceptions of Cambridgeshire and Westmorland again. The reason for this association may be that most of the large authorities are more highly urbanized than most of the small authorities rather than that large authorities *per se* have better facilities for the education of young children. Table A.5 showing nursery provision against per cent population living in urban districts and metropolitan boroughs indicates that this is a likely explanation, although once again the Welsh counties distort the picture. When these are removed from the table, the more rural counties are found to have low provision, whereas the more urbanized counties have higher provision. There are prominent exceptions to this: Westmorland is a 'rural' county with high total provision; Durham is an 'urban' county with low provision. The Welsh counties also do not fit into the expected pattern with reference to the employment of married women. In spite of the limited employment of women, high nursery provision predominates. In England there is some evidence for the predicted relationship (see Table A.3). However, this is by no means a powerful association as there is considerable spread in the middle range of the distribution. This spread also applies to the frequency distribution of social class against nursery provision (see Table A.4). There is a slight tendency for counties with a low proportion of semi- and unskilled manual workers to have more facilities for the education of children under 5, and those with a high proportion to have fewer facilities. Nevertheless too many of the authorities are clustered in the 21–25 per cent, 26–30 per cent manual workers groupings for this table to be of much use. The criticism that the distribution of observations for the independent variable is too clustered, applies with even greater force to Table A.6. None of the Welsh counties has any day nurseries and twenty out of forty-six English counties have none. There is no pattern for those authorities which have some day nursery places. In turn there is little relationship between the proportion of primary school classes which are oversize and the provision of nursery schools. It might be expected that those counties with a large number of oversize classes might have the fewest maintained nursery schools and classes, since they would not be able to spare teachers from the compulsory age range for the under-5s. Table A.7 shows the relationship between total nursery provision and oversize classes, and does not demonstrate that the above suggestion is false. The presence of the rural areas also makes this hypothesis difficult to test, since they tend to have small classes, yet nursery education is often not feasible. It will be more appropriate to examine this question in the county boroughs.

Here there is a tendency for the large authorities to have low nursery provision, although there are a number of exceptions, particularly Bristol and Manchester; small authorities tend to have high provision, but again the exceptions, such as Merthyr and Burton, are quite numerous (see Table A.8). This contrasts with the administrative counties, but Table A.9, showing the distribution of nursery provision against the proportion of women working, shows a similar weak association between the two variables to that in the counties. The higher the proportion of manual workers in the area, the lower is the proportion of children obtaining nursery places, although again there are exceptions and the association is weak (see Table A.10). Table A.11 shows that population density, which is not independent of the proportion of manual workers in the population, has little relationship to the amount of nursery provision. Nor has the proportion of children obtaining day nursery places (see Table A.12). However, Table A.13 shows an association between the number of oversize classes and the provision of nursery places consistent with the suggestion made earlier in discussing the administrative counties: where there is a severe shortage of teachers, leading to oversize classes, there is little nursery provision.

Correlation coefficients

Although these frequency distributions can give only an impression of associations between the extent of nursery provision and other characteristics of local education authorities, some of them do indicate relationships which seem worth following up at a more sophisticated level. For this purpose, some additional independent variables were selected which might have explanatory value for the variation in the provision of nursery education. For the frequency distributions it was only feasible to consider the total number of nursery places per 1,000 child population in each authority, whereas in the analysis below the subgroups of independent and maintained places are used as well. There are therefore three separate dependent variables, whose association with each of the independent variables is measured by calculating correlation coefficients. The multiple effect of these independent variables is investigated by doing a step-wise multiple regression. The regression equations derived from this are discussed after considering the correlation coefficients. Table 6.7 lists the variables.

The independent variables can be classified into three broad categories: socio-economic, demographic and educational. They have been selected on the grounds that a relationship might be expected between them and the dependent variables. However, the nature of the association will not be the same for all three dependent variables. For example, high socio-economic

Table 6.7. **List of variables* to be related to the extent of nursery provision**

Dependent Variables

1. Total provision of pre-school education per 1,000 child population, 1965
2. Maintained provision of pre-school education per 1,000 child population, 1965
3. Independent provision of pre-school education per 1,000 child population, 1965

Independent Variables

4. Males in administrative, managerial and professional occupations as a proportion of economically active males, 1961
5. Males in non-manual occupations as a proportion of economically active males, 1961
6. Males in semi- and unskilled occupations as a proportion of economically active males, 1961
7. Economically active females as a proportion of economically active males, 1961
8. Males employed in industry as a proportion of occupied males, 1961
9. Per cent of population living in Urban District and Metropolitan Borough areas, 1961 (Administrative Counties); Population per acre, 1961 (County Boroughs)
10. Proportion of persons living at more than 1½ persons per room, 1961
11. Family size: children aged 0—14 as a proportion of all married women 25—54, 1961
12. Per cent change in population, 1951—61
13. Proportion of private households with exclusive use of amenities, 1961
14. Net expenditure on day nurseries per 1,000 population, 1964/5
15. Number of places in day nurseries per 1,000 child population, 1965
16. Pupil—teacher ratio in primary schools, 1962
17. Oversize classes in junior schools: per cent over 30, 1964/5
18. Total cost per primary school pupil (excluding nursery), 1961/2
19. Net expenditure on special schools per 1,000 population, 1961/2
20. Net expenditure on facilities for recreation per 1,000 population, 1961/2
21. Per cent selective school places, 1959/60
22. Per cent 13 year-olds in all age schools, 1964/5
23. Per cent seats Labour after 1962 local elections (County Boroughs only)

* Sources: Variables 1—3 (see Ch. 5); 4—13, 1961 Census; 14, Institute of Municipal Treasurers and Accountants' Health Statistics, 1964—5; 15, (see Ch. 5); 16, Department of Education and Science, Statistics return 26 (unpublished); 17, Department of Education and Science, List 71 1964—5; 18—20, Institute of Municipal Treasurers and Accountants' Education Statistics 1961—2; 21—22, Department of Education and Science, List 71 1959—60, 1964—5; 23, Municipal Year Book, 1963.

class is likely to be associated with high provision of independent places, but not necessarily with high provision of maintained places.

In some cases the *expected* direction of the association is not in doubt. For example, in urban areas of high density with overcrowded housing, it would be expected from the consideration of such issues in Chapter 4 that maintained provision would be high. However, the situation is not always so simple. For example, a number of variables have been selected as indicators of the quality of other educational provision in the area. Two conflicting hypotheses can be examined about these: where the quality of education at various stages is high, the provision of maintained nursery education will also be high, as a result of a progressive outlook and high spending on education by the authority; or where the quality of education in general is high, there will be fewer resources to spend on the provision of nursery education, which is sometimes regarded as an extra service since it is not catering for children of compulsory school age. It is not easy to put forward hypotheses concerning the effect of measures of qualitative variations.

Tables 6.8 and 6.9 show that most of the correlations between the measures for nursery education and the other variables listed are low. Although the observations are not a sample but consist of all local education authorities, the coefficients can be tested for significance on the assumption that the observations on which they are based are sample data.

This provides a simple objective guide to which coefficients are high enough to merit consideration as indicating associations and which are not. For the administrative counties r is significant at a 1 per cent confidence level when equalling 0·33 or above, and in the case of the county boroughs r is significant at the 1 per cent level when equalling 0·28 or above. The coefficients which are significant are marked (S) in Tables 6.8 and 6.9. Out of a total of 117 coefficients excluding the inter-relationships between the dependent variables, thirty-one are significant, and of these twenty-one refer to the administrative counties and ten to the county boroughs. The breakdown of the significant coefficients between types of provision is, total four; maintained eight; independent nineteen. The higher coefficients for independent provision are probably due to the closer relationship between the social class indices and this form of provision, social class being related in turn to a number of the other variables. In the same way, the more important role of independent places in the counties may account for the higher coefficients there.

The coefficients for total provision are of less interest than those for the separate breakdowns of independent and maintained. The two frequently conflict and consequently cancel each other out in the relationship between total provision and the independent variables. For example, the correlations between maintained and independent provision and the proportion of males in non-manual occupations are respectively −0·13 and 0·70, which become 0·27 when the two forms of provision are added to make up total provision. This explains the small number of significant coefficients for the latter.

Table 6.8. **Correlation coefficients: Administrative counties**

Independent variables	Dependent variables: Number of nursery places per 1,000 child population aged 2—4		
	1 Total	*2 Maintained*	*3 Independent*
1. Total pre-school education	1·0	0·83	0·38
2. Maintained pre-school education	0·83	1·0	−0·18
3. Independent pre-school education	0·38	−0·18	1·0
4. Males in administrative professional and managerial occupations	0·32	−0·12	0·77 (S)
5. Males in non-manual occupations	0·27	−0·13	0·70 (S)
6. Males in semi- and unskilled occupations	−0·15	0·09	−0·41 (S)
7. Economically active females	0·26	−0·03	0·52 (S)
8. Males employed in industry	0·03	0·11	−0·14
9. Per cent population living in U.D.s and Met. Boroughs	0·19	0·00	0·34 (S)
10. Overcrowding	0·01	0·10	−0·16
11. Family size	−0·39 (S)	−0·20	−0·36 (S)
12. Per cent change in population	−0·10	−0·36 (S)	0·42
13. Households with exclusive use of amenities	0·01	−0·24	0·43 (S)
14. Expenditure on day nurseries	0·21	0·07	0·26
15. Places in day nurseries	0·06	0·03	0·07
16. Pupil—teacher ratios in primary schools	0·11	−0·40 (S)	0·47 (S)
17. Oversize classes in junior schools	−0·09	−0·30	0·63 (S)
18. Cost per primary pupil	0·20	0·44 (S)	0·34 (S)
19. Net expenditure on special schools	0·27	0·09	−0·38 (S)
20. Expenditure on facilities for recreation	0·35 (S)	0·40 (S)	−0·04 (S)
21. Per cent selective school places	0·35 (S)	0·57 (S)	−0·33 (S)
22. Per cent 13-year-olds in all age schools	0·08	0·12	−0·06

(S) = significant at 1 per cent level.

Table 6.9. **Correlation coefficients: County boroughs**

| Independent variables | Dependent variables: Number of nursery places per 1,000 child population aged 2—4 | | |
	1 Total	2 Maintained	3 Independent
1. Total pre-school education	1·0	0·87	0·34
2. Maintained pre-school education	0·87	1·0	−0·16
3. Independent pre-school education	0·34	−0·16	1·0
4. Males in administrative, professional and managerial occupations	0·10	−0·14	0·48 (S)
5. Males in non-manual occupations	0·09	−0·21	0·59 (S)
6. Males in semi- and unskilled occupations	−0·21	0·04	−0·50 (S)
7. Economically active females	0·24	0·27	−0·02
8. Males employed in industry	0·03	0·30 (S)	−0·52 (S)
9. Population per acre	−0·15	−0·06	−0·16
10. Overcrowding	−0·31 (S)	−0·17	−0·30 (S)
11. Family size	−0·13	−0·06	−0·14
12. Per cent change in population	−0·17	−0·31 (S)	0·27
13. Households with exclusive use of amenities	−0·03	−0·13	0·19
14. Expenditure on day nurseries	0·05	0·14	−0·18
15. Places in day nurseries	0·19	0·28 (S)	−0·15
16. Pupil—teacher ratios in primary schools	−0·10	−0·12	0·04
17. Oversize classes in junior schools	−0·26	−0·18	−0·17
18. Cost per primary pupil	0·16	0·07	0·21
19. Net expenditure on special schools	0·04	0·13	−0·16
20. Expenditure on facilities for recreation	0·11	0·17	−0·11
21. Per cent selective school places	−0·02	−0·01	−0·02
22. Per cent 13-year-olds in all age schools	−0·24	−0·19	−0·11
23. Per cent seats Labour after 1962 local elections	−0·03	0·19	−0·43 (S)

(S) = significant at 1 per cent level.

The social class of the area and maintained provision are not associated according to these measures in either the administrative counties or the county boroughs. Nor is the proportion of working women in the labour force.* In the county boroughs the correlation between levels of industrialization and the extent of maintained nursery provision is significant, and in the expected direction. However, although positive, it is not significant in the administrative counties. The correlations between maintained provision and population per acre in the boroughs and the proportion of the population living in urban areas are negative, which is unexpected, but the coefficients are not significant. Nor, according to this evidence, are the other need indices of overcrowding, family size and adequate housing associated with maintained nursery education in either type of authority. Change in population is negatively correlated with maintained nursery education, but it is difficult to interpret this result, as declining population is not distinguished from rising population.

Turning to the relationship between the provision of maintained nursery education and other local authority services from which children benefit, there appear to be some marked associations in the administrative counties, but not in the county boroughs. The exception to this is places in day nurseries where there is a significant positive correlation in the boroughs, but in the counties day nursery provision appears to be unrelated to educational provision for children under 5. In the counties, the more local authorities spend on primary school pupils and facilities for recreation the more nursery places they provide;† the larger the number of oversize classes, and the higher the pupil–teacher ratios in primary schools, the lower the provision of nursery education. This seems to indicate that certain authorities have more extensive facilities with higher standards for children of primary age and

---

* However, there are correlations of 0·70 and 0·39 in the counties, and 0·37 and 0·40 in the boroughs between the proportion of working women and expenditure on day nurseries, and the number of places provided in day nurseries. Since the aim of day nurseries is unambiguously to provide care for the children of working mothers, these correlations are not as high as might be expected, particularly in the county boroughs. Although the aim of nursery education has not been to provide for the children of working mothers, various historical factors in the setting up and continuance of nursery schools and classes, and some ambivalence in the minds of the authorities and the public indicated that there might be some relationship (see Chapter 3). This is not borne out by the above evidence, especially in the counties where the correlation is negative.

† Care must be taken in interpreting any results which involve measures of expenditure. Bleddyn Davies (1968, p. 20) states the difficulties: '. . . expenditure can often be a bad indicator of other aspects of standards. This can be because prices of inputs vary, or because local authorities sometimes use (for various reasons) needlessly expensive techniques. . . . It is often clear that authorities are inefficient at relating the benefits of alternative techniques to their costs. The accounts of local authorities may also yield bad indices of standards because attempts to establish uniform accounting conventions have met with a doubtful degree of success until recent years.'

below.* It would be interesting to know whether this results in poorer secondary education or whether progressive and efficient local education authorities are able to maintain high standards in both spheres. County authorities providing a high proportion of selective school places† in 1959–60 also provide a high number of nursery school places, but there appears to be little relationship between the proportion of children in all-age schools and nursery provision.

As would be expected, the association between social class and independent nursery education is high, particularly in the counties. A number of the other significant associations may be spurious in that they can be explained in terms of social class, for example in the boroughs the proportion of Labour seats held after 1962 is inversely related to independent nursery provision. The explanation for this is the high inverse relationship between Labour-held seats and the proportion of the population in social class I and II, which in turn is associated with independent nursery education. Similarly, in the counties, the significance of the correlations between the extent of this form of education and indices of overcrowding, standards of housing and pupil–teacher ratios in primary schools is due to the connexion of these variables with social class. The highest correlation is one of 0·63 between oversize classes in junior schools and the provision of independent nursery education in the counties. This may indicate that in areas where the quality of state primary education is particularly poor, at least in terms of class size, about which parents appear to worry a great deal, the investment in private education for young children is especially high.

Many of the differences between the coefficients for independent provision in the counties and boroughs can probably be accounted for in the following way. Independent nursery education is made up of a number of strands: there are voluntary organizations designed to provide for children with inadequate home environments or unsatisfactory amenities in the areas in which they live; cooperative groups run by parents; and private concerns run for profit. The last of these is comparable to other forms of independent education, the others generally are not. It would be easier to predict

---

* Yet Bleddyn Davies found little correlation between expenditure on the various educational welfare services, which would indicate that, for example, those authorities which spend most on medical services do not also spend most on special schools. The following table indicates that the coefficients for the provision of nursery education with educational welfare services are small, though usually positive.

Number of nursery school pupils per 1,000 population January 1962 with:

1. Meals and milk	+0·09
2. Special education	+0·17
3. Aid to pupils in secondary schools	−0·11
4. Medical inspection and treatment	+0·14
5. Recreational facilities	+0·18

(See Davies, 1968, p. 272.)

† This variable also correlates highly and positively with other indices of educational standards.

associations with characteristics of areas were it possible to separate out these different strands accurately. For example, the first of them ought to be sensitive to need indices such as overcrowding, whereas the third ought to be closely related to the proportion of the population defined as middle class. The latter is inversely related to overcrowding, and therefore will intervene in any relationship between pre-school education and overcrowding. In the county boroughs there is more voluntary provision than in the counties, which explains the lower coefficients in this type of administrative area. There is other evidence that in both types of authority an increasing proportion of provision takes the form of collective effort by parents. The assumption that this form is largely a middle-class monopoly receives support from the close association between high social class and high provision, particularly in the administrative counties.

According to this evidence it is also high in the counties where a large number of women go out to work. However, it may not be correct to deduce from this that independent nursery education has developed in these areas because female employment is high. The latter variable is also correlated with social class (with males in administrative, managerial and professional occupations 0·55, with males in non-manual occupations 0·42). In the boroughs where the association between the extent of female employment and social class is much less marked (0·19 and 0·15) there is a small negative association between independent nursery provision and female employment.*

Regressions

Finally Tables 6.10 and 6.11 show the results of the regression analysis. So far the simple correlations between each independent variable and the three dependent variables respectively have been shown. A stepwise multiple regression tries to discover which combinations of independent variables account for the greatest part of the correlation with the dependent variable. In other words it seeks to show the multiple effect of a number of independent variables on a dependent variable, the regression being the best line of fit for the relationship between the former and the latter. The first variable given in each of the tables below has the highest correlation coefficient with

---

* In conclusion the total number of significant associations is low, but since the product—moment correlation coefficient is a measure of linear association, and there was a possibility that some of the associations involved might be non-linear, the data were transformed into their logarithmic equivalents. However, most of the log-transformed values were very similar to those given in Tables 6.8 and 6.9. Those affected strongly enough by logarithmic transformations to become significant at the 1 per cent level are listed below. In no case did this apply to the coefficients for maintained nursery education.

    (a) Administrative counties: Total nursery places with (9.), per cent of the population living in urban districts and metropolitan boroughs = 0·35.
    (b) County boroughs: Total nursery places with (22.), per cent of 13-year-olds in all age schools = −0·29, independent nursery places with (12.), per cent change in population = 0·28, and (13.), households with exclusive use of amenities = 0·38.

the dependent variable. However, those that follow will not necessarily be those with the second or third highest coefficients, since many of the independent variables are intercorrelated and therefore add relatively little towards accounting for the variation in the dependent variable. As in previous sections the local education authorities are divided into administrative counties and county boroughs and separate analyses have been completed for maintained, independent and total nursery places in each of these. Table 6.10 shows the results for the administrative counties.

Only those variables whose F values are significant at the 5 per cent level have been listed above. The number having a significant effect is small and the proportion of the variation explained by them is also low. For the total number of nursery places the variable with the highest correlation coefficient (r), that is family size explains only 15 per cent of the total variation. With the introduction of three more variables the square of the multiple correlation (R^2) rises to 0·44. Thus the 'model' explains 44 per cent of the variation. For reasons given when discussing the correlation coefficients, the separate analyses for maintained and independent provision are more interesting. In the case of the former the fitting of three variables explains 54 per cent of the variation. It is surprising that the percentage of selective school places is the best predictor of the number of local authority nursery places, and it is hard to interpret this result. The emergence of the level of industrialization reinforces the findings that rural counties, where agriculture is still an important industry, are very poorly provided with state pre-school education. As expected, the most important predictor of the extent of independent provision is the proportion of males in administrative, professional and managerial occupations. This explains nearly 60 per cent of the variation.

Turning to the county boroughs, Table 6.11 shows that the models are even less successful in explaining variation in nursery provision in this type of authority.

In the case of total provision only 20 per cent of the variation is explained. Very little significance should be attached to such inconclusive results. Nevertheless, it is worth noting that the proportion of people living at more than one and a half persons per room, i.e. overcrowding, is negatively associated with provision for pre-school education, and explains a higher proportion of the variation than any of the other variables fitted. If the need for nursery education is associated at least partly with poor housing, then it is clear from this evidence that existing provision is distributed in a way which favours areas with better housing. This has important policy implications. The proportion of the variation in maintained places explained is 21 per cent, less than half of that explained for the administrative counties. Demographic factors, that is population change and population density, emerge as the most important variables, followed by the percentage of children in all-age schools. The emergence of the latter might indicate that those authorities which have been unable to rid themselves of a type of school which is regarded as

Table 6.10. **Variables explaining variation in nursery provision in the administrative counties**

		R^2	F-value	r
Total number of places				
	Variables			
11	(family size)	0·15	10·3	0·39
21	(per cent selective school places)	0·28	10·6	0·35
20	(expenditure on facilities for recreation)	0·37	7·9	0·35
4	(males in social class I and II)	0·44	6·1	0·32
Maintained places				
	Variables			
21	(per cent of selective school places)	0·33	27·8	0·57
20	(expenditure on facilities for recreation)	0·47	16·1	0·40
8	(level of industrialization)	0·59	8·5	0·11
Independent places				
	Variables			
4	(males in social class I and II)	0·59	82·5	0·77
21	(per cent selective school places)	0·68	17·4	0·33

Table 6.11. **Variables explaining variation in nursery provision in the county boroughs**

		R^2	F-value	r
Total number of places				
	Variables			
10	(overcrowding)	0·09	8·7	−0·31
15	(day nursery places)	0·16	6·1	0·19
22	(per cent of 13-year-olds in all-age schools)	0·20	4·2	−0·24
Maintained places				
	Variables			
12	(per cent change in population)	0·10	9·1	−0·31
9	(population per acre)	0·15	5·1	−0·06
22	(per cent 13-year-olds in all-age schools)	0·21	6·1	−0·19
Independent places				
	Variables			
5	(males in non-manual occupations)	0·35	43·6	0·59
18	(cost per primary school pupil)	0·38	4·8	0·21
21	(per cent selective school places)	0·42	5·7	−0·02

obsolete are unable to provide education for children prior to compulsory schooling. The proportion of males in non-manual occupations explains the highest proportion of the variation in independent places. As in the counties, the role of the middle-class population asserts itself. However, it is more broadly based in the boroughs including all non-manual occupations, rather than just the higher echelons of these, and explains a much lower proportion of the variation. This is probably due to the larger number of voluntary organizations providing pre-school education in working-class areas in the boroughs than in the counties.

The attempt to explain the high variation in the provision of nursery education in different parts of England and Wales in terms of measurable characteristics of local authority areas has not been successful. Although this chapter has shown that there are some associations between certain of the objectively defined characteristics of the local education authority and the extent of pre-school education in any area, apart from one or two exceptions such as the relationship between independent places and a middle-class population, these associations are too weak to be interpreted as plausible measurable causes of the extent of provision.*

The difficulties encountered in this study were also experienced by Jean Packman in her study of the variation in the proportion of children in care in local authorities (Packman, 1968). Faced with an almost identical problem, the need to explain a curiously large variation in the number of children in care in different areas, which did not seem to coincide with other variations in the characteristics of the area, the author set about carefully measuring the number of children in care per 1,000 population under 18 in a sample of one authority in three. She found that in 1962 the national average was 5·1, but that the figure for Oxfordshire was 9·7 and for Bootle 1·9, which is the reverse of what would be expected when taking into account the notion of children at risk with the greatest need.

There are considerable problems in identifying need for any social service, and nursery education and child care are no exceptions to this. Packman carefully measured need by identifying the circumstances in which it occurs,

* In the National Survey carried out by the Government Social Survey and Mr G. F. Peaker for the Plowden Report (Central Advisory Council for Education, 1967, Vol. II), one of the variables included in a regression model designed to identify predictors of attainment was whether the child had attended a nursery school or class. It did not in fact emerge from the regression analysis as significant. But more important from the point of view of this chapter, when correlated individually with forty-two other independent variables in the model for five different age and sex groups only twenty-three coefficients were significant out of a total of 210. The other variables covered many aspects of the child's background ranging from parents' education, occupation and income, to the physical amenities of the home and parental attitudes to various issues. Where a coefficient was significant it was not consistently so for each age and sex group, the only exception being the obvious relationship between age of starting school and whether the child went to nursery school or class. This accounted for five out of the twenty-three significant variables. Thus attendance by the individual child does not appear to be related to any aspect of its home background, any more than the supply of provision is closely related to any aspects of individual areas.

and using the incidence of these as a measure of need. But the indices of social conditions which emerged were not correlated with the proportion of children in care. Her findings in this respect were therefore similar to those of this study, and the results of her investigation of the relationships between voluntary and maintained provision were identical, in that she also found no consistent relationship. In some areas they seemed to be complementing each other and in others they seemed to be substitutes for each other. Nor did she find a clear relationship between alternative services to taking children into care such as approved schools, adoption or special schools for the maladjusted, although they obviously play a part in accounting for variations as did the extent of preventive services.

Any analyses of this kind are bedevilled by the problem of time. It is not altogether satisfactory to relate political control in 1962, or family size in 1961 to the number of nursery places in 1965. It may well be more meaningful to take political control in 1952 or family size in 1945. Decisions to develop pre-school education or to stop providing it have been taken at different times over many years, and in the maintained sector there has been virtually no expansion since 1956. Had it been possible to collect data on the number of places for pre-school education in 1945 and 1955 and include this in the regression analysis, the amount of variation explained would have been very high, as a result of the inclusion of these variables. Jean Packman also found considerable continuity over time, those authorities with the highest proportion of children in care in 1952 reappeared in the list for 1962, as did those with the lowest proportion. Bleddyn Davies found that 'a striking feature of patterns of local authority provision was their continuity. This was as true of education as in general it was of local health, welfare and children's services' (Davies, 1968, p. 263). He found for example that for primary education, 'one could predict over a third of the variation in teachers' salaries per pupil in 1961–2 from the pattern in 1950–51 and over four-fifths of it from the pattern in 1958–9. Similarly one could predict more than a quarter of the variation in total costs per pupil from the variation in 1950–51 and three-quarters of it from the variation in 1958–9' (pp. 263–4).

In the case of maintained nursery education this continuity has been reinforced by the central government's embargo on any expansion in preschool provision. The role of the central government in the administration and development of the educational service is increasing, and part of the rationale for this is that a more satisfactory allocation of resources between different areas will be achieved in this way. The Department of Education and Science's control over school building and the quota system for teachers are the best examples of this. The Department's decision to disallow any increase in the number of places for children aged 3 to 5 was largely an attempt to ensure that resources should be concentrated on the compulsory sector. But in doing this, existing inequalities within the nursery sector have been maintained. Thus the 'league tables' given earlier in this chapter for

1965 would not look very different for 1955 and possibly even for late 1945 or 1946.

While mentioning the relative positions of local education authorities with respect to the provision of nursery education, it must be stressed again that this only refers to quantitative standards. The quality of nursery provision may well be much higher in some authorities that have very few places than in other authorities with large numbers of places. Unfortunately there are no output indices available for nursery education. It would be very difficult to find a measure of performance for such young children, whether academic attainment, personality development or social adjustment, which might be used as a valid index of output. It might have been possible to develop indices of the quality of services rendered such as teachers' qualifications, and pupil—teacher ratios in nursery education, but this has not been attempted.

The failure to identify either individual variables, or a combination of variables, which adequately explain the variation in the provision of state nursery education might be due to the fact that the model as constructed is not an effective means of revealing any underlying uniformities. This might be due to the omission of vital variables, the inclusion of others which confuse the picture, or to inherent problems such as intercorrelations amongst the independent variables, the identification problem of variables which have more than one kind of effect, or even to difficulties in defining the dependent variable. On the other hand, there simply may be no uniformities in the provision of maintained nursery education. The unequal distribution of maintained places may in itself be the result of decisions being taken over the last thirty years in a haphazard way; that is unrelated to demand variables such as social class or to need variables such as overcrowding, or to expenditure on other kinds of educational provision. This does not invalidate the suggestion made in Chapters 2—4 that over time various forces of political, economic and demographic change have put strain on the resources of the family, which are utilized in the socialization of young children. Nor does it invalidate the suggestion that these strains have led to the provision of nursery education. It does, however, mean that the response to such changes has been far from uniform from one area to another as well as from one time to another.

Although it has been suggested that the central government leaves fewer and fewer decisions to local authorities on educational provision, which leads to more equal standards of local provision in the main educational services, than in for example the social work services, nursery education occupies a unique position. For twenty-six years, from 1918 to 1944, there were permissive powers for local education authorities to set up nursery schools and classes. The 1944 Education Act made it mandatory to provide education for children from the age of 3 to 5. However, for reasons given in Chapter 4, this was never enforced. Hence local authorities have had somewhat more autonomy in the initiation and carrying through of decisions to increase or decrease the number of places in nursery education in their areas, than in many other aspects of educational policy. The role of unique historical factors in decision-making at the local level might therefore play an important part in determining the extent of nursery provision in different local authorities. Packman found in her study that the policies pursued by different children's departments was an important source of variation, and some children's officers believed it to be the most important single cause. The difficulty of attributing the variation to the kind of factors considered in this chapter possibly indicates that a consideration of less clearly defined, more subjective forces, such as the attitudes and interests of local officials and politicians at certain periods, may be a more fruitful approach to the problem of why nursery education is distributed so unevenly. It may also provide further insight into why it has developed so slowly with the exception of two or three periods when numbers increased rapidly, and it may aid the attempt to account for this differential rate of growth.

7. Decision-making on pre-school education in four local authorities

This chapter attempts to trace the history of nursery education, and the way decisions were taken on it, in four local authorities since the Second World War.* The choice of authorities was determined by the need to compare pairs of authorities which are broadly similar in size and other characteristics, yet which make dissimilar provision of pre-school education. It also depended on their willingness to provide the necessary information. These conditions were met by two large, affluent and rapidly expanding counties in the South-east, Hertfordshire and Kent, and by two small, heavily working-class county boroughs with relatively static populations in the Midlands, Smethwick and Burton-on-Trent. In 1965 Hertfordshire had twenty-three maintained places per 1,000 child population aged 2 to 4, and Kent five, compared with an average for administrative counties of fourteen; Smethwick had ninety-three and Burton twelve, compared with an average for county boroughs of fifty-two.† Hertfordshire and Smethwick are amongst the authorities with a relatively high ratio of places to population in their respective types of authority, whereas Kent and Burton are amongst the lowest.

The following pages will illustrate the evolution of one educational service, touching on the administrative processes only insofar as they affect its volume, character or distribution. It should be stressed that all the people involved are concerned with other aspects of education too, that they operate within a given framework of legislation, that there is rarely any appreciable

* It draws on the written papers of the administration of these authorities, including minutes and reports of the education committees or their sub-committees, and files of correspondence between the officials and teachers, Her Majesty's Inspectors, elected members, the Ministry of Education and the general public. In Kent, where at one time the provision of nursery education was a controversial issue, the local press provides further material. Relying on such written evidence did not prove as fruitful as was hoped, since the minutes and reports of local authority departments are always brief and consequently often uninformative. Even the argument at full council meetings is not reported, only the final decisions being recorded. Files of correspondence were more worth-while sources; however, two of the authorities did not keep these for more than two or three years. For this reason, interviews were sought with some of the people who had been involved. This also proved difficult since many of the officials had moved to jobs in other authorities or retired, and elected members were even harder to trace, many of them having retired or died. There are also dangers in drawing on the memories of participants in the events described. First, only a small selected group of those involved could give their accounts, which might give rise to bias; secondly, the accounts themselves might be biased or inaccurate, or both. However, such difficulties are inherent in any attempt to study decision-making processes over a long period.

† These averages are based on totals excluding Wales and the Metropolitan area.

reserve of unused resources, and that the opportunities for securing additional resources, or for manipulating the resources they already have, are limited. Throughout, it will be necessary to return to these constraints in explaining decisions about nursery education. Yet the fact remains that every authority is operating under more or less similar restraints. Nevertheless, as Chapters 5 and 6 have shown, there are big differences in the extent of provision made which cannot be satisfactorily explained by, for example, variation in need. Why the differences have arisen can be more interesting than the differences themselves. Comparative statistics cannot tell us anything about the people who provide the service, and it is perhaps they rather than any others who ultimately shape it. It is the demands that are met rather than the demands themselves which determine whether a child will be able to have nursery education. In discussing the social services Donnison and Chapman (1964, pp. 253–4) suggested that

the development of these services does not proceed as a continuous equilibrium-seeking response to marginal changes in external, impersonal forces (as economic analysis of organisations often suggests). It is begun and driven forward by people, within the groups providing the service, its progress is partly self-sustaining – growth promoting further growth – and it is not uniform and continuous, but passes, like a drama, through succeeding 'acts' of uncertain duration and differing character.

The development of nursery education is no exception. Unfortunately, there is never a single individual or group on whom every move depends, and it is, to quote Wilson (1961, p. 128), hard to get at 'the details of councillor participation, the internal political manoeuvrings, within and between committees, and the influence of particular individuals or groups' because the minutes and working papers give no clue to individual influences.

As a further preliminary, it is necessary to describe briefly the administrative structure of the local education authority. It is made up of three tiers in the counties and two tiers in the county boroughs. The first tier consists of the county or county borough council and its education committee, which controls the policies implemented by the officials who are headed by the chief education officer. The second tier in the counties consists of the Divisional Education Executive and the divisional education officer and his staff, or, in the case of the 'excepted districts',* a District Education Committee partnered by the borough education officer and his staff. The third tier (the second tier in the county boroughs) consists of the schools themselves with their governing bodies or management committees, partnered by the teaching staff. All important matters of policy are decided at the first-tier level, and

* The 1944 Act abolished the powers of the second tier in local government in the sphere of education. However, those municipal boroughs or urban councils with a population of 60,000 or more, or those with an elementary school population of 7,000 or more, could on application retain their powers. These authorities became known as the 'excepted districts' and their powers are similar to those of the divisional executives.

consequently most of the ensuing discussion will deal with this level. However, the delegation of some functions to the divisional executive under schemes which vary from authority to authority, laid down by the county councils, makes it necessary to refer to them from time to time. The role of the third tier is of little significance in the decision to provide places for pre-school education; however, it may be important in the deliberations involved in abolishing such places.

The local education authority is obliged to establish one or more education committees to fulfil its duties. The majority of its members must be members of the county borough or council, but it should also include persons with a special knowledge of education. It is usually the largest and always the most powerful committee of the county or borough council. Because of the wide range of provision it must cover, it operates through a number of specialized sub-committees. Amongst these there is usually a primary sub-committee responsible for junior and infant schools and nursery education, which deals with priorities in school building and school improvement programmes at the primary level, with current expenditure in the schools and the appointment of head teachers, and which occasionally may implement changes or additions to the curriculum or recommend the adoption of new teaching techniques.

This sub-committee makes most of the decisions about the provision of nursery education.

The two administrative counties — Hertfordshire and Kent — will be considered first, followed by Smethwick and Burton. This in turn is followed by a discussion of the similarities and differences in the policies for nursery education in the four areas. The amount of material available for the counties is far greater than for the county boroughs, since the latter cover less extensive areas and smaller populations.

Hertfordshire

In January 1965 there were eighteen maintained nursery schools* in Hertfordshire, which provided 711 full-time and 576 part-time places, and four nursery classes with approximately 100 places making a total of 1,099 full-time equivalent places, which constitutes provision for 2·2 per cent of children aged 2 to 4.† This is reinforced by 2,960 independent places, which provide for a further 5·8 per cent of the age group.‡ When the forty-seven

---

* Two of these came under the London Borough of Barnet after April 1965.

† The discrepancy between the number of nursery classes given here and the number under Hertfordshire in Appendix 4 which is also quoted on p. 123 is due to the Department's special definition of a nursery class (see Chapter 5, p. 93). The figure given here is the local authority's and the percentage of children provided for is based on this. However, the rankings given later involve comparison with other authorities and are necessarily based on Department of Education and Science figures.

‡ This includes places in ten voluntary nursery schools which are grant aided by the local education authority.

English administrative counties are ordered according to the ratio of maintained places to child population, Hertfordshire ranks eleventh, and it ranks third for independent places. There were also seven day nurseries under the auspices of the local health authority. The maintained places were not distributed evenly throughout the authority — for example, St Albans had two nursery schools and two nursery classes, whereas Stevenage had none — the more populated western half of the county being somewhat better off than the eastern half; however, there was at least one nursery school in each of the divisions, so no large area was left devoid of places. The great majority of independent places were in registered premises under the medical officer of health. They accounted for 2,036 places and registered child-minders accounted for a further 824 places. These small independent nursery schools and playgroups have grown up all over the county, although there seems to be a tendency for them to proliferate in bunches, some towns having a consistently larger number of groups than others, indicating that the establishment of a group, for which there may well be excess demand, leads to the establishment of more groups. There were only five independent nursery schools under the Department of Education and Science, four of which were in the western half of the county. They provided 100 places.

Before the war there was no nursery education in Hertfordshire. The war saw the establishment of one nursery school and two nursery classes, largely as a result of evacuation, and forty-two wartime nurseries. When the war ended the grant procedure for wartime nurseries was discontinued, and authorities reverted to the pre-war system of separate responsibility for day nurseries and nursery schools and classes by the local health and education authorities respectively (as described in Chapter 4). By the end of 1945 the number of wartime nurseries had dropped to thirty-five, and another five closed down in the first three months of 1946. The primary sub-committee minutes gives inadequate buildings as the reason for these closures. Many of the nurseries had been inadequately housed in requisitioned property. Before the suitability of the accommodation of the remaining nurseries was assessed, it was necessary to decide whether they should be taken over by the education or health department or, indeed, whether they should be abolished altogether. An interim report of the primary sub-committee on the provision of nursery education pointed out that, under the order of priorities agreed by the county council for building, nursery schools had been classified as B2. Since priorities A1, 2, 3 and B1 would not be completed for at least six years, there were no plans for nursery schools in the immediate post-war period. Therefore, existing war nurseries should be taken over where possible to be used as nursery schools. Behind the somewhat dubious rationale of this lay a difference in power between the administrators involved. The powerful chief education officer at the time was convinced of the value of nursery provision and believed that it belonged to the province of the education department rather than to that of the health department. He also presumably believed that his own department could organize this service more effectively than the existing health department. The medical officer of health was considerably less powerful in the hierarchy of chief officers and consequently his own department's bid to take over the wartime nurseries was quashed early on without a prolonged fight, although it did succeed in wresting three of them from the education department's grasp, which subsequently became health department day nurseries. The sharing out of war nurseries merely shows that the power wielded by the officials concerned can affect the nature and extent of provision in a demonstrable way. Since expansion was to be so difficult later, what happened at this juncture was crucial.

At the time those involved were optimistic about the future. The primary sub-committee laid down a long-term policy which would 'aim at securing comprehensive and suitable provision for the whole county for children of nursery school age' (Sub-Committee Report, 1 June 1945). Meanwhile, it had to be content to adapt those wartime nurseries whose existing accommodation was adequate. Where this was not the case, it hoped to replace them with houses which might be either bought or rented. The Committee argued that the home-like atmosphere of such buildings actually provided a better transition from home to school than formal school buildings. A further rationalization was its belief that, where a war nursery was already in existence, there would be enough local support for a nursery school, but where this was not the case there would not be enough support to warrant setting up a school, even where it did not involve new building. No evidence was offered to support this. In fact, with the exception of one wartime nursery where a questionnaire was sent to parents in order to discover whether there would be adequate support for a nursery school — the response indicated the affirmative — the committee had no information on demand for this service.*

In nearly every case the sole criterion as to whether a nursery school should be established out of a wartime nursery was the nature of the building in which the latter was housed. For example, a nursery in East Barnet served a poor area where it was recognized that a nursery school was needed; yet because of its building it was not recommended for adaptation and the alternative of buying or renting a house was not suggested. The primary sub-committee recorded the necessity for better information on need. An ill-defined concept such as 'the needs of the district' was used sometimes, but in practice the decision to start a school was based on the suitability and availability of existing accommodation. The exceptions were three wartime nurseries with unsuitable buildings, which were to be replaced by nursery

---

* During 1945 the St Albans local education committee asked for a grant to study the need for pre-school education in the area. Although they had asked for this in 1944 and it had been turned down, permission was granted the following year, subject to permission from the Ministry of Education to include the item for grant purposes. Whether this permission was ever given is unclear, but it has not been possible to trace a report of the study. However, the request is a rare example of an attempt to increase information about the need for this service.

wings built on to infant schools. Eighteen of the wartime nurseries were converted into nursery schools, a few of which were in prefabricated huts or on requisitioned land, which meant that replacements might have to be considered at some time in the not too distant future. Along with the existing nursery school and class these provided places for approximately 1,000 children between the ages of 2 and 5. The history of the intervening twenty years is one of a struggle to maintain the nucleus created in 1945 by on the one hand dismissing attempts to close the schools down, and on the other hand securing replacements for schools whose buildings necessitated this. The number of full-time equivalent places* in 1965, 1,004, indicates that the local education authority was successful in this.

At the end of 1947 the possibility of increasing the provision of nursery education was discussed by the primary sub-committee. It decided that no further provision was possible, although no reasons were given. Since it discussed the costs of nursery schools at the same meeting, it seems likely that their high cost per pupil may have been a major influence on the decision. The costs of nursery education were taken up again in 1948, a member of the committee having expressed concern about them. The high costs were defended on the grounds that they were inevitable in small units, where good staffing ratios were essential. There were no further developments† until late in 1951 when the lease of the building housing a nursery school ran out. There was a strong case for a new building and the Ministry of Education's approval was sought. The Ministry replied that it would not consider it as a project for inclusion in the major building programme but that it had no objection to the authority providing alternative premises for less than £5,000 under the minor works programme. When consulted on this the county architect thought that a new school for forty children for under £5,000 would be very difficult. However, the education committee proceeded and the Finance and General Purposes Committee approved the purchase of a site. By this unusual use of the minor works programme, Hertfordshire was able to replace those nurseries whose buildings were no longer adequate with new schools, and thus maintain its numbers, where a less imaginative authority might have closed down the schools. This is an example of the way a local authority with foresight can manipulate the resources available to it in order to protect the services it offers.

* A part-time place equals half a full-time equivalent.

† Every local education authority was required under Section II of the 1944 Act to submit a Development Plan on or before 1 April 1946. The authorities were 'to estimate the immediate and prospective needs of the area as regards primary and secondary education, including arrangements for children under five years of age' (Circular 28, May 1945). The Hertfordshire Development Plan published in 1949 made provision for twenty-six nursery schools and thirty nursery classes, which amounted to 3,200 places. This allowed for the admission in the urban areas of 14 per cent of the expected annual entry to schools. But the Plan pointed out that 'since there is little information on which the future plans ought to be based it is probable that expansion of the facilities proposed will be necessary in some districts'.

Early in 1953 the new Conservative government put pressure on the local education authorities to economize (Ministry of Education Circular 242). Earlier chapters have shown that in such circumstances nursery education is always vulnerable, and the situation in Hertfordshire in 1952 proved to be no exception. The primary sub-committee began by considering the possibility of excluding the rising 5s from the infant schools. These children cost nothing in terms of expenditure on teachers' salaries or the maintenance of buildings but they did increase the size of the general allowance, a *per capita* sum for expenditure on books and materials. Consequently, the committee decided not to seek this allowance for them, but to leave the arrangement standing whereby such children were admitted when there was room. In this way they kept children in the system, yet contributed to the required cuts in expenditure.

Then the education committee decided to reduce the expenditure on nursery education by £3,500, which they believed would involve closing down certain schools. The size of this saving was probably agreed upon by the chief education officer and the county treasurer beforehand. However, no schools were closed down, in spite of one attempt, and for the year 1952/3, surprisingly, the committee approved the spending of an extra £1,200 on nursery education. Possibly the authority saved money on capital equipment on which expenditure could be postponed for a couple of years. The following quotations on the attempted closure are from the minutes of the primary sub-committee (10 March 1952):

Since the school serves no large centre of population, as do all our other nursery schools, and as the Welwyn Parish Council had recommended very strongly that it should be closed, it was felt that the school should cease. . . . Following the report of the proposed closure of Oaklands many letters of protest have been received. A memorandum signed by 110 householders in the area urges the continuance of the school; letters have also been received from the local doctors, the Welwyn and District Labour Party, and the Mid-Herts Teachers' Association.

all of which apparently urged that the school should continue. Thus 'the opinion of the people of the area' is that it 'is fulfilling a very important function', and for this reason it was kept open. The success of this outcry can be partly attributed to the quality of the school's head teacher, who was held in high regard, and partly to the leader of the opposition to close it, who was an extremely articulate parent, whose handicapped child had benefited enormously from attending the school.

Opportunities arose in 1954 to take over day nurseries which the health department wished to close down. A nursery school sharing a building with a day nursery was expanded in this way. A divisional executive proposed that a second day nursery should be taken over; the officers at county hall were in favour of this and the Ministry was prepared to approve it. However, the primary sub-committee decided that it was unable to recommend that the education committee should support this proposition. No reasons are given for this decision in any of the documents. But the matter was not allowed to rest there. The county councillor for Welwyn Garden City took up the matter in the education committee, but his motion to have the proposal referred back was narrowly defeated. He then raised it at a county council meeting, where he was successful. At the following primary sub-committee, at which the referred item was discussed, the arguments against the proposal were recorded. Although a building needing no adaptation was available, and there was a waiting list of 100 at the existing nursery school on the other side of the town, the committee stated that it had considered the question of additional facilities for nursery education before, and owing to other commitments come to the conclusion that expansion was impossible. It added that the extension of nursery education in one area would lead to demands elsewhere. The 'if we allow this, where shall we draw the line next time?' argument is a common one in situations where a decision is taken to turn down a proposal. In this case it may have been further strengthened by the fact that a number of committee members served areas where there was either no nursery school or no prospect of one, so why establish a precedent in this case, from which there was little chance of the electors in their own areas benefiting in the future? In surveying the distribution of places in the county the committee had noted that of twenty-six centres of population Welwyn was better provided for than fourteen of them and worse off than eleven. Although the committee kept to its decision not to take over the day nursery, it did ask for a review of nursery education in the county.

This review, which was completed in 1955, brought to light some interesting facts and gave rise to ambitious plans for the future; it revealed from the size of waiting lists considerable excess demand; that the county made provision for approximately the same proportion of its child population as was made nationally; and that over half the children attending nursery schools in the county came into special need categories. It recommended that the possibility of part-time nursery education, which would allow a larger number of children to benefit from existing provision, should be investigated. It expected the number cf children in some primary schools to fall, in which case the authority would start setting up nursery classes. The six existing nursery schools on requisitioned land were to be found new sites after derequisitioning. In urban areas, where there was no nursery school and no likelihood of a nursery class for some years, consideration was to be given to the provision of nursery accommodation — sites with the development corporations had been earmarked for this purpose — and in the light of local needs and economic expediency nursery classes might be built on to existing primary schools.

The first move to implement this was the obtaining of approval in principle from the Ministry to replace two of the schools on requisitioned land. This was given, subject to the cost being within the minor works limit of £10,000, after which the committee decided that, because of the high running costs of nursery schools, it should replace them with nursery classes instead.

A high-handed letter from the Ministry followed (Sub-Committee Minutes, 5 March 1956). It pointed out the educational advantages of nursery schools over classes, suggesting that the desire for economies should not outweigh these, that Section 8(2)b of the 1944 Act states that local education authorities were to establish nursery classes where they considered nursery schools to be inexpedient, that the provision of classes rather than schools would eliminate 2-year-olds. It asked whether the establishment of nursery classes was a matter of general policy in Hertfordshire and whether, since the authority was abandoning provision for 2-year-olds, the demand for this age group had actually fallen off.

This was an extraordinary letter in the light of the Ministry's policies at the time. Apart from the fact that it had been urging the local education authorities to economize, its interpretation of the 1944 Act that nursery classes should only be established in rare circumstances, where a nursery school was not possible, was entirely new. In any case, as the primary sub-committee pointed out, the County's Development Plan, which was accepted by the Ministry, intended that the authority should have more classes than schools. The point made by the Ministry on 2-year-olds was equally unjustified. It knew that most authorities were giving priority to 3- and 4-year-olds in a situation of excess demand. Finally, with the increasing relaxation of formal methods in the infant schools, the nursery class was no longer regarded as educationally inferior to the nursery school by most educationalists.

It is often argued that rigidity and inefficiency in bureaucratic organizations are the result of over-emphasis on formal depersonalized relationships to the exclusion of interaction of a more personal and informal kind. In the case of the above intervention by the Ministry the opposite situation had occurred: personal factors had intervened in a somewhat unusual way, disrupting the smooth running of a bureaucracy. The head teacher of one of the existing nursery schools was well liked by parents. For various reasons, many of the latter thought the school to which the new classes were to be attached inappropriate for the incorporation of two nursery classes. Furthermore, the popular head of the existing nursery school would lose her autonomy and status as a head teacher if her school were to be replaced by classes. She therefore decided to leave. Amongst the parents who were up in arms over this situation, there happened to be a civil servant of some seniority at the Ministry of Education, who then used his influence to reverse the local education authority's decision to run classes instead of a school.

The outcome of all this was that three years later the school was replaced by classes and in the meantime a petition by parents, and a request from the education committee, was submitted to the owners asking for an extension of the lease, which was granted. It is difficult to say for whom this represents victory.

Similar reprieves were given to the other nursery schools on requisitioned land with one exception in 1958 where no suitable premises could be found to replace it. Since this was the only closure of a nursery school in Hertfordshire between 1945 and 1965 it is necessary to inquire into the circumstances further. Why, for example, did the school at Welwyn, which was threatened with closure, survive while this one did not? There appear to be a number of reasons: first, nearly all its pupils were from working-class homes; second, the head teacher was less forceful in opposing the closure than in the other instance; third, the school was on the borders of the county cut off from county hall by poor communications, which probably hindered the organization of a successful pressure group in the little time that was available; fourth, and perhaps most important, the town was represented on the education committee by a man whose general attitudes towards the social services did not predispose him to support nursery education, whereas the councillor at Welwyn believed strongly in its value.

The second move in response to the review discussed earlier was to ask the divisional executives to submit proposals for nursery education in their areas. Those which suggested setting up nursery classes were to have their plans rejected. During 1956 the Ministry ruled that there was to be no increase in the number of children under 5 at school. However, the primary sub-committee decided to consider provision in north and east Hertfordshire, which were especially badly off. There was little that it could do other than purchase the occasional site on which accommodation for pre-school education might be built later. The problem was particularly acute in Stevenage where there was a rapidly growing child population, entrance to the infant school frequently had to be postponed until after the child was 5, and there was no local authority nursery school or class. Recognizing that there were a number of children in special need of nursery education who, had they lived elsewhere in the county, would have obtained a place, the primary sub-committee decided in 1959 to give financial help to a private, non-profit-making nursery school at a Community Centre. The school was suffering from a shortage of funds; its superintendent was paid below Burnham; and it needed new equipment. Consequently it applied to the local education authority for help, and since the authority felt there was a strong case for a nursery school in the town, it sought a method to award a grant. The officers discovered a loophole by which they could do this under Section 9(i) of the 1944 Act, whereby a local education authority may pay a grant to individual pupils at certain independent special schools and independent secondary schools. They decided a grant to the school would be more appropriate in this case, and £75 was paid towards the teacher's salary. A year later this was renewed and a second voluntary nursery school in Stevenage was aided in the same way. The following year, in 1961, the grant was increased to 25 per cent of the teaching staff's salary in order to ensure that they might be paid Burnham and Whitley scales. By the end of 1963 the local authority was aiding five schools in this way. It was also continuing to purchase sites for future maintained provision should the Department of Education and Science lift its embargo on the expansion of nursery education.

The only other change during this period was the expansion of one of the nursery schools in 1959 as a result of a classroom being freed by the local junior school. The view of the officials was that it would be ridiculous to leave it empty, there was pressure in the area to use it and so the Ministry was asked for its approval, which it gave. They were also able to replace a school on an inadequate site as a result of receiving a gift of land, which was to be used to accommodate a nursery school.

Had the number of places in the voluntary schools aided by the authority been included in the figures for maintained education, Hertfordshire would have been close to the top of the list of administrative counties given in Chapter 5. Between 1963 and 1965 another five voluntary nursery schools were receiving grants. By 1967 there were eighteen such schools. The original loophole had been informally sanctioned by the Department of Education and Science over the telephone. Later the Department was forced to withdraw this as a result of a letter from another local authority pointing out what Hertfordshire was doing and asking whether it was illegal, since the clause referred to secondary schools. The officials in Hertfordshire were then ingenious enough to discover another loophole, to which the Department again turned a blind eye, and which has so far proved impregnable. They turned to the 1937 and 1958 Physical Training and Recreation Acts, which enable grants to be made to voluntary bodies by local authorities. The powers of the council under these Acts were delegated to the education committee; and since 1963, 25 per cent of the salary bill of the schools concerned has been paid under this. The local education authority also gave a licence to a voluntary committee to build a temporary school on the site of a junior and infant school, giving them a 15 per cent grant towards the capital cost and a loan under the same Acts. The existing primary school was on a large site, its managers welcomed the addition of a nursery school and the primary sub-committee minutes stated that 'with the considerable housing development which has taken place in the neighbourhood of these schools, the eventual provision of a nursery school or nursery classes by the county council would seem to be eminently desirable'. They went on to say that it would be possible for the education committee to take over the school when the Department's restrictions were removed. They suggested that this might be a useful precedent in other parts of the county, where existing sites are large enough, or where an eventual nursery school is included in the Development Plan. The local education authority intends taking over all the voluntary schools with one exception, a school which prefers to remain independent. In this way the authority has built up a large nucleus which will form a basis of expansion later, without opposition from any of the officials or from elected members.

The conclusions that can be derived from this study of nursery education in Hertfordshire and further comment on the influences behind these decisions will be presented after the development of nursery education in Kent, Smethwick and Burton has been discussed.

Kent

There were three nursery schools* and three nursery classes (see note †, p. 125) in Kent on 1 January 1965. There were ninety-seven full-time places and eighty-four part-time places in the schools and approximately fifty-five full-time equivalent places in the nursery classes. There were, in addition, 4,716 independent places, of which the vast majority were in schools or playgroups registered with the health authority, as in Hertfordshire.† There were thirteen independent schools under the Department of Education and Science providing 327 places. Maintained places provided for 0·2 per cent of the 2 to 5 age group, and independent places for 5·9 per cent of this age range. Kent ranks thirty-fourth out of forty-seven in the provision of maintained places and sixth in the provision of independent places. There were no day nurseries in the county. Thus large parts of Kent were devoid of state nursery education or, indeed, any kind of maintained provision for the under 5s.

As in Hertfordshire, there were no nursery schools or classes in Kent prior to the Second World War. By 1945 there was one nursery school and forty-two wartime nurseries, exactly the same number as in Hertfordshire. In Kent some of these wartime nurseries had been attached to primary schools and were really the equivalent of nursery classes, bar longer hours. On receiving Circular 221/45 on the adaptation of the wartime nurseries, discussion began, as in Hertfordshire, between the parties concerned.

In Kent at this time the county council was not always the health and welfare authority, which complicated the situation in that, in addition to the health and education committees, representatives from the district councils were involved. The latter were asked to inform the county council which nurseries they proposed to run for welfare purposes and which were to be made available to the local education authority. This is strikingly different from what happened in Hertfordshire, where the chief education officer, rather than accepting what came to him after other departments had decided which nurseries they wished to run, went out to get all that he could, and won the lion's share. However, there was a more clear-cut division of responsibility between two departments at county hall. In Kent the county education department had no means of forcing the transfer of buildings and land from the former Part III authorities. Nevertheless in Kent the primary sub-committee was much less enthusiastic about the prospects of taking over the

---

* Two of these were taken over by London Boroughs on 1 April 1965.
† 3,338 of these places were registered under premises and 990 under persons.

wartime nurseries and introduced conditions which the nurseries must satisfy, before it would run them: for example, they had to cater for children over 2 years of age and they had to be on a site where they could be associated with an existing infant school, from which the head teacher could give regular supervision, since they had decided that provision generally should take the form of nursery classes. As a result of this, only three wartime nurseries were taken over by the education committee, and they continued to run seven nurseries which had been attached to primary schools. Twenty-two went to the welfare authorities, the future of five was undecided and five were to close. There is no mention in any of the documents of the criteria determining these closures.

A little later, in 1946, one of the borough councils asked the education committee of the county council to take over two wartime nurseries. Initially the committee refused on the grounds that the accommodation was unsatisfactory. However, after pressure from the borough, which stressed the high demand for nursery education in the area, it agreed to take over one of the nurseries and to set up classes at two nearby infant schools to replace the other. Probably the reluctance to take over these schools could be genuinely attributed to the poor accommodation of the nurseries concerned. There appears to have been a general view that it was a mistake to remain committed to wartime arrangements which were thought to be sub-standard or not truly educational in conception. But sometimes this kind of reasoning can be used to mask members' lack of interest and officials' unwillingness to increase their burden in a particular area.

Meanwhile the education department had received many inquiries on whether the extent of nursery education in the county could be improved. Some of these letters came from such organizations* as local Labour Parties or their women's sections, Trades Councils, Teachers' Associations, Parish Councils, Housewives' Leagues, and in one case a local branch of the Communist Party. Most of the requests were from individual middle-class mothers who, for example, wrote that they had a 'bright, energetic child in need of a lively environment where he could meet other youngsters'. There were one or two letters from working-class mothers. For example, one writing on behalf of several others asked if a nursery school might be opened in their district since their husbands were all working short-time owing to fuel cuts and the mothers wished to help by working part-time: 'we know you have difficulties, but we do not expect expensive nursery furniture, just somewhere to leave them'. Occasionally letters went via Members of Parliament†

* There was an unusual request for a village nursery school from the village Parents and Old Scholars Association whose representative had canvassed the village and stated that fifty children would attend. He stressed the need for a school since many mothers were working on the land in 'inclement weather unsuitable for accompanying children'.

† One such letter to an M.P. was obviously from a working-class mother. She wrote: 'it [the nursery] is needed very badly; the children are playing in the roads and there is so much danger for them playing on the streets', ending touchingly, 'Sir we wish you all the best of success and good luck'.

to the Ministry of Education then back to the local education authority. These requests were fobbed off, always politely, by referring to the Development Plan, which would provide for considerable nursery school provision.

The divisional executives also pressed for nursery classes occasionally in the immediate post-war years. In 1946 the Orpington Branch of the Communist Party produced a petition for nursery classes with 200 signatures, for which the divisional executive went on to press, though without success. One of the three wartime nurseries which were taken over by the local education authority had been the subject of considerable discussion at the divisional level, which was reported in the local newspaper. One of the councillors for the area had pressed for its adaptation as a nursery school. This local pressure may have affected the education committee's decision to take over this nursery. Whether there was similar local pressure behind the decision to take over the other two nurseries has not been possible to ascertain.

The Development Plan referred to above reaffirmed the committee's preference for nursery classes, arguing that they afford a useful stimulus to the infant schools and provide a better distribution of facilities in that they are closer to the children's homes. However, it foresaw the need for some nursery schools serving areas with populations of between 50–100,000 and which set standards for the nursery classes in that area. They envisaged the county having twenty-one nursery schools and 186 nursery classes. Unfortunately the Plan does not state what proportion of the child population in the relevant age group would be catered for, but it would appear that it is more ambitious than Hertfordshire's 14 per cent. Details of these Plans are included since they are still the statutory basis for expansion, and if authorities depart from them the Ministry asks for an explanation. However, in practice, the local education authorities use them only where it suits. They are also revealing on the lack of information available to local government. Officials in both Hertfordshire and Kent described the ratio of places to children arrived at as *ad hoc*. There was certainly no reliable estimate of the demand or the need for nursery education, and the estimates of population were difficult to calculate and proved to be very unreliable. The introduction to the Kent Plan comments that 'the ingredients of optimism and intelligent guesswork have had to be employed in generous measure'.

During the five years from 1946–51 provision for children under 5 in Kent was constantly threatened. The history of two nursery classes at Sheerness illustrates this. They were taken over by the education committee and adapted from a wartime nursery in 1946. Local pressure and the activities of a councillor influenced this decision, as already mentioned. In addition the building and grounds were adequate, there were fifteen 'need' cases and three teachers' children attending, and the staff were keen to cooperate in the change-over. In 1948 the health committee asked to take the classes over for use as a day nursery, which was 'urgently required'. Since it was open for day nursery hours and served the needs of working mothers, the education committee acquiesced.* However, in March 1950 the health committee cancelled its decision, on grounds of economy. The divisional executive, which had almost ceased to regard the classes as part of educational provision in the long uncertainty over their future, then recommended closing them. The local education authority officials considered this along with the possibility that the Urban District Council would refuse to renew the lease on the premises. Unfortunately this easy way out did not present itself, so they asked the divisional executive to reconsider their proposal to close the classes and to consider running a nursery school with extended hours to satisfy the needs of parents. The divisional executive reaffirmed their original decision on the grounds that the local education authority's proposal would give rise to staffing problems, with reference to qualified teachers. After more to-ing and fro-ing the divisional executive eventually won and the classes were closed, and since it could not suggest an alternative educational use for the premises the lease was not renewed.

The authority considered closing other schools. For example, in 1948 the chief education officer wrote to the divisional executive officer at Northfleet, asking whether the provision of nursery classes in the area was necessary. The divisional executive itself had already considered closing them in 1947, since they were on requisitioned land. However, it had decided that they served an important social need for the children of working mothers and other special cases, and this was reaffirmed by the divisional education officer the following year in his reply to the chief education officer. The authority therefore continued to requisition the land and the classes were saved. Eventually, the Ministry urged an alternative to requisitioning and in 1954 the owner sold the land to the Kent Education Committee. However, by this time there were very few nursery schools or classes left in Kent. The collapse of pre-school education in this county came about in 1951/2. The above examples of closures and attempted closures are evidence that it had been virtually under siege for some years. The pressures from the county council to cut educational expenditure in 1951, followed by the demand for economies in educational expenditure from the central government in 1952, meant it was unable to hold out any longer.

In November 1950 the county council asked for lists of possible cuts in educational expenditure. These were prepared by the education committee and presented at the next county council meeting in February 1951. The cuts

* Although there is no evidence in the papers of this, it is possible that officers in the education department offered it to the medical officer of health first since the Inspectorate and the Ministry had been pressing that the classes should be reorganized as a school since September 1947; the officials considered fighting the Ministry on this, since they believed that staffing costs were lower for classes and that the latter could be more easily adapted for infants' use. In May 1948 the local education authority received another letter from the Ministry awaiting comments on its letter of September 1947. It appears that delaying tactics were being used! In early 1949 the local education authority wrote to the Ministry pointing out that the organizational changes which the latter required had not been carried out and seeking approval for the classes to go to the Health Department. The Ministry gave their approval.

suggested were classified as those which were regrettable in the committee's view, but which would not vitally affect the service, and those which contained reductions which would vitally affect the service.* Nursery education came into the former category. The reasons behind its inclusion here will be considered later. Meanwhile, the controversy which it created will be discussed. Although there was opposition to the cuts in education expenditure in general and protest meetings were called by, for example, teachers' organizations about this, the only proposed cut which provoked a major outburst of protest was that concerning nursery education.

The budget debate at the county council meeting was a stormy affair. The total reduction in spending suggested by the education committee's first group of cuts amounted to £239,000. The council decided to implement all these, along with an additional £5,000 worth of cuts from items in the second category. There was a move by an alderman, supported by ten other members, to cut the remaining items, which was defeated.† He argued that this would reduce the county rate by 2½d. A wing-commander seconded, describing the ratepayer as bloodless and emaciated, and stating that it was impossible to squeeze any more out of him. 'Show that Kent, as ever, rebels against the blood-sucking activities of Whitehall. Kent is seething with indignation over these estimates', he said (Kent Messenger, 23 February 1951). A lieutenant-colonel, supporting the motion, stated that the education committee had not been honest in cutting down costs. He had found that a load of fertilizer was carted thirty-five miles from Sevenoaks to Faversham for school allotments, which he described as a disgrace. This was countered by another member who said criticisms of the education committee were being addressed to the wrong place, they should be sent to Whitehall. When put to the vote the resolution was heavily defeated, yet its sponsors demanded a

* The first category consisted of:
1. Upkeep of buildings and deferment of minor improvements (£30,000).
2. Postponement of the replacement of obsolete furniture (£18,000).
3. Books, stationery and apparatus, restriction of the increase in allowances for this (£49,000).
4. Swimming ended (£1,000).
5. Music and drama, curtailing of concerts and dramatic performances for schools (£5,500).
6. FE grants to voluntary bodies ended (£2,000).
7. Evening classes, abolition of these in certain subjects (£3,000).
8. Salaries of teachers, reduction of the number of teachers (£30,000).
9. Physical training clothing (£10,000).
10. Nursery schools and nursery classes, the abandonment of the service (£13,000).
11. Additional cuts to the above in the upkeep of buildings and grounds, furniture and equipment, books, stationery and apparatus, and aids to pupils in further and higher education.

The second category consisted of:

The abandonment of the youth service, reduction in cleaners and caretakers wage bill, and a further reduction in evening classes, higher education grants, and teachers' salaries.

† Later in the debate he demanded an increase in spending on civil defence.

count, which evoked from a clergyman member, 'Look at Ajax defying the lightning.' The individual item in the list of cuts which created the most controversy was the abandoning of nursery education. One Labour member, recalling that day nurseries had already been cut by 50 per cent, described this as the greatest tragedy proposed, saying, 'Whatever we may think of parents going out to work, they will still go out to work if you abandon the nursery schools. I do suggest you are abandoning the child.' This was met by cries of 'Rubbish' and 'No', and the lieutenant-colonel shouted, 'The mother's place is in the home looking after the children. What we cannot afford we cannot have, and we cannot afford these schools' (*Kent Messenger,* 1951).

After completing the debate on the education committee's report, a resolution was passed with an overwhelming majority stating:

That this council, after considering the burden of expenditure on education borne by the ratepayers of the County, most strongly urges His Majesty's Government to take such action centrally as may be necessary to reduce such expenditure until such time as the financial resources of the nation are adequate to meet the full implications of the 1944 Education Act.

This was followed by the passing of cuts in the estimates of the health and children's committee. One councillor attacked the committee for spending just under £5 per week on the maintenance of children in care, which he regarded as an 'impossible figure'. The afternoon's proceedings are an example of the classic conflict between those who favour considerable expenditure on the social services and those who wish to keep it to a minimum. The latter group is usually obsessed with the idea that rates must be kept down and frequently blames the central government for making excessive demands on the local authorities. On this occasion there was a large Tory majority and consequently the cuts imposed by the finance committee on education and the other social services were bound to go through at a county council meeting. However, heedless of the accusation of blood-sucking, Whitehall, or more accurately Curzon Street, intervened and the fight to preserve nursery education in Kent began.

A letter from the Ministry stated:

I am directed by the Minister of Education to state that he deplores the decision to close all existing nursery schools and classes regardless of their particular circumstances and asks the Authority to reconsider it. In the Minister's view the circumstances of each closure should be considered individually, and the Authority should satisfy themselves that the economy proposed in each case outweighs the loss of facilities to which the population served has grown accustomed.

As a result of this letter the finance committee recommended that the decision to close the classes should be deferred until after further investigation. This was adopted by the county council at its meeting in May. Meanwhile the local education authority received many protests and no support* for the move to close the schools and classes. Nearly all the divisional executives which had a nursery school or class in their area expressed concern about the decision, as did the managers of the schools involved. A number of teachers' organizations wrote condemning the cuts, most of them drawing special attention to the closing of nursery schools and classes.† The parent–teacher associations of several of the schools with classes wrote in very strong terms deploring this decision, as did local branches of the Nursery School Association. A number of organizations not directly concerned with education also appealed to the education committee to rescind its decision, such as local Labour Parties, Trades Council, Women Citizens' Associations, branches of various trade unions and Urban District Councils. Large numbers of individuals also wrote protesting about the closures. (Amongst these letters was one from parents offering to pay for the nursery education their children were receiving rather than see it abolished.)

A number of Kent Members of Parliament were drawn into the dispute, one of whom, Norman Dodds, M.P. for Dartford, asked a parliamentary question. He asked if the Minister was aware of the widespread concern in Kent at the decision of the education committee, pointed out that this had been decided without consulting the divisional executives, and asked if he would intervene in order to have the decision reconsidered. The Minister replied that he deplored the local education authority's decision to close its nursery schools and classes regardless of the particular circumstances and that he was asking for a reconsideration of this decision. The Member of Parliament's implied condemnation of the local education authority's failure to consult its divisional executives is an interesting example of the defence of the right of second-tier authorities to contribute to educational decision-making. The next step taken by the local education authority was to write asking the divisional executives to do just this, by providing information and advice on the nursery schools and classes in their areas. In this way the local education authority hoped to answer the points in the second sentence of the Ministry's letter quoted on p. 139.

While the divisional executives were preparing their reports, the officials in the education department received a number of requests from county councillors who, like the Kent Members of Parliament, had received numerous letters of protest, asking for more information about the service. One retired naval commander asked for this from the Chairman of the education committee 'as there is a tremendous row going on in Beckenham over the closing of nursery schools. Would you please be good enough to let me have the facts on this subject to refute the Socialists' argument'. The reply gave

---

* One exceptional letter was received saying that 'it is time most of the nursery schools were closed. They encourage many parents in laziness and shirk their responsibilities.'

† These included the Kent County Advisory Committee of Teachers and the Kent Federation of Head Teachers' Associations, as well as local associations of the National Union of Teachers.

details about the saving incurred in abolishing the schools and classes. It amounted to one sixth of a penny rate in a full year. The county councillors' letters revealed ignorance of the aims and structure of state provision for children under 5. For example, they wrote letters to the medical officer of health for information on nursery classes and to the chief education officer for information on day nurseries. One better informed councillor wrote to the chief education officer saying that he believed that Kent could not afford nursery classes under the present conditions, that he was not fully convinced that they were necessary, but that a 100 per cent grant from the Ministry of Education would probably alter his view!

Pressure from a different direction and of a different kind was exerted on the officials in the form of a letter from the Ministry of Education to the chief education officer, which was described as an 'off the record' paper on the 'value of nursery schools and nursery classes as we see it'. It went on to say that the nursery provision catered for working mothers and was meeting welfare needs as well as industrial needs, so that their closure would lead to child-minding, which it deplored; and that they performed a valuable role in training NNEB students and in providing a small but effective nucleus which would be hard to recreate; and finally that they doubted whether the accommodation of some of them could be used for infants without expensive alterations.

The response of the chief education officer was that the first point was not valid since the need was for day nurseries and that it was the health authority's responsibility to avoid child-minding. This viewpoint underlines the 'buck-passing' to which separate responsibility by two departments for the same age range of children, although supposedly different types of children in terms of their needs, can give rise. The chief education officer did not agree with the suggestion that much of the accommodation freed would be difficult to use for infants, but he accepted the other points raised.

The question of infant school provision was probably crucial in the re-affirmation of the decision to close the schools and classes. 1951 was the year 'the bulge' entered school and there was undoubtedly pressure on infant school places. In writing to the divisional executives for information, the chief education officer asked them to take this into account. He pointed out that infants of statutory school age might be excluded owing to lack of accommodation, but this might be avoided by using nursery accommodation. 'This, in some cases, may be a deciding factor, irrespective of the merits of the case for nursery provision.'

The replies from the divisional executives indicated that in all but two cases the accommodation might be used for older children either immediately or within the next two years. However, the need did not appear to be pressing in the three nursery schools in the county and the executives concerned in each case stressed the importance of the facilities they provided to the area and the hardship their loss would cause. There were four classes whose accommodation could not be used to any advantage for infants in the near future; two of these were attached to schools in Beckenham. The divisional executive stressed that these schools served an area with poor, overcrowded housing and that the headmistresses were under constant pressure from health visitors and other social workers to admit children to the nursery class. Only thirteen of the sixty children attending had been admitted on educational grounds alone. This was also true of a third class at Penge, where admissions were restricted to children needing places on welfare grounds. The fourth class where there was no pressing need for the infant school places was in Bromley. Places here were also restricted to welfare cases and the divisional executive presented a forceful case for retaining the class.

This was to no avail. In July, after a full discussion in which the education committee informed the council that there was a good case for the retention of every class and school, and that they would be glad if all of them could be continued, the county council decided to accept the advice of the county finance committee and close all the classes, with the exception of those in Beckenham, but retain the schools with the exception of that in Beckenham. The reason the Beckenham classes escaped the axe whilst all the others did not is complicated. It can be summarized as strong opposition to closure from the headmistresses concerned, well organized protest from the parents, a powerful plea from the Borough Education Officer who, amongst other things, mentioned 'the jibe of lazy mothers is not, in my opinion, to be sustained in our schools', and the intervention of various other local groups, along with the fact that since there was no pressure for infant places the classes would be left empty. But this might be described as a hollow victory since it was won at the expense of the nursery school in the town, which was sacrificed since it served a more affluent area than the classes. This might appear illogical in the light of the chief education officer's earlier reasoning, that the responsibility for provision for children with special needs belonged to the health department — i.e. one of the reasons given for abandoning nursery education in general was also given for keeping two classes in particular.

The county council's decision was accepted by the Ministry and the closures took place at the end of the autumn term. The controversy attracted the attention of the national press and *The Times* published a leading article (*The Times*, 17 September 1951) attacking Kent's policy. This did not convince those concerned in Kent and in February 1952 the county council adopted a recommendation that the remaining nursery schools and classes should be discontinued as an economy.* The grounds for these proposals for further closures were similar to those given earlier: first that the accommo-

* These proposals were part of a £300,000 cut in the estimates similar to those made a year earlier. On this occasion a lower proportion of the cuts were sustained by education than in 1951. Cuts in the social services included the demand for the closure of all day nurseries and a reduction in expenditure by the children's committee. In a four-hour debate the Labour group tried unsuccessfully to have these cuts deleted.

dation was needed for primary school places; second that although the schools were fully used and meeting local needs, they were largely fulfilling the role of day nurseries and that the health committee had recently decided to abolish all day nurseries as an economy; and finally that the committee had not made systematic provision for nursery education of 50,000 or more children in the county; only 190 were in these schools or classes.* The uneven distribution of nursery education in the county had not gone un noticed either. All the schools and classes were in north-west Kent. On this occasion, however, those who wished to close the schools and classes were less successful. The Ministry immediately objected to closing the two schools, although the closure of the classes was acceptable as long as this relieved pressure on the infant schools. A month later the Ministry wrote again re-affirming this and pointing out that the Minister had received numerous representations about the closures. Amongst these was 'a resolution from the divisional executive, asking for the Minister's intervention'. As a result of this and further protests, the two schools and one of the classes remained open. This constituted nursery provision in Kent till late 1964, when a class was established to release married teachers under Addendum I to Circular 8/60. The four local authorities' response to the Addenda to this Circular will be described in a short appendix to this chapter since most of the classes were established after January 1965, the date which marks the end of the period considered in this study. Meanwhile, what has been discussed so far will be illustrated further by turning to the county boroughs.

Smethwick

In 1965 there was one nursery school in Smethwick containing eighty-one children, and there were seven nursery classes with 195 children, according to the Department of Education and Science definition. Five of these were regarded as nursery classes by the local authority and had places for approximately 140 children. This provided state places for 7·4 per cent of the population aged 2 to 4. There were no independent places. Smethwick ranks fifteenth out of thirty-one English county boroughs for maintained places per child population aged 2 to 4, but bottom for independent places.† There was one day nursery run by the health authority.

All the classes and the school had been in existence since 1946 with one exception. This is a class which was established at a new school in 1958. However, the nursery class was not entirely new but a transferred class from a nearby infant school, whose accommodation was thought unsuitable for

* This number refers to the position after the closure of the eleven classes and one school in 1951. Prior to these closures 500 children attended a nursery school or class — i.e. less than 1 per cent of children aged 2 to 5.

† As in Kent and Hertfordshire, the percentages are based on the local education authority's figures for nursery classes, but the rankings on the department's figures for these classes.

F*

nursery children, since they shared a room with girls from a secondary modern school. The inspector concerned commented on the undesirability of such an arrangement and as a result the headmistress wrote to the chief education officer. He suggested the transfer scheme since he felt that the committee would not wish to see a nursery class closed down in that part of the town. The class which it replaced was set up during the war, as were two of the others, in order to release mothers for work. Another class dates from before the war and the nursery school is also pre-war in origin. A site was acquired for it as early as 1930, during which year the director of education made a long report to the education committee favouring nursery schools and suggesting sites should be bought in areas where housing was least satisfactory. This may have been in response to the circular sent out in 1929 by the new Labour government's Minister of Health and President of the Board of Education, encouraging authorities to exercise their powers to establish nursery schools and classes. However, soon after the purchasing of the site came the financial crisis of 1931. For the next four years there was very little school building anywhere and it was not till 1936 that Smethwick submitted plans for the nursery school to the Board of Education for its approval. The Board wrote back asking for details of the number of children aged 2 to 5 living within half a mile of the school. The authority replied saying that a census had been undertaken which showed that 111 parents wished to send their children to the school. After further correspondence it was eventually agreed that a works canteen should be adapted for the school, and in 1938 Viscountess Astor opened it amidst considerable publicity.

In 1945 the health authority took over all the wartime nurseries in Smethwick. The present chief education officer explained this in terms of the personalities involved. There was a powerful health committee chairman and an outstanding medical officer of health who had great influence at the time. So the reverse of what took place in Hertfordshire appears to have happened in Smethwick. However, the education committee retained the nursery classes they had run during the war and in 1946 established two more. The reasons for the decision to establish the latter are not clear. The education committee minutes in September 1945 state that the closure of three wartime nurseries might lead to an increased demand for nursery class accommodation, so it is possible that pressure of this kind existed and coincided with space in two of the infant schools. However, one of these classes was closed down in 1952 at the time of the demand for economies, although pressure for infant school places rather than cuts in expenditure was the reason for the closure. None of the other classes was closed. Alternative cuts were made, since there was a high demand for nursery education in the borough, a number of councillors were particularly interested in it and the committee as a whole would not have wished to save money in this way.

Until the early 1960s the Labour Party had had a large majority on the borough council. In an industrial, working-class town of this kind with high density of population and little open space the need for nursery education was pressing, and it was recognized as such by a number of Labour councillors, who understood the difficulties facing the family in trying to rear young children in this kind of environment. The Tories in this borough, with one or two exceptions, have shown much less interest in nursery education.

The Development Plan in 1946 proposed nursery places for approximately 25 per cent of the population in the relevant age group. Although this catered for a higher proportion of children than in either Hertfordshire or Kent, the Ministry wrote that owing to the predominantly industrial character of the area it was not satisfied with provision 'on this limited scale'. This shows a surprising adherence to the notion of planning for nursery education according to the needs of the area.

The local education authority then produced a Revised Plan, published in April 1949, which nearly doubled the number of nursery places. In devising the original Plan the officials had attempted to estimate demand by calculating the number of children on the waiting list in the catchment area of the existing nursery school. This suggested that between a quarter and a third of children aged 2 to 5 would require nursery education. However, the waiting list would have been an under-estimate of demand and they based their plans on the lower estimate of a quarter. Thus, although Smethwick attempted to avoid the *ad hoc* nature of Kent and Hertfordshire's estimates for their Plans, it was not very successful. The authority showed a preference for nursery schools; however, it was forced to plan for a higher proportion of its places in nursery classes, owing to the difficulty of obtaining sites in one of the most built-up local authorities in England.*

This is an example of the way educational policy is determined by existing bricks and mortar, not only of the school buildings but of the area in general. One author describing secondary education in a working-class industrial borough says: 'one of the predominant influences on the history of education in West Ham is the obsolescence of the area' which needs a 'vast programme of urban renewal' (Peschek and Brand, 1966). In Smethwick the attitude of the chief education officer was that the department had vast problems and it did not want to take on more than was absolutely necessary. Thus, although he did not wish to abandon existing nursery schools and classes, he had no wish to take on any more. He was grateful to Circular 8/60, behind which he could shelter, when he was pressed by a member to provide more nursery places.

* When building a new primary school, the local education authority sometimes wrote to the Ministry to try to persuade it to accept a smaller site than the regulations permit, giving for example the 'proximity of Warley Woods' as a rationalization for this request. This provides an interesting contrast to a large administrative county such as Hertfordshire where the authority tried to buy sites larger than the size laid down by the regulations and to plan for a nursery class was one way of obtaining a larger primary school site.

Burton-on-Trent

The smallest of the four authorities discussed in this chapter and, indeed, one of the smallest in the country, is Burton-on-Trent. Its size contributes to the brevity of the following description. In 1965 there were no nursery schools in the borough and one nursery class containing sixteen children.* There were no independent places and no day nurseries (see note †, p. 143). The class provided for 0·7 per cent of the child population aged 2 to 4. Burton ranks seventy-fifth out of eighty-one in the provision of maintained places and bottom in the provision of independent places, along with twelve other authorities.

As in Smethwick, the first maintained provision was established prior to the war. When a new director of education was appointed in 1938, he found on arrival that a primary school was about to be modernized and asked whether a nursery class might be attached to it. Two more classes were established during the war and run on wartime nursery lines. In 1946 these two classes were taken over and run solely by the education department and it retained the class, which had been set up earlier. It has not been possible to discover further details about this, nor whether there were any other wartime nurseries in the borough and their fate.

The Development Plan for Burton was more ambitious on pre-school education than those of the other three authorities. It proposed to attach nursery classes to every infant school except one, which was to be served by a nursery school, and there were to be two additional nursery schools. This made a total of eleven classes and three schools. The Plan expressed a preference for nursery schools since they could have their own supervisors specially trained in nursery education, which was not true of most infant head teachers. However, in spite of this, like the other three authorities they opted for nursery classes as the major source of provision, but hoped to rectify the above defect by having a nursery class organizer who would be responsible for all the classes.

However, like the rest of the Plan, this never came into operation and only a few years later, in 1952, the authority closed down its three nursery classes. The chief education officer at that time, now retired and a town councillor in the same county borough, stated that the shortage of infant school places was the main reason for the closures and the demand for economies from the government a considerably less important one. He maintained that had it just been a need for the latter he would never have made the cuts in this way, since he was an advocate of nursery education, believing it could prevent juvenile delinquency and adult crime, and that surely it was preferable to run nursery classes than reform schools.

* In 1964 there were two classes with fifty-two children on the department's definition. In 1966 there was one class with sixteen children, hence the 1965 mean given in Appendix 3 is two classes with thirty-four children. However, the 1964 classes were reception classes with a high proportion of 'under-5s'.

If he believed so stiongly in these classes it is perhaps surprising that he and his committee were unable to make alternative arrangements for the increasing population in the infant schools, such as temporary classrooms under the minor works programme. A Labour member of the education committee who was 'heartbroken' at this decision believed that alternative infant school accommodation would not have been forthcoming from the Tory government. However, probably the most important reason behind the decision to close the classes was a simple matter of priorities. After the war Burton had only four secondary schools, and was therefore faced with the intractable problem of all-age schools, which had to be replaced as soon as possible. Consequently, nearly all the new building was confined to this sector. In fact, there appears to have been comparatively little opposition in the town to the closures, unlike in Kent. This may be because the closures were made more gradually in Burton and because a much smaller number of children was involved.

As a result of these cuts there was no maintained nursery education in Burton until 1965 when a class was set up under Addendum I to Circular 8/60.

General comments

These descriptions provide evidence, at a more micro level than what has gone before, about the attitudes and events which influence the provision of nursery education.* The aim was to search for information about the key people involved, and to identify the crucial periods for pre-school education and the various actions local authorities might take at such times. What contrasts between the authorities emerge from these descriptions? The most useful comparisons will be between authorities of the same administrative type, though some contrasts between the types will also be commented on. Some of the differences in the extent of provision in these authorities can be explained by differences in the attitudes of the policy-makers, by the distribution of power amongst the officials, by their desire and ability to manipulate scarce resources, making use of any opportunities to extend provision quickly and efficiently and, up to a point, by the effectiveness of pressure groups for nursery education. These factors operate in two contexts: where expansion is attempted and where reductions were threatened. In the

* A study of decision-making in the children's service is at present being carried out at the universities of Birmingham and York by a team of six. Since it is tracing the process of decision-making by studying 200 individual referrals, it is at a more micro level than this study. This has been facilitated by the fact that these decisions are being studied as they take place rather than some years after. The study has two major aims: to highlight the differences between policies and practices in four children's departments (two administrative counties and two county boroughs with varying records in the proportion of children taken into care), and to study the process of decision-making. There are therefore some similarities in the design of the study and the one described in this chapter, and it will be interesting to compare their findings, when the Child Care Research is complete.

particular case of nursery education since the war, the latter is more important than the former, owing to the central government's embargo on expansion in the second half of this period.

To begin with the attitudes of the policy-makers, it would be an over-simplification to say that members and officials in Hertfordshire and Smethwick believed in the value of nursery education in satisfying certain social needs, whereas those in Kent and Burton-on-Trent did not. But one could argue that at crucial times when the future of the service was under scrutiny, in Hertfordshire, particularly amongst the officials, and in Smethwick, particularly amongst the elected members, a viewpoint prevailed that this service was of sufficient importance to justify its continuance or expansion, even if this meant that other kinds of educational provision might suffer. (In fact, its maintenance or development rarely impinged directly on other services, so that the problem of determining new priorities which might threaten the existing patterns of provision hardly arose.)

The philosophy and aspirations of those who provide this service are important and are linked to the way in which they seize on opportunities and perceive future needs. It is therefore useful to discover their identifications, their attachments to goals and organizational units and their awareness of the social changes, which give rise to an increased demand for the social services. The question of the attitudes of the producers of the service was raised at the end of Chapter 4, where it was stated that those involved at central government level always expressed positive attitudes about nursery education. This is also true of most of those involved at the local level, who are concerned with the day-to-day running of the educational service. But although none of them denied the value of nursery education, the amount of value they placed on it did vary. The question was raised as to how far the classical conflict between those who wish to extend the social services and those who take a *laissez-faire* attitude, seeing their extension as the denial of individual responsibility, plays a part in the provision of nursery education. There is some evidence from the facts presented in this chapter that a conflict of this kind can arise when pre-school education is debated. There are some elected members in local authorities who are fundamentally opposed to the provision of nursery schools or classes and at times they have been influential enough to affect the supply of places.

In this study the chief example of this is the closure of the Kent schools and classes. Initially the Tory majority was in favour of abolishing some of the provision, whereas the Labour minority was not. At the council debates, the right wing of the Tory Party pressed for the abolition of all the provision and the arguments they used were of a traditional kind, suggesting that the private individual was being too heavily taxed in order to provide public services ('the rate-payers will never tolerate this'), and that individual responsibility was being whittled away ('this encourages mothers to neglect their children').

The latter indicates that the notion of the nursery school as an extra-familial aid to the socialization of children has not been finally routinized. There are still sections of the population whose norms do not permit them to accept this institution and the letter from a Kent citizen suggesting that nursery schools encourage laziness amongst parents is a further example of this. The final stage of Smelser's model of structural differentiation (that is routinization) had not been completed.

There are other examples of the classical conflict such as the failure to prevent the closure of a school in Hertfordshire, the only case in the county during twenty years, where one of the influences was the right-wing Tory views of the county councillor for the area concerned.

Those who hold negative attitudes of the kind expressed in the Kent debate tend to be men, elderly or in late middle age, Conservative and opposed to expanding the social services. These, with the exception of the last one, characterize most local authority elected representatives, therefore some might argue that this tells us comparatively little about those people who oppose nursery education. There is truth in this, yet the fact that those who express public disapproval are hardly ever young, Labour or women councillors is meaningful.* Although attitudes are changing, the traditional Labour Party view of nursery education as an equalizer has remained; and the recognition of the new pressures on the family is greater amongst women, who are more intimately involved in the socialization of children than men are.

An analysis in depth of the attitudes of officials was not possible. The danger of inferring from decisions about nursery education that their attitudes and values must be different and then using the different attitudes as an explanation of different decisions taken on nursery education is obvious. But some differences in attitudes did emerge independently from policies on pre-school education: for example, the view that many mothers ought to be relieved of their children for part of the day, since frustrated women make bad mothers, expressed by an officer in one authority, against the view that since psychologists have shown that children suffer from being removed from their mothers, we should be wary about providing nursery schools extensively, from an officer in another. An awareness of the changing social structure appeared to be greater in Hertfordshire, partly as a result of the New Towns there, whose population structure was a constant reminder of the needs of families with young children. Personal factors such as whether an assistant education officer had several young children himself also affected attitudes. But finally it must be stressed again that these differences were subtle. No local authority official stated that nursery schools were of little value and as such a waste of public money, and no one said that they are so vitally important that they must take first priority. More than one official did

* An assistant education officer maintained that practically all the pressures for expansion came from Labour members, who he felt were more likely to understand the real role of nursery education, whereas most of the Tories saw it as a way of letting mothers work.

suggest that the possibility of giving the expansion of nursery education higher priority than the raising of the school-leaving age should be considered seriously, but others reflected the central government's viewpoint that the compulsory sector must take higher priority. It is these small differences that are crucial when the question of closing a nursery class or school has been raised, and more important they will be crucial in determining the rate of expansion of different authorities when the embargo is lifted.

However favourable, the attitudes of the providers are of little avail, unless they are powerful enough to act on them and efficient enough to do this effectively within the constraints of scarce resources. There are examples of the effect of powerful personalities in the foregoing description, such as the division of wartime nurseries between the health and education departments after the war. There are even more examples of the way in which the manipulation of scarce resources is important. Kent and Burton's failure and Hertfordshire and Smethwick's success in keeping all their nursery schools and classes intact in 1951/2 was due to the ability of the latter two to discover alternative cuts of a less irreversible kind than the abolition of pre-school education. Using the minor works programme to replace old buildings with new schools is another example, as is the use of loopholes in the legislation to help voluntary organizations providing pre-school education.

The pressure groups formed to try to prevent the closures had varying degrees of success. The chance of success is increased considerably by support from an elected member or from an official at the divisional level. The survival of the classes at Beckenham, where the borough education officer pleaded for the retention, is an example of this. The personality and ability of the organizer of the group is also vital, and the quality of the head teacher of the school concerned helps too. Whether a pressure group forms at all is probably more dependent on the existence of an articulate, middle-class group of parents than on any other condition. Where this does not exist, a pressure group is unlikely to appear. The way in which the local authority handles closures can also be important. One reason for the lack of pressure-group activity in Burton may be the fact that closures were made gradually; no child already in a class was sent home, as happened in Kent.

The constraints of shortages of teachers and buildings, and the central government's edict forbidding expansion have been the context in which the influences described above have operated.* This is the reason why the pro-

---

* This applies to other areas besides nursery education. Peschek and Brand in their study of secondary education in West Ham and Reading summarize this: 'Few authorities have the sites, the money and the teachers for radical operations and, as both authorities point out, central government finance is a sorry story of cut-backs, postponements and denials. Indeed when one considers that neither Reading nor West Ham are financially very poor authorities, it is a sobering thought that in these last 20 years of unprecedented prosperity, Reading has built only five new secondary schools and West Ham three. The differing party controls seem irrelevant for both authorities have to the very best of their ability urged the Ministry on in all possible ways' (Peschek and Brand, 1966, p. 6).

vision of pre-school education has remained a non-controversial issue in local education authorities. When the public or its elected representatives have asked for increased provision, the education department officials have reminded them of the embargo on expansion and the discussion has gone no further in most cases. Some officials have been glad of the opportunity to shelter behind this, others have done so regretfully and look forward to the day when the embargo is lifted. When this does happen, some chief education officers will be reluctant to implement new provision; others, from the evidence in this chapter, will try to exploit every opportunity to expand. Certainly pre-school education will become a controversial issue when priorities have to be considered. The arguments put forward in Kent in 1952 will reappear, although probably the opposition will be less extreme as the idea of extra-familial aid to the socialization of young children becomes more acceptable. The degree to which it becomes a party political issue may affect the extent and nature of the opposition. The Labour group on the education committee considered here has been anxious, when in the minority, to keep nursery education as a non-political issue, since to do otherwise would mean that any proposals it made would be rejected.

The role of the local politicians in initiating new developments is small as far as nursery education is concerned; consequently, although it was agreed in an earlier chapter that the Labour Party was an influence on the expansion of pre-school education nationally, particularly when it took office in 1929, it has been less important at the local level. To quote Donnison and Chapman (1964, p. 249), 'no one would deny that elections do sometimes bring about important changes in the policies of local social services: we only wish to establish that such changes usually originate from other sources...'. Their principal role is 'to approve, modify or reject decisions which commit the providers to significant changes in their objectives, to courses of action which involve risks, or impinge on other services, and to significant expenditures or redistributions of resources'. It is in this rather than an initiating role that a Labour majority, rather than a Conservative one, might be crucial.

One can summarize briefly the points that emerge from the studies of the four authorities. Their policies have had to concentrate on preserving existing provision rather than expanding it. In this context decisions taken at two periods have been crucial in determining the present level of provision: first the change-over from war nurseries to nursery schools and day nurseries in 1945; and second the way cuts were made from 1951/2. Less crucial but still important are the response to the Addendas to Circular 8/60 and the degree to which aid has been given to voluntary schools. Various influences on the way the local education authority dealt with each of these can be detected. Taking the above issues in turn, the events of 1945 were influenced by the interest of the officials concerned in running services for the under-5s, and the power wielded by interested officials. Those of 1951/2 were influenced by attitudes of the majority of elected members on the education committee and sometimes on the council as a whole, and by the efficiency and resourcefulness of officials in finding other less drastic ways of reducing expenditure. Whether the local education authority has started nursery classes since 1964 has been influenced by the need for teachers within its area and the degree to which its officials believe classes can free married women to return to teaching, and by whether they believe the authority has too many commitments to take on extra tasks. Finally whether the local education authority is prepared to make grants to independent nursery groups depends on how far it believes in the value of such provision and its potential for development into maintained schools later, and how cautious it is about using public funds for projects which risk the accusation of *ultra vires*.

Packman in her study also points out that, whether a children's department defines the Children's Acts narrowly and stresses the immaculate administration of the law, or whether it defines them broadly, stressing the need to stretch the law to its utmost where necessary, affects the number of children in care (Packman, 1968, Chapters 12 and 13). She suggests that fundamental attitudes towards the conflicting issues of the protection of the child and the maintenance of the family intact will also affect the numbers in care. These attitudes will affect practices on all manner of issues ranging from the use and timing of adoption to the encouragement or discouragement of fit person's orders for offenders. Variations in policy in this field can also be attributed in part to the influence of elected representatives and the attitude of the finance committee in particular, which in turn may be under pressure from other sources to keep costs to the minimum. In emphasizing the above factors, she stresses, as has been stressed here, that the officials of local departments are not simply free agents to change policies and practices at whim.

This chapter has pointed out some of the diverse pressures and motives that help to shape a social service, and has indicated the kind of barriers that stand in the way of its growth. It has shown what kind of influences determine the speed of the response to the changing needs of the family with reference to the socialization and education of young children in an industrial society, at a lower level than discussed in previous chapters. It picks out some of the salient factors concerning the nature of the opposition at this level. The variation in the extent of provision of pre-school education in England and Wales is attributable in a large measure to the providers of the service in the local education authorities and how they perceive the needs to be met and the standards of service that they believe are required. This, in turn, rests on their past experience and the attitudes derived from this, and their ability to make the most out of very little, rather than to succumb to a fatalism about the scarcity of resources and the central government's restrictions.

8. Conclusion

In the introduction to this study three questions were raised about the development of nursery education. What were the causes of the growing demand? Why had provision developed so slowly? Why were some areas better supplied with nursery education than others? In describing the growth of pre-school education in England and Wales during the twentieth century, and its distribution today, the study has tried to answer these questions. For this a number of secondary sources have been used. It was not possible to undertake fresh empirical research, such as a survey of parents' attitudes, which would have been helpful for testing some of the assumptions made. It is to be hoped that someone will think it worthwhile undertaking this task. Instead, the study has drawn on various kinds of documentary evidence. It has traced the development of public policy by way of Ministry circulars and parliamentary statements. It has followed through the work of pressure groups, such as the Nursery School Association, by using their Annual Reports and minutes of their meetings. It has used government statistics to measure rates of growth and the present distribution of provision. And, in considering the role of ideas the literature on change in education has been drawn on, as has that on the sociology of the family in order to understand the way the pressures of industrialization have affected the family. Lastly, the study has used the documents of local education authorities in trying to understand how decisions are taken to allocate resources to nursery education at the local level.

The pages which follow summarize the answers given to the three questions posed, and identify which influences have been most important, which evidence most useful, and which aspect of theory most relevant. This will be followed by a short discussion of future trends and policies.

The demand for nursery education has grown because the family cannot meet the requirements for the socialization of young children. There are various reasons for this. The standards demanded of parents have grown as knowledge about the importance of the early years for children's later emotional and intellectual development has spread. Thus, even in ideal material conditions, mothers may feel unable to meet these standards, which require the devotion of energy, patience and initiative, to the care, education and entertainment of their young children. In many cases, material conditions, using the term in its widest sense, are of course not ideal. First and most important, mothers may not be available to carry out these tasks because they have jobs outside their homes. The reasons why they work vary from financial necessity to a desire to use whatever special skills they possess. The first reason is most likely to be applicable to unskilled manual groups with low incomes; the second to middle-class professional groups. Between these extremes there is a range of positions, many of which combine elements of each extreme. Whatever their reasons for working, mothers must make arrangements for the care of their children. These are not always adequate, and even when they are, there is evidence from the USA to show that mothers would prefer arrangements which provide education as well as care. (Care must of course be taken in applying American evidence to Britain. But it seems safe to assume in this case that the findings would be similar (Rudermann, 1968).)

The second material factor is the difficulty created by the physical environment of urban living. Housing conditions in our cities are frequently not conducive to high standards in rearing young children. This is true both of sub-standard old houses and of the high blocks of flats which are replacing them. The next factor concerns the structure of families in terms of size and spacing of children. There may be only one child or, where there is more than one, the age difference may be such that siblings would provide little companionship for each other during the pre-school years. This leads parents to seek nursery schools or playgroups for their children, partly because they believe such companionship is important for their children's development and partly because the task of amusing and occupying one child alone may be more difficult than with two or more children. Other aspects of the structure of the family are significant, in particular the decreasing opportunity for relying on female relatives for regular help. A woman's mother or sister may be at work herself or live too far away to be able to relieve her of her children from time to time. Finally, the emancipation of women has thrown open many doors that were previously closed to them with respect to education and job opportunities. They are more aware of the alternatives to house-keeping and child-rearing and many of them find these alternatives more attractive, since they offer financial reward, companionship, and even social status, all of which are lacking in the role of housewife (Gavron, 1966).

The chief reason why provision has developed so slowly is that nursery education is seen as a potential threat to the family, whose fundamental role is the socialization of the young. In a climate in which many people believe that the institution of the family has been undermined in a serious way, any innovation which might be interpreted as removing responsibility from parents for their children has been suspect. Thus, although public expenditure on nursery education was first made possible by an Act of Law in 1918, which in 1944 was extended to cover all children whose parents desired nursery education, scant funds have been appropriated to it. It has had low priority throughout the period, except in one or two special circumstances. These were as follows. The election of a Labour government in 1929, which briefly encouraged the expansion of nursery education as a socialist measure designed to help the under-privileged and to equalize opportunity, marked the first occasion on which nursery education was given higher priority. Demographic change in the late 1930s was the second influence, which made possible some expansion. But the most important influence was the Second World War. Because of the need for married women in the labour force, the expansion of nursery education became a high priority during the war. Those who are responsible for taking policy decisions about the allocation of resources would probably deny that a belief in traditional values and norms surrounding the family plays a part in shaping their attitudes to nursery education. But the fact remains that resources for nursery education can be provided when certain political or economic pressures are operating, such as those of wartime. Yet the simple grounds that the 'normal' family cannot meet the expectations defined in its role as socializer of the young, are not acceptable as a reason for giving nursery education enough priority to expand it at other times.

Vaizey has argued the importance of the economic situation for educational development, peak rates of expansion 'coinciding with years of high economic activity' (Vaizey, 1958, p. 22). The effects of cuts in public spending through various economic crises have already been described in earlier chapters. The lack of financial resources to provide for innovation and growth in pre-school education has been an important factor in its slow development. However, this explanation is inadequate on its own. Why has there been a consistent, if slow, expansion in the provision of special schools for example, whereas maintained pre-school education has remained at a standstill for a number of years? It is necessary to ask what priorities have dictated that those limited financial resources available have been spent on other spheres of education. It appears that the most important of these is that the compulsory sector must be given precedence.* This statement appears in almost every post-war circular restricting the growth of nursery schools and classes. Second, education is increasingly seen as an investment towards greater productivity, and it would be extremely difficult to measure the value of nursery education in such terms. Its products are many years away from the labour force, and it therefore has no obvious and easily measured rewards. It is perhaps this kind of situation that Titmuss envisaged when he said:

Generalising from historical experience we may believe that we can produce a technical elite without any great improvement in the social foundations of education just as in the past we produced an administrative elite without bothering our heads overmuch about the education of the masses (in Vaizey, 1958, p. 9).

To summarize, a major reason for the slow growth of nursery education is a lack of normative consensus on its value. In examining the reasons for its

* The clauses referring to County Colleges in the 1944 Act, like those referring to nursery education, have never been implemented.

growth and in considering why there has been a demand for it, the emphasis has been on groups and individuals with favourable attitudes towards it, to the neglect of negative and hostile attitudes. But in every series of correspondence in the press making a plea for more nursery schools, there is a sprinkling of letters deprecating their development. The reason usually given is that children under 5 should remain at home in the care of their mothers. Theories of maternal deprivation have provided ammunition for this attack. Bowlby's work on children in institutions, whom he found suffered long-term effects on their personalities as a result of maternal separation and deprivation of maternal love, has become widely known. However, it has been much misunderstood and vulgarized by the popular press, women's magazines and journals on child care. Conclusions about children in institutions have been applied to children living at home with their parents in a totally different environment. This has led to the belief that the child should not be separated from its mother before it is 5. More extreme arguments have been advanced against the provision of nursery schools. For example, the National Campaign for Nursery Education set up in 1965 received a letter from the British Housewives League expressing the view that nursery schools would encourage more mothers to go out to work and thus contribute to an increase in juvenile delinquency.*

The answer to the question as to why some areas are much better supplied with nursery education than others is not independent of the answers to the first two questions. The long-term changes in the family as a result of the pressures of industrialization do not proceed at identical rates in all areas of industrial societies, simply because the pressures occur neither simultaneously nor with the same degree of strain in all areas. Thus demand for working women or the standards of housing vary. However, the evidence in Chapter 6 shows that the extent of provision is not as closely related to objective measures of such pressures as might be expected, although some of the associations between the characteristics of areas and the number of nursery places do conform to expected patterns, for example, the distribution between rural and urban areas. But where associations do exist they are frequently not as strong as expected. The situation is complicated by the issues raised in the answer to the second question. Those with the power to alter the existing situation vary in how much they adhere to traditional values about the family, and at times when pressures for expansion or cut-backs are being exerted at the national level, the values of those who occupy such positions at

---

* This argument has been used in reverse by the proponents of nursery schools. Thus some years ago Nancy Astor wrote to *The Times*, 'I wonder if people realise what juvenile delinquency costs the country? The cost of keeping a boy or girl in a remand home is £260 a year or £5 a week, and sending a boy to an approved school costs as much as sending him to Eton. The problem of nursery schools should be gone into from a common sense point of view, and not sentiment, to do what you can to encourage happy childhood. Family allowances may not prove to be the best way of helping children before school age. Nursery schools have been proved beyond any doubt. They do not break up homes but help to keep them. . .'. (*The Times*, 18 August 1951.)

the local level are crucial. However, it would be wrong to lay too much emphasis on underlying values. The evidence presented in Chapter 7 showed that administrative efficiency and foresight in making the optimal use of scarce resources, particularly at times of economic difficulties, can be crucial in determining the levels of provision.

These conclusions clearly over-simplify the situation. In fact, one of the tasks of this study has been to show how complex is the effect of industrialization on educational systems. In the long term, many of the economic and social factors which accompany industrialization may operate directly on the provision of the social services, but in the short term this influence is tenuous. The anomalies in the provision of pre-school education from area to area illustrate this.

One of the theoretical questions raised is the extent to which new social policies are formulated and implemented in response to changing social needs. Indeed the analysis relies on the notion that institutional change, in this case the expansion of establishments for pre-school education, takes place in response to certain 'needs' of society. This emphasis on the functional needs of society, which lies behind Smelser's model of structural differentiation, may lead to a simplistic and one-sided analysis of the causes of a particular set of events. In arguing that pressures on the family, particularly those concerning the performance of maternal roles, have been the prime motivating factors in the demand for nursery education, other important causative factors may have been neglected. For example, the demand for nursery education may be more closely related to a gradual increase in parents' aspirations for social mobility on behalf of their children, than to a demand based more directly on the frustrating experience of attempting to reach high standards in socializing children at home.

There is a common view among parents that nursery education will give their children a start over their contemporaries in preparing them for primary school. However, the rationale that nursery education will increase educational attainment and thereby enhance the chances of upward mobility does not undermine the earlier argument, because it also rests on the belief that extra-familial agencies can perform the necessary tasks more effectively. The difference is that it relies more on pull factors relating to the good qualities of the extra-familial institution and less on push factors relating to the undesirable qualities of the family for the performance of certain functions. Unfortunately, there is no evidence enabling one to weight satisfactorily these possible underlying causes. For example, has the decline in domestic service for the middle classes been more or less important than increased opportunities for the employment of married women? Is the growth of high flat living in urban areas more or less important than reduced contact with kin?

Although it would not provide all the necessary evidence, a survey of attitudes among parents of pre-school-age children would make possible more conclusive statements. However, at the cost of some speculation it is necessary to avoid a descriptive catalogue of legislative changes, with no explanation, theoretical framework or reference to wider changes.

In approaching the development of a particular social policy in terms of 'needs' it is necessary to clarify what is meant by this concept (see Gold-thorpe, 1962). A failure to satisfy such needs does not imply social collapse, but it may mean that certain ends held in common by members of society are less likely to be achieved. For example, the rejection of nursery education by leaving children to the vagaries of the family may reduce the possibility of equality of opportunity for all children. In tracing the history of nursery schools, an attempt has been made to avoid analysis simply in terms of an *ad hoc* response to needs. Thus, the growth of a more humanitarian outlook towards the child and its physical development, and more recently its psychological and social development, have been considered too. At the same time, modes of thought have not been treated as virtually autonomous but as themselves part of wider social changes. The explanations put forward are, however, at a fairly high level of generality, and they do not explain the particular nature of these educational institutions, for example, their characteristic rejection of instruction and classification, or the development of part-time as opposed to full-time accommodation.

Some attempt has been made earlier in this study to consider the purposive actions of particular individuals and groups involved in the fight to establish pre-school education, although this has remained perhaps at too superficial a level. Boskoff has suggested,

the level of innovation or deviation is directly related to the perceived failure of existing practices in meeting the functional problem. In general the effective motivation for innovation in this situation is more likely to be found among the 'producers' of the 'service', than the 'consumers', though there is varying communication between consumers and producers. A tentative explanation for this locus of motivation may be the greater awareness of the availability of workable alternatives among technical and managerial units . . . (Boskoff, 1964, p. 229).

It is important to consider this statement in relation to the question posed earlier: why has the growth of state provision been so slow? It is necessary to do more than identify the needs and the structural conditions favourable to innovation in response to such needs. The specific categories of persons who are the predominant sources of this innovation must be identified. For example, it has been suggested that the middle-class mother of young children has played a vital innovatory role in the growth of private pre-school education in recent years. Further research is necessary to discover why some women who belong to this category become involved in this role, and others do not. Cultural and psychological factors are significant in explaining such differences. At the more general level, they are 'variables which intervene between a social activity or structure, and its consequences for other parts of the social system' (Smelser, 1962, Vol. 4). Thus the changes in the family and their consequences for the growth of pre-school education will also be modified by such factors.

In trying to say why the enactment of social policy by the state in response to what appear to be fairly obvious needs has been so slow, three related areas have been considered: lack of resources, conflicting values, and how these two affect the attitudes of the 'producer'. One of the questions asked by Goldthorpe is how far extensions to the social services can simply be seen as part of an ever-growing policy of state intervention to ensure better standards for all. Even if this interpretation were feasible (it might be argued that it fits certain periods in the development of pre-school education, such as the 1930s), it explains nothing about the nature of the particular policies, nor their rates of growth. In fact general principles are subject to every conceivable change of circumstance. As Titmuss has stated,

since its beginnings in the nineteenth century English education policy has not been characterised by any distinctive positive philosophy. . . . Historians of education have shown how the schooling of the mass of the children came to be regarded as a painful necessity tempered in times of war and emergency, by short lived phases of indulgence (in Vaizey, 1958, p. 6).

This describes exactly the pattern of growth in state pre-school education. War, depression and the discovery that increased provision for children under 5 might alleviate the crisis in the supply of teachers have all played vital roles. Titmuss goes on to say that, 'What progress has been made over the whole period [1929—54] can be attributed more to a declining birth rate among the working classes than to any political decision to invest more in education' (in Vaizey, 1958, p. 8). The expansion of nursery classes in the 1930s has been traced to this factor. Thus, within the general framework of studying the supply of nursery education in the context of certain social needs, it is essential to avoid seeing its growth as an *ad hoc* response to such needs.

The second theoretical question raised in the introduction and discussed in Appendix 7 is the usefulness of Smelser's model of structural differentiation and its limitations. Further discussion of the value of the model is also confined to the appendix, so that those not interested in the theoretical issues involved may read on without the text being interrupted.

The third is the role of ideas in influencing the changes described. Their influence has largely been confined to the content of the education of young children. The nature school of education, backed by a more humanitarian outlook towards children, influenced Froebel, whose emphasis on learning through play has had a lasting influence on the content of nursery education. The work of John Dewey and the progressives exerted a further influence during the first three decades of the twentieth century. The work on child development of Susan Isaacs, Arnold Gesell and others has been influential in stressing the need for young children to spend time with others. More directly, the psychologists' work on group dynamics with reference to small children usually showed gains in sociability and maturity among children attending nursery schools. But many of these studies lacked careful statistical design, using neither controls nor representative samples. Bowlby's work on maternal deprivation had a countervailing effect during the 1950s in stressing the importance of the relationship between mother and child for the latter's development. But none of these examples has operated independently because the influence they exert is determined by other issues such as the availability of resources or the economic need for nursery education. Such ideas are frequently used as rationalizations for either hostile or positive attitudes towards nursery education.

More recently, the study of educational deprivation has had an important influence on the provision of pre-school education. The rediscovery of poverty in the affluent society, and of child poverty in particular, and the dilemmas created by immigrant or minority groups, which are underprivileged and culturally disadvantaged, has led to a search for methods to alleviate these problems. Nursery education has been one of the remedies prescribed and because it is able to attack the problems 'before it is too late', it has received widespread support recently from those anxious to deal with such difficulties. In the United States it has been implemented on a large scale as part of the Poverty Programme. The Office of Economic Opportunity has distributed federal funds to Operation Headstart, a nation-wide programme designed to bring culturally disadvantaged children into the schools before starting compulsory schooling at 6. Although initially designed primarily for underprivileged minority groups, such as Negroes and Puerto Ricans, entrance is normally based on the size of the family income, so that any child from a family whose income falls below a certain level qualifies. Most of the early programmes were confined to six weeks during the summer before the child entered the elementary school. Since then, many of these have been extended to run throughout the year and further attempts are being made to extend some of these to two- or even three-year programmes. They are also being slowly extended upwards into the elementary schools, where follow-through projects are being undertaken.

In the last five years educational research has shown consistently that various characteristics of children's home environment, particularly parental attitudes, strongly influence children's achievement at school. Such variables as parental aspirations have been found to be better predictors of attainment than variables related to the school such as size of class or teachers' qualifications. This has led to the belief that in order to equalize opportunity it is essential that some children should be given extra help, which will counteract the failings of their homes, before they start elementary schooling.

New research on the development of intelligence has indicated that the early years are vitally important in determining later test scores, in that the growth of intelligence is much more rapid at this stage than later. Not surprisingly, the effects of deprivation have been found to be greatest during the period of most rapid growth. Bloom shows that approximately 50 per cent of the child's final intelligence and about 33 per cent of his performance on achievement tests can be predicted from measures of his intelligence at the age of 5 or 6, whereas such predictions cannot be made from measures relating to 1-year-old children (Bloom, 1964). This has usually been interpreted to mean that the pre-school stage is a critical period in the development of intelligence, and sometimes to mean in addition that at this stage the child is more responsive to intellectual stimulation than later and that consequently any deprivation in the environment of the child is likely to have especially damaging and even irreversible effects.

In a recent article, Lawrence Kohlberg has criticized this. He attacks the work of Spitz and Bowlby and their 'impressionistic conclusions ... as to massive irreversible cognitive and developmental retardation due to maternal and stimulus deprivation in infancy', and he questions the notion of a critical period with respect to intellectual development, suggesting that the improvement of children's intelligence quotients by special teaching before they start primary schooling may not be feasible. He believes that the reason for the unquestionable increase of predictability between infant tests and tests at school entrance is 'largely the result of the fact that infant tests do not reflect the hereditary contribution to adult intelligence and is only in part the result of the filling in of intellectual skills by environment in these years' (Kohlberg, 1968).

Nevertheless the findings of Bloom and of Hunt, amongst other things, are influencing policy-makers and their advisers to consider the expansion of nursery education more seriously than at any other time during the last twenty years. For example, the Plowden report recommended a massive expansion of nursery education, advocating that by 1980 part-time places should be provided for all children whose parents wish them to attend. It is estimated that this would involve 35 per cent of 3- to 4-year-olds and 75 per cent of 4- to 5-year-olds, and that 15 per cent in each age category would require full-time nursery education, the rest requiring part-time provision only. Such estimates, both of the overall proportion of children wanting pre-school education and of the proportion needing full-time provision, were largely guesswork and may underestimate the demand for the former and the need for the latter. It proposed that nursery provision in educational priority areas should be established before expansion took place elsewhere. In this respect it gave priority to establishing nursery education in order to alleviate deprivation, although this was only one of a number of grounds for expansion listed by the committee (CACE, 1967, Vol. 1, Chapters 9, 31). Its proposals involved an increase in spending from £36 million in 1965 to £85 million in 1980. The ensuing discussion resulted in 1968 in a decision to spend £3 million on pre-school education in urban areas designated as deprived* during

* See Circular 225/68 (Home Office), 19/68 (Department of Education and Science), 35/68 (Ministry of Health).

the remaining months of that financial year and the financial year 1969—70. The urban programme announced by the Home Secretary in Parliament on 22 July 1968, asks the thirty-four relevant authorities to submit bids for projects for nursery schools and classes, day nurseries or residential homes. By early in 1969 bids for nursery education had been received from the authorities concerned. The Department of Education and Science then selected those that were to be allocated funds. During the next four years it is planned to authorize expenditure of £20—25 million. The process of submitting bids and allocating funds has been repeated and presumably will be repeated again at further stages.

This leads to the question of what is likely to occur in the future and what kind of policies ought to be implemented. In the light of the United States' experience it seems likely that the belief in the efficacy of nursery education in reducing educational deprivation is more likely to grow than wither away; but whether the present government or its successor will feel able to allocate more funds is an open question. One result of the present policy could be that hopes are dashed with respect to the effects of nursery education on the children concerned. A failure to improve their later performance might lead to a withdrawal of any further plans for expansion.

Those who hope for miraculous results are probably being over-ambitious in the light of existing evidence. For example, Douglas and Ross found that attendance at nursery school did not give long-term advantages to those children in their national sample who had had this experience (Douglas and Ross, 1964, pp. 83—94). They discovered that at 8 the nursery school children did better than the control group, but that by the time they were 11 they had lost this advantage, and by the time they were 15 they had fallen behind. But they rightly comment that these findings are not conclusive since the original selection of children requires careful study before conclusions can be made. In their sample many of the children had been sent to nursery schools or classes as a result of health visitors' recommendations.

Yet the failure of nursery education to have any *lasting* effect is not altogether surprising. The present content of nursery education is not designed to give children a formal advantage over their peers who have not attended. The stress is on learning through play rather than accomplishing the skills of reading and writing. Although many small studies indicate that the children's intellectual ability develops rapidly as a result of this, these early years constitute a period of rapid growth anyway, so without adequate control groups one cannot tell how much more ready to learn they are than those who have not attended nursery schools. Once formal education begins, the latter may be able to catch up fairly quickly. Thus by the time children are 11, the advantage of an extra year or two of organized play added on to six years of formal schooling may be small.

If deprived children are going to obtain long-term benefit from this experience it is necessary to develop new ways of structuring the content of nursery education. For example, it may be necessary to start teaching such children to read, in order that they should keep up with their middle-class contemporaries later. American investigators are conducting such experiments currently. For example, Bereiter and Engelmann prescribe a set of teaching procedures and curricula for disadvantaged children, which cover language, reading, arithmetic and music, as well as the 'management of the pre-school'. They argue that learning at above normal rates must be achieved by such children if they are to catch up, and that this demands special programmes. One of the major problems of the plans that they outline is that they require a very high level of skill from the teachers who will implement them (Bereiter and Engelmann, 1966).

Traditional approaches to the content of education are hard to uproot and this seems especially true of nursery education which has changed little in this respect over the last fifty years. The attempt to introduce such reforms into the curricula of pre-school education will meet with resistance. Those who have started some experiments in the implementation and subsequent evalua-tion of structured programmes in this country have already met with opposition from practising teachers, many of whom firmly believe that deprived children in particular should have an unstructured timetable. After all, as Chapters 2 and 3 of this study show, the first time nursery education was prescribed by a public body (the Consultative Committee of the Board of Education in 1908) the chief ground was the need to remove young children from the pressures of formal education. Ever since then teachers have been anxious to avoid forcing children into more formal pursuits before they are ready for them. However, as Bruner has argued, readiness can be taught (Bruner, 1966). Nevertheless, the advocacy of a more structured programme, consisting of intensive courses in language development, for example, must be accompanied by experimental studies which investigate any possible emo-tional strain such courses may impose on the participants, as well as their effects on the children's intellectual development.

Structural programmes may prove to be as disappointing in this respect as more traditional approaches which start from the view that children should be allowed to mature at their own pace in an environment designed to let this take place freely without adult pressures. On the basis of a review of studies in this field, one American expert suggests:

that there is no compelling evidence for the long-term effectiveness of short-term educational intervention at the preschool level. Many preschool programs for disadvantaged children have shown that they make relatively large gains in intelligence test performance during the first year of the pro-gram; but this characteristic acceleration in intellectual growth is not always maintained during a second preschool year or when the children enter first grade (L. Morrisett in American Social Science Research Council Report, 1966).

It is possible that follow-through programmes throughout primary education combined with pre-school intervention might improve the children's later performance more effectively. There is a great need for more general research on the long-term effects of pre-school education on all children, not only the deprived. We also need to improve our understanding of the nature of cognitive development in young children, including the conditions under which children learn effectively, and the kind of tasks that can be learned more appropriately at this period than later.

Various projects are now under way and more are being planned, although none of these intends following children up for more than two or three years. The most large-scale study being undertaken at present is an Action-Research project on Educational Priority Areas, directed by A. H. Halsey. It is not confined to pre-school education, although this is the most important subject to be investigated at a national level, in four of the five areas where action programmes are being undertaken, namely London, Liverpool, the West Riding of Yorkshire and Birmingham. In each of these areas, and in Dundee, a research officer is responsible for collecting information about parents, teachers and children in designated educational priority areas. But most important from the point of view of this study, a research project has been devised to test a structured language programme for pre-school children. It aims both to test the feasibility of implementing intervention of this kind, and to evaluate the success of the programme when implemented. A language programme was selected as the form of intervention most likely to be acceptable to teachers and because there is good evidence to suggest that language development is central to cognitive growth in general at this age. It will be some time before any results are available from this research, although the action programme, involving the setting up of playgroups and the giving of financial and other encouragement to existing nursery schools and classes in slum areas, should yield results earlier.

The National Foundation for Educational Research is also working on a structured language programme in nursery schools in Slough. It is piloting the American Peabody language programme and adapting it for British use and is also investigating ways of testing young children. The Schools Council is sponsoring research of a rather different kind: a study of current good practice in nursery schools, which will isolate and describe these practices, using the inspectorate to help identify them. The hope is then to encourage teachers to replicate them elsewhere. Not directly concerned with nursery education, but of undoubted relevance to it as far as the deprived child is concerned, is the Compensatory Education Project, which is sponsored by the Schools Council at the University of Swansea. A major part of this study is concerned with devising a method for identifying 5-year-olds in need of compensatory education. There seems no reason why the methods that emerge should not be adopted for use with 3- or 4-year-old children for the purpose of identifying those children who should be given priority when nursery places are being allocated.

Were the findings of such research to indicate that there are no lasting benefits to be derived from pre-school education from the point of view of the child's emotional and intellectual development, should policy-makers abandon proposals such as those put forward by Plowden? The answer would not necessarily be 'Yes', since there are other reasons why nursery education is desirable, some of which have been discussed at length in this study. Subjective assessments indicate that it is an experience which children enjoy, and such limited research as has been done indicates that, in the short term at least, children benefit from it. The advantage to parents and teachers in the infant school of children who have matured emotionally and learnt to mix with peers and adults other than their parents could itself justify expenditure on nursery education. In other words, nursery education may prove beneficial for socialization as such, if not in the long term for educational performance as such. It may present alternative models for identification; provide outlets for aggression and the constructive expression of phantasy; provide an opportunity for orientation towards peers; and provide a situation for involvement in joint activities, which makes possible a sense of wider collective identification. Secondly, a more imaginative use of pre-school education in educating parents, and involving parents in their children's education may in the long run have a more powerful effect on the later educational performance of children, than intervention which concentrates directly on the children only. There is a need for experimentation and careful evaluation of the role it could play in this respect. Thirdly, the provision of full-time nursery education would release mothers for work, thereby contributing to the economy's need for extra manpower. It would provide more appropriate facilities for the care and education of children whose mothers are already working, in place of the *ad hoc* and often inadequate arrangements made for such children at present. As this study has indicated, many people would not regard the former and some would not regard the latter as valid reasons for the establishment of nursery education. However, if present trends continue it will no longer be appropriate to regard working mothers as a small deviant minority, whose needs can be ignored by governments pursuing *laissez-faire* policies. Finally, and perhaps most important, there is increasing evidence to suggest that parents want nursery education for their children. This study has argued that the pressures and strains of rearing and socializing children in industrial societies, of which the employment of mothers in jobs outside the home is just one example, are such that there is a strongly felt need for extra-familial agencies to aid in this process.

If expansion does take place there are several unresolved policy questions about the form it should take. The Plowden Report's proposal to begin with areas with pronounced social needs seems right, but in the short run this may increase the variation in the extent of provision from area to area. Chapter 6 of this study showed that much of East Anglia is devoid of nursery education and it will not benefit from the new scheme under the urban programme. Is it fair on the tax-payers in such areas that their opportunities in this respect should remain so limited? Should the children of agricultural workers be neglected whilst those of the urban working class are catered for? The traditional nineteenth-century attitude towards early school education as a method of rescuing children from the slums of our big cities still lies behind many of our present-day attitudes. Although the difficulties of bringing up young children in urban areas are greater in the sense that access to safe open spaces is often unavailable, the presence of green fields does not alleviate all the strains on the family that have been described. On the other hand, an expectation that all areas should provide for identical proportions of children would be wrong. The principle of territorial justice defined by Davies is relevant here.

In the services for which the most apparent appropriate distribution between individuals is 'to each according to his need', the most appropriate distribution between areas is 'to each according to the needs of the population of that area'. Since the former criterion is synonymous with social justice, we can call the latter 'territorial justice'. The statistical definition of territorial justice is a high correlation between indices of resource use or standards of provision, and an index measuring the relative needs of an area's population for the service, the relative inequality of the standards being the same as that of the need index. Territorial justice is a necessary condition but not of course a sufficient condition, for achieving social justice (Davies, 1968, p. 16).

One of the most important difficulties in implementing such a concept is the problem of defining need, which will be determined partly by values about the role of the service in question. But, however need is defined with respect to nursery education, it is doubtful whether the Department of Education and Science's allocation of money for extra nursery schools and classes will go far to implement the principle of territorial justice. For example, in the first stage of the urban programme the local authority bidding for the third largest number of projects (seventeen), only exceeded by the Inner London Education Authority and Birmingham, was Leicester. As shown in Chapter 6, this is already the authority with the highest number of places per thousand child population aged 2 to 4 in England and Wales.

Although the Department have considered the extent of existing provision in the allocation of funds, there are still many urban authorities with very few places, and a few who have more new projects than would be expected, given that this is taken seriously into account. And the problem of the rural areas remains untouched.

Another important question is the relationship between day nurseries and nursery education. Since day nurseries have been set up to provide care rather than education for young children, they have not been included in this study. However, in some senses this is a theoretical distinction. It ought by now to be clear that the reasons for providing nursery education include the provision of facilities to care for the children of working mothers, of which the most obvious example is teachers. Should there be a large-scale expansion of nursery education, would it be right to continue to separate out from their peers some of the most underprivileged children in our society, those from homes where the family income is particularly low or where there is only one parent? There is a strong case for unifying the two services for all children over 3, in order to avoid a socially divisive system and to rationalize administrative procedures, and it is a pity that, when an obvious opportunity to do this occurred in 1945, it was not grasped. The major barriers to unification in the past have been the need to provide care in day nurseries for longer hours than those worked in the educational system at present, and the need to cater for children under 3, including infants as young as 6 weeks. The first difficulty could be solved by supervised daily minding schemes, whereby the children who need all-day care could spend the period between the end of the school day and the end of the working day with the non-working mothers of other pupils. The second problem could be solved by maintaining the present day nurseries as crèches for babies and very young children.

Chapter 2 of this study described two strands in the origins of pre-school education, a middle-class strand in the form of the first kindergartens and a working-class strand in the form of the nursery schools set up to improve the health of young children. There has been some convergence of these strands. But on the one hand the growth of playgroups, a mainly middle-class movement, and on the other the re-emergence of deprivation – this time concerning education rather than health – as the major reason for expanding maintained pre-school education, represents a reversal back to these differentiated strands. Until nursery education is universally provided for all children in maintained schools, this distinction is likely to remain and may even become more significant. One alternative to publicly financed and administered nursery education which has been put forward* is the encouragement of cooperative groups run by mothers on playgroup lines, which would be given some help from public funds but which would mainly be financed and run independently. Although such a scheme might have the advantage of drawing on the resources of parents' willingness to provide this service, it would have unfortunate results with respect to working-class children. Chapter 6 showed that provision of this type tends to exist in middle-class areas. The chances of it taking root on a large scale in working-class areas are at present remote.

The final question of policy to be considered is whether or not to charge for nursery education. A minority recommendation of the Plowden report was that charges should be levied on a means-test basis, since there had been no expansion for twenty years in spite of the 1944 Act and, therefore, its future prospects were bleak. However, the validity of the reasoning behind

---

* This method was favoured by a Conservative councillor in Hertfordshire, who believed that such groups would render the present nursery schools and classes redundant and relieve local education authorities of the burden of running them.

G

this recommendation is doubtful. The major resource constraint over the past twenty years has been the shortage of infant school teachers, which would not be alleviated by the imposition of such charges. There are also many unanswered questions to be considered before such a recommendation can be taken seriously. Will such charges cover the full economic costs of providing nursery education? If not, what proportion of costs will they cover? How will the means test scheme be devised and which groups will be eligible for free places? What effects might charges have on the demand for nursery education? Would they deter parents in certain categories, such as those who would not qualify for free places, yet would feel unable to afford charges, however small, from sending their children? Would middle-class parents decide to educate their young children in independent nursery schools, since there would be no financial advantage in sending them to state schools, thus restricting the amount of money that could be collected from charges based on a means test? The proposal to charge also raises the more fundamental questions which surround the controversy of universal or selective social services. Without reiterating the case for one or the other, it does seem necessary to consider whether there is any justification for providing free education from 3 to 5 selectively and from 5 to 15 universally. Those who advocate charges have not done this yet.

For many years the catchphrase of educational reformers was 'secondary education for all'. Today there are signs that the demand for nursery education for all will be heard more frequently. But this demand must compete with other claims of which the most important is further education for all. So far it has done badly in this competition, since the expansion of further and higher education since 1944 has been unprecedented. Chapter 7 of this study tried to throw some light on the motives of those taking decisions about nursery education in local authorities, in order to have a clearer idea why nursery education has fared so badly. But to understand more clearly why priority has been given to further and higher education, rather than nursery education, it is essential to study decision-making by central as well as local government. Such attempts are also more likely to be revealing if they study the way decisions are taken, as they are being taken, rather than by tracing them back over many years as in this study. To return to priorities there are signs that the rapid expansion of further and higher education may be checked in the next few years. Perhaps this will provide the opportunity to move towards the routinization of nursery education, the final stage in the process of differentiation described in the preceding chapters. Many claims have been made about the benefits to be derived from universal nursery education. As early as 1926, Bertrand Russell wrote:

the nursery school; if it became universal, could, in one generation, remove the profound differences in education which at present divide the classes, could produce a population all enjoying the mental and physical development which is now confined to the most fortunate, and could remove the terrible deadweight of disease and stupidity and malevolence which now makes progress so difficult (B. Russell, 1926, p. 181).

Although it is hard to share Russell's optimism about such far-reaching benefits of pre-school education to humanity, it is perhaps not rash to predict that the pressures for it will become so overwhelming that eventually it will be supplied for all children. When this is achieved every child will improve his chances of having a fair start.

Appendix 1: The sources of the data

The data on which the aggregates in the tables in Chapter 5 are based are given in Appendix 4, which gives the actual number of places in each of the categories set out on pp. 84–92 of this Chapter, for every local education authority. In considering the sources of the data and their limitations it is proposed to follow the order of the categories given in Appendix 4. These are as follows:

Maintained Sector
1. Number of day nurseries.
2. Number of places in day nurseries.
3. Number of nursery schools.
4. Number of full-time places in nursery schools.
5. Number of part-time places in nursery schools.
6. Number of nursery classes.
7. Number of full-time places in nursery classes.
8. Number of part-time places in nursery classes.

Independent Sector
9. Number of independent nursery schools.
10. Number of full-time places in independent nursery schools.
11. Number of part-time places in independent nursery schools.
12. Number of children in registered premises.
13. Number of children with registered child-minders.

The first two columns give the number of day nurseries and the number of places in them. They have been included in the totals since their aim is to provide care for the children whose mothers are unable to look after them, rather than to educate them. They have been included in the table for the purpose of comparison with the numbers of nursery schools and classes. The data were obtained from the Statistics Branch of the Department of Education and Science, which provided unpublished data on the number of nursery schools and classes and the number of children in them in each local education authority. Columns 3, 4 and 5 refer to nursery schools and exclude children over 5 in nursery schools, which form a separate category in the Department figures. They are already of compulsory school age and ought to be receiving pre-school education. Their numbers are, in any case, small.

Columns 6, 7 and 8 refer to nursery classes. Unfortunately owing to an error, the Department obtained no information on the number of nursery classes for the year 1965. Consequently the figures in columns 5 and 6 are the mean number of classes and places for the years 1964 and 1966. It is assumed that this will give the nearest approximation possible to the 1965 figures. However, they will obviously not be completely accurate.* Columns 9, 10 and 11 in Appendix 4 refer to the number of institutions registered as independent nursery *schools* and the number of places in them. These schools are distinguished from other independent nursery schools by the fact that they contain five or more children over the age of 5, but they are nevertheless primarily nursery schools with the majority of their children aged under 5. A few of these schools are recognized as efficient, the rest are simply registered with the Department of Education and Science. All other independent nurseries, which do not qualify as schools because they do not have five or more children over 5, register with the local health authorities. These come into columns 12 and 13 of Appendix 4 and are registered with the health authorities under the Nurseries and Child Minders Regulation Act, 1948. Paragraph 1 (1) of this Act states:

Every local health authority shall keep registers:

(a) of premises in their area, other than premises wholly or mainly used as private dwellings, where children are received to be looked after for the day or a substantial part thereof or for any longer period not exceeding six days;

(b) of persons in their area who for reward receive into their homes children under the age of five to be looked after as aforesaid.

The Act gives them power to impose certain requirements in conjunction with this registration. These concern the maximum number of children who may be received in the premises or the house concerned, the qualifications of those in charge of the establishment, the staffing with respect to qualifications, experience and numbers, and medical supervision of the children. They may also impose standards of accommodation and equipment, feeding and diet. Those who fail to register or to comply with any order of the above kind are breaking the law.† There is no information on the number of prosecutions made in conjunction with this Act, nor of the number of registrations that have been cancelled through failure to comply. It seems that most local authorities would be reluctant to resort to litigation, and it has been impossible to trace an example of such a case. Many local authorities may be able to bring sufficient pressure on those concerned to prevent the need from ever arising. Where they have failed, it would be difficult to prove an offence, owing to the large number of loopholes left in the Act. Frequently the offender will argue that the children under her care are those of a relative, or are being looked after free of charge, or that she is looking after the children temporarily for a sick friend or for a short time while the mother is shopping.

* In all cases where the mean was not a round number it has been rounded *upwards*. In cases where there was one nursery class in 1964 and none in 1966, and vice versa, it has been assumed that this class was in existence in 1965.

† Para. 4, sections 1 and 2. Section 2 applying to persons states, 'Where at any such time as aforesaid a person receives as mentioned in paragraph (6) of subsection (1) of Section 1 of this Act children of whom he is not a relative, and (a) the number of children exceeds two, and (b) the children come from more than one household, then if he is not registered under Section 1 of this Act, or if he contravenes or fails to comply with any requirement imposed under section two thereof, he shall be guilty of an offence.'

Medical Officers of Health are not unaware of such efforts to evade the law. Speaking at a symposium of the Society of Medical Officers of Health in March 1966, Dr Preston stated, 'It is extremely frustrating to find children kept in the squalid, often dangerous, conditions and be powerless under the present legislation to do anything about it' (quoted in Yudkin, 1967). As a result of growing criticism the Act has been amended in the Health Services and Public Health Act, 1968.

The Act was extremely unsatisfactory in two respects. First, it was unenforceable for the above reasons. Second, it allowed the local authority wide interpretation of its responsibilities. A few health authorities have refused to accept their responsibility to uphold the law. Thus one medical officer of health wrote in reply to a circular letter sent out in order to obtain figures for this study, 'this authority neither enforces nor encourages registration'. In other cases the Act had become ineffective through a failure to appreciate its main purpose, which is to eliminate unsatisfactory conditions for the care of young children outside their own homes. Another medical officer wrote that the policy of his department was to encourage registration where there was compliance with certain requirements, otherwise to discourage it, thus allowing the existence of unregistered establishments with lower standards than those set by the local authority, and outside the control of the authority.

The chief cause of ambiguity and lax interpretation, however, was the clause which refers to the looking after children 'for the day or a substantial part thereof'. A substantial part of the day may mean two hours to one authority, ten to the next. In the latter case many agencies may not be required to register, or may even be refused registration, on the grounds that they do not conform to the qualification of running for 'a substantial part' of the day. Many private nursery schools and pre-school playgroups operate for two or three hours in the morning or afternoon only, and hence may not be registered with the authority, if it so chooses. This had important consequences for the attempt to measure the extent of private pre-school provision, to which reference has already been made in the text. The Act as amended in 1968, has been improved in the following ways: 'substantial part' has been changed to 'two hours or longer'. Several children from one household are no longer discounted for the purposes of registration. The local health authorities have been given powers to impose regulations on the number and qualifications of the adults caring for the children, on the premises, on the feeding arrangements, and on the records to be kept on the children. All this should involve a more rigorous test before registration is granted. The maximum fines for illegal child-minding have been doubled and the period of imprisonment for second and subsequent offences increased from one month to three months.

Reference has also been made to the problem of separating children who are being minded from children who are being educated. The 1968 Act does not deal with this problem. It would be a false assumption to maintain that all those groups classified under the premises category are serving educational goals, and those classified under the persons category are not, although it would be true to say that a far larger proportion of those in the latter category have primary aims of a non-educational kind.

To deal with the 'persons' category first, some method had to be devised to sort out educational agencies, such as playgroups organized by women with houses large enough to accommodate a considerable number of small children, from child-minders caring for a few children, usually working mothers. The only feasible method was to use the number of children involved as a criterion. Thus all groups consisting of eight or more children in the 'persons' category have been regarded as agencies for pre-school *education* and all those with less than eight children have not. This is crude and inadequate in many respects. The rationale behind its use is as follows: it is debatable whether some of the most important aims of the pre-school education movement, that is, the possibility of interaction with other children of a similar age, and group activity to promote cooperation and social learning, can be carried out for the individual child with much less than seven other children present;* it is doubtful whether a child-minder taking on the task of caring for children in most cases for the whole day, while their mothers are working, and responsible for providing them with meals, would accept responsibility for eight or more children — indeed, few authorities would allow her to do so unless she employed one or more regular assistants† and had an adequate amount of accommodation measured in terms of square footage per child, neither of which is likely for the working-class women who form the bulk of those child-minders performing the protective rather than educational role; thirdly, this was the only possible criterion on which all authorities could be expected to have readily available information.

In dealing with registered premises, the assumption was made that all children in these groups would be undergoing education. This assumption is also subject to criticism. Some of the cases coming into this category are private day nurseries comparable with the maintained day nurseries rather than the nursery schools. However, extra information sent by a number of local authorities on all registered premises in their areas, on such aspects as the number of hours per day, which children attended, indicated that the vast majority of the registrations concerned were the equivalent of private nursery schools or playgroups usually running for the morning or afternoon only. However, there are included in the figures a number of organizations which ideally ought to be excluded. But it can be argued that the children are undergoing an educational experience, in that they take part in various activities with a number of other children. This is also true of the small number of groups in the 'persons' category, where eight or more children are involved, yet whose primary aim is protection rather than education. Further, the over-estimate of the extent of educational provision involved is likely to be more than counteracted by a similar under-estimate through excluding groups of six or seven in the category of 'persons', a number of which may have as their primary aim the educational benefit of the children.

---

* The Pre-school Playgroup Association regards a group of six children as the minimum number feasible to fulfil its educational purposes.

† Many restrict the number of children to a ratio of five children to every adult. In many areas the ratio is dependent on the age of the children. For example, the London Borough of Camden lays down a maximum of five children aged 0–2 per adult, and eight children aged 2–5 per adult.

This data was collected by circulating a letter to the 145 local health authorities asking for:

1. The number of children in registered premises on 1 January 1965.
2. The number of children in groups of eight or more being cared for by registered child minders on 1 January 1965.

The date was selected in order to fit in with statistics for other forms of pre-school education, provided by the Ministry of Health and the Department of Education and Science, whose statistical returns for each year refer to 31 December and 1 January respectively.

Replies were received from eighty-nine of the 145 local health authorities to whom letters were circulated. This represents an initial response rate of 61 per cent. The further follow-up letters increased the number of replies to 141. However, two authorities refused to cooperate, one gave incomplete information and another failed to reply to either of the follow-up letters.* The final response rate was 97·3 per cent. For the four authorities from whom information could not be elicited and for London and Middlesex, who could not provide it owing to the re-organization of local government in London, it seemed worth calculating estimates of the number of children concerned rather than eliminating the authorities from the analysis altogether.† This made possible a complete national analysis.

Two final general points need to be made concerning imperfections in the definitions and omissions in the data. First, the majority of the categories refer to the number of children on the registers at a specific date. However, either the average daily attendance or the maximum number of places possible is given sometimes by institutions registered with the health authority. These different definitions could give rise to large differences in the final figure obtained. The most usual definition of the number of children on the register ought to give a realistic picture of the actual number of children involved, although this will not be perfect from the point of view of a measure of provision by the authority. The figure collected from local health authorities on the number of children in private nurseries may well be a measure of the extent of registration by the health authorities under the 1948 Nurseries and Child Minders Act, rather than a measure of the extent of actual provision. Second, the major omission is that of children under 5

* These were Bath, Croydon, Hampshire and Dorset.

† It proved possible to obtain the number of children in registered premises in each authority from the central department, the Ministry of Health, thus avoiding the need for estimates of this. The estimates for nursery groups in the child-minder category were made by obtaining information from the Ministry of Health on the total number of registered child-minders in each of the authorities concerned. The problem was then to estimate how many children these child-minders cared for and what proportion of these were in groups of eight or more. The average proportion for small groups of authorities of a similar kind to each of those authorities where the information was lacking was calculated. It was assumed then that this proportion would apply to the authority, and the estimate was made accordingly. This method is deficient in that it assumes uniformity in a situation where in fact variation prevails. However, the category concerned constitutes only a small part of the total provision of pre-school education in any one area. Thus some inaccuracy in these estimates will not seriously affect the totals.

attending nursery classes in independent schools. There were just under 15,000 children under 5 in independent schools in 1965. However, it is not possible to separate out those children, who are early entrants to classes primarily for children of 5 and over, from those in specially constituted nursery classes. Since this study is concerned with the development of pre-school education, children under 5 receiving education which is not specifically designed as pre-school education have been eliminated from the figures for the maintained sector. For this reason it seemed advisable to omit all the children under 5 in independent schools. If they are added into the national figures, on the unlikely assumption that they are all in the equivalent of maintained nursery classes, the percentage of the children in the age group receiving pre-school education rises from 9·9 to 10·8 per cent.

There is no possibility of improving the accuracy of these figures until changes are made in the way the official statistics are collected and collated. At present there is no published table showing national figures for pre-school education.* This is largely due to the division between the Ministry of Health and the Department of Education and Science on the registration of independent establishments. However, neither of the Departments presents adequate information. The Ministry of Health publishes one table in its annual report. The categories in this are based on legal definitions set out in the 1948 Nurseries and Child Minders' Act, which are inadequate in that they fail to distinguish totally different kinds of provision from each other. It collects no information on the age of the children concerned, the size of the establishments or the nature and extent of staffing in the independent sector. The Department of Education and Science produces considerably more extensive statistics. However, the tables it publishes are confined to nursery schools. There are some useful figures giving age and sex breakdowns for all types of school (see Statistics of Education, Vol. II), which show the number of children under 5 receiving some kind of education and indicates that the proportion of boys is somewhat higher than girls, but there is no separate table for pre-school education giving figures for both nursery schools and nursery classes. There are a few separate tables for nursery schools showing, for example, the frequency distribution for the size of nursery schools (see Table A.1). In addition there are tables on pupil—teacher ratios, salaries, and

* This was attempted by the Plowden Report (see *Children and their Primary Schools*, Central Advisory Council for Education, Vol. I, pp. 108—10, Tables 4 and 5). But this attempt makes the deficiencies of the official statistics apparent. The Council attempted to compare provision in 1965 with that of 1932. The value of this exercise is diminished by the fact that there is no data on independent education for 1932 in any of the relevant categories. The inclusion of children under the supervision of the Home Office in residential nurseries in the 1965 figures seems misguided, since in no circumstances can the purpose of their placement in such homes be interpreted as educational. In addition this category is not applicable to 1932. In the second of its tables giving pre-school provision in 1965, it has gathered together all the available data from the departments concerned, yet this does not present a coherent picture of provision. Once again nursery classes are not given as a separate category, and the table is cut in two with figures from the health departments given separately. The report mentions in the text the high variation in the amount of provision from one area to the next, yet has not quantified this variation. This problem is dealt with in Chapter 6 of this study but the deficiencies of the statistics presented in Chapter 5 apply also to it, and consequently any interpretation of the data must take this into consideration.

Table A.1. Size of nursery schools in UK, 1965

Type of school	Number of schools with the following numbers of pupils on the registers								
	up to 20	21 to 30	31 to 40	41 to 50	51 to 60	61 to 80	81 to 100	over 100	Total
Maintained	3	21	181	107	55	48	26	20	461
Direct grant	4	2	3	2	2	2	1	–	16
Independent recognized as efficient	3	2	1	1	2	–	–	–	9
Other independent	99	36	24	16	9	8	1	3	196
All nursery schools	109	61	209	126	68	58	28	23	682

Source: Statistics of Education 1965, Vol. II, Table 27, p. 60.

current and capital expenditure (Statistics of Education, 1965, Vol. II, Tables 27(ii), 43 and 37). Again it would be more useful to have information on expenditure on all maintained nursery education, instead of on schools only, which provide fewer places than classes. Finally, a regional table shows the number of nursery schools in each region. As it stands it is of very little value since it simply gives the number of schools with no information on the number of places in them or of the population of the regions.

Appendix 2: Note on the child population estimates

The only information on the size of the child population in each local authority in any one year, with the exception of the Census year, are estimates made by the General Register Office. Unfortunately these estimates are not made for yearly cohorts, but for three groups consisting of children aged 1, 1 to 4, and 5 to 15. This has necessitated making certain calculations to obtain the number of children aged 2 to 4 inclusive, that is, in the age group receiving nursery education. A simple procedure was adopted of subtracting the number of children aged under 1 on 30 June 1963* from the number of children aged 1 to 4 on 30 June 1964,† which would amount to the appropriate number of children aged 2 to 4 in 1964. A dilemma arose on whether to take a two-year group of 3- to 4-year-olds or whether to include 2-year-olds as above. The latter was chosen for two reasons: firstly, a number of 2-year-olds receive pre-school education of one kind or another; secondly, the error resulting from the above calculation, which fails to take into account migration and deaths of children under 1, during their second year of life, would be doubled on subtracting two consecutive groups of under 1-year-olds from the 1 to 4 total. Although the error resulting from this may be small as a national aggregate, it could be considerable for certain local authorities. The effect of internal migration is not spaced evenly over the country with each area gaining as much as it loses in population. Nor can the effects of emigration and immigration apply with the same force to each local authority. Since it is intended to study the extent of variation in the amount of pre-school education in local authorities, it seemed important to keep this error as low as possible.

* Quarterly Return to the Registrar General, Fourth Quarter 1964, Appendix A (HMSO).
† Quarterly Return to the Registrar General, Fourth Quarter 1965, Appendix A (HMSO).

Appendix 3: Frequency distributions

For a more precise description of the independent variables in these tables see p. 107.

Table A.2. Frequency distribution of size of child population by nursery places per 1,000 child population aged 2–4. Administrative counties

Size of c.p \ Nursery provision	61 and over	41–60	21–40	Under 21
Under 7,500	Breconshire Caernarvonshire Carmarthenshire Montgomeryshire Westmorland (5)	Merioneth Cardiganshire (2)	Anglesey West Suffolk Herefordshire Pembrokeshire (4)	East Suffolk Isle of Wight Lincolnshire (Holland) Rutland Radnor Lincolnshire (Kesteven) (6)
7,500–15,000	Cambridgeshire Denbighshire Flintshire (3)	Yorkshire (East Riding) (1)	Oxfordshire Bedfordshire Cornwall Huntingdonshire (4)	Cumberland (1)
15,000–30,000	East Sussex West Sussex (2)	Monmouthshire Devon Berkshire (3)	Wiltshire Yorkshire (North Riding) Somerset Norfolk Worcestershire Northumberland Dorset (7)	Northampton- shire Shropshire Lincolnshire (Lindsey) Leicestershire Gloucestershire (5)
30,000–60,000	Buckinghamshire Glamorgan Hertfordshire Warwickshire (4)	Hampshire Staffordshire Cheshire (3)	Derbyshire Nottinghamshire Co. Durham (3)	(0)
Over 60,000	Middlesex Surrey London (3)	Lancashire Kent Essex (3)	Yorkshire (West Riding) (1)	(0)

Table A.3. Frequency distribution of proportion of economically active females by nursery places per 1,000 child population aged 2–4. Administrative counties

Working women \ Nursery provision	61 and over	41–60	21–40	Under 21
25–30	(0)	(0)	Pembrokeshire Anglesey (2)	Radnor (1)
31–35	Breconshire Carmarthenshire Glamorgan Montgomeryshire (4)	Cardiganshire Monmouthshire Merioneth (3)	West Suffolk Yorkshire (North Riding) Co. Durham Huntingdonshire Cornwall (5)	East Suffolk Lincolnshire (Lindsey) Rutland Lincolnshire (Kesteven) (4)
36–40	Cambridgeshire Denbighshire Flintshire (3)	Yorkshire (East Riding) Hampshire Devon (3)	Wiltshire Oxfordshire Herefordshire Norfolk Northumberland Derbyshire (6)	Cumberland Shropshire Lincolnshire (Holland) (3)
41–45	Buckinghamshire Caernarvonshire Warwickshire (3)	Kent Berkshire Cheshire (3)	Yorkshire (West Riding) Bedfordshire Somerset Nottinghamshire Dorset (5)	Isle of Wight Gloucestershire (2)
46–50	Hertfordshire East Sussex West Sussex Westmorland (4)	Staffordshire Essex (2)	Worcestershire (1)	Northampton- shire Leicestershire (2)
51 and over	Middlesex Surrey London (3)	Lancashire (1)	(0)	(0)

Table A.4. Frequency distribution of semi- and unskilled males by nursery places per 1,000 child population aged 2–4. Administrative counties

Manual workers / Nursery provision	61 and over	41–60	21–40	Under 21
15–20	Middlesex Surrey (2)	(0)	Bedfordshire Derbyshire (2)	(0)
21–25	Buckinghamshire Hertfordshire East Sussex West Sussex Westmorland Warwickshire (6)	Kent Berkshire Cardiganshire Devon Essex Cheshire (6)	Somerset Worcestershire Huntingdonshire Cornwall (4)	Northampton-shire Isle of Wight Leicestershire Gloucestershire (4)
26–30	Cambridgeshire London Caernarvonshire Carmarthenshire Denbighshire Montgomeryshire (6)	Yorkshire (East Riding) Hampshire Monmouthshire Merioneth Lancashire Staffordshire (6)	Yorkshire (West Riding) Wiltshire Oxfordshire Yorkshire (North Riding) Herefordshire Dorset Nottinghamshire Northumberland Durham Pembrokeshire Anglesey (11)	Shropshire Radnor (2)
31–35	Breconshire Flintshire Glamorgan (3)	(0)	(0)	Cumberland East Suffolk Lincolnshire (Lindsey) Lincolnshire (Kesteven) (4)
36–40	(0)	(0)	West Suffolk Norfolk (2)	Lincolnshire (Holland) Rutland (2)

Table A.5. Frequency distribution of per cent population living in Urban Districts and Metropolitan Boroughs by nursery places per 1,000 child population aged 2–4. Administrative counties

Pop. density \ Nursery provision	61 and over	41–60	21–40	Under 21
40 and less	Breconshire Carmarthenshire (2)	Berkshire Cardiganshire (2)	West Suffolk Oxfordshire Norfolk Anglesey (4)	Lincolnshire (Holland) Rutland Radnor Lincolnshire (Kesteven) (4)
41–50	Buckinghamshire Denbighshire Montgomeryshire Westmorland (4)	Merioneth (1)	Herefordshire Somerset Pembrokeshire Derbyshire (4)	Cumberland East Suffolk Leicestershire (3)
51–60	Cambridgeshire East Sussex Caernarvonshire Flintshire (4)	Yorkshire (East Riding) Devon Hampshire (3)	Wiltshire Cornwall (2)	Northampton- shire Lincolnshire (Lindsey) Shropshire (3)
61–70	West Sussex Warwickshire (2)	 (0)	Bedfordshire Nottinghamshire Dorset Huntingdonshire (4)	Gloucestershire (1)
71–80	Hertfordshire Glamorgan (2)	Kent Cheshire Staffordshire (3)	Yorkshire (West Riding) Worcestershire Northampton- shire (3)	Isle of Wight (1)
81–90	Surrey (1)	Essex Monmouthshire Lancashire (3)	Co. Durham (1)	 (0)
91–100	Middlesex London (2)	 (0)	Yorkshire (North Riding) (1)	 (0)

Table A.6. **Frequency distribution of proportion of day nursery places per 1,000 child population by nursery places per 1,000 child population aged 2–4. Administrative counties**

Day nursery places \ Nursery provision	61 and over	41–60	21–40	Under 21
0	West Sussex Westmorland Breconshire Caernarvonshire Carmarthenshire Denbighshire Flintshire Glamorgan Montgomeryshire Warwickshire (10)	Kent Berkshire Yorkshire (East Riding) Devon Cardiganshire Monmouthshire Merioneth (7)	West Suffolk Yorkshire (North Riding) Norfolk Worcestershire Huntingdonshire Pembrokeshire Anglesey Cornwall (8)	Cumberland East Suffolk Northampton- shire Isle of Wight Lincolnshire (Lindsey) Lincolnshire (Holland) Rutland Radnor Shropshire (9)
0·1–5	Buckinghamshire East Sussex (2)	Essex Hampshire Staffordshire (3)	Yorkshire (West Riding) Wiltshire Oxfordshire Herefordshire Bedfordshire Dorset Somerset Nottinghamshire Northumberland Co. Durham (10)	Gloucestershire Leicestershire (2)
0·6–10	Cambridgeshire Surrey Hertfordshire (3)	 (0)	Derbyshire (1)	Lincolnshire (Kesteven) (1)
11 and above	Middlesex London (2)	Cheshire (1)	Lancashire (1)	 (0)

Table A.7. Frequency distribution of per cent over-size classes by nursery places per 1,000 child population aged 2–4. Administrative counties

Over-size classes / Nursery provision	61 and over	41–60	21–40	Under 21
0	(0)	Cardiganshire Merioneth (2)	(0)	Isle of Wight Radnor (2)
1–5	Breconshire Caernarvonshire Carmarthenshire Denbighshire Glamorgan Montgomeryshire Westmorland (7)	Yorkshire (East Riding) Monmouthshire (2)	Herefordshire Norfolk Anglesey Pembrokeshire (4)	Cumberland East Suffolk (2)
6–10	Cambridgeshire East Sussex West Sussex Flintshire (4)	Kent Devon (2)	Yorkshire (West Riding) Wiltshire West Suffolk Somerset Worcestershire Dorset Northumberland Shropshire Cornwall (9)	Dorset Lincolnshire (Holland) Rutland Lincolnshire (Kesteven) Gloucestershire Shropshire (6)
11–15	Buckinghamshire London Hertfordshire (3)	Berkshire Hampshire (2)	Yorkshire (North Riding) Derbyshire (2)	Northampton- shire Lincolnshire (Lindsey) (2)
16–20	Middlesex Surrey Warwickshire (3)	Lancashire (1)	Oxfordshire Nottinghamshire Co. Durham (3)	Leicestershire (1)
21 and over	(0)	Essex Cheshire Staffordshire (3)	Bedfordshire (1)	(0)

Table A.8. **Frequency distribution of size of child population by nursery places per 1,000 child population aged 2—4. County boroughs**

Size of c.p. / Nursery provision	121 and over	91—120	61—90	31—60	Under 31
Under 3,000	Wakefield Dewsbury (2)	Chester Eastbourne Hastings Smethwick (4)	Canterbury (1)	Gt Yarmouth (1)	Merthyr Burton (2)
3,000—4,500	Oxford Burnley Darlington Northampton Southport (5)	Barrow Warrington (2)	Rochdale Doncaster Gloucester (3)	Bath Exeter East Ham Worcester Carlisle Lincoln Tynemouth (7)	Wigan Sunderland Bury (3)
4,500—6,000	Rotherham (1)	Derby Norwich Newport (3)	Oldham York Halifax Barnsley (4)	St Helens Bournemouth Grimsby Preston Gateshead (5)	Bootle W. Hartlepool Wallasey S. Shields Blackpool (5)
6,000—9,000	Reading (1)	Portsmouth Blackburn Ipswich Brighton (4)	Salford West Ham Wolverhampton Southend Swansea (5)	Walsall Birkenhead W. Bromwich (3)	Huddersfield (1)
9,000—15,000	Leicester Stoke Bolton (3)	(0)	Croydon Cardiff (2)	Newcastle Plymouth Middlesboro' Southampton (4)	Stockport (1)
Over 15,000	Bristol Manchester (2)	(0)	Birmingham Bradford (2)	Leeds Coventry Sheffield Liverpool Kingston upon Hull Nottingham (6)	(0)

Table A.9. Frequency distribution of proportion of economically active females by nursery places per 1,000 child population aged 2—4. County boroughs

Working women \ Nursery provision	121 and over	91—120	61—90	31—60	Under 31
35—40	Rotherham (1)	Barrow Newport (2)	Doncaster Barnsley Swansea (3)	Sheffield Grimsby Plymouth Middlesboro' (4)	W. Hartlepool Merthyr (2)
41—45	Darlington (1)	Derby Portsmouth Ipswich (3)	Canterbury (1)	Southampton Gt Yarmouth Lincoln Tynemouth (4)	Sunderland Burton S. Shields (3)
46—50	Wakefield Reading Bristol (3)	Chester Warrington (2)	Wolver-hampton Southend Cardiff Gloucester (4)	Kingston upon Hull St Helens Gateshead Coventry Newcastle Walsall Birkenhead (7)	Wallasey (1)
51—55	Oxford (1)	Norwich Smethwick (2)	West Ham Croydon (2)	Bath East Ham Exeter Worcester Carlisle W. Bromwich Dudley (7)	Bootle Wigan (2)
56—60	Stoke Dewsbury Manchester Southport Northampton (5)	Hastings Brighton (2)	Birmingham York (2)	Leeds Bournemouth Liverpool Nottingham Preston (5)	Stockport Huddersfield Blackpool (3)
61—65	Leicester Bolton (2)	(0)	Salford Bradford Halifax (3)	(0)	Bury (1)
66—70	Burnley (1)	Eastbourne Blackburn (2)	Oldham Rochdale (2)	(0)	(0)

Table A.10. **Frequency distribution of semi- and unskilled males by nursery places per 1,000 child population aged 2—4. County boroughs**

Manual workers \ Nursery provision	121 and over	91—120	61—90	31—60	Under 31
15—20	Southport (1)	Eastbourne (1)	Croydon Southend (2)	Bournemouth Bath (2)	(0)
21—25	Darlington Wakefield Reading Northampton (4)	Barrow Chester Hastings Norwich Brighton (5)	Canterbury Cardiff Gloucester (3)	Leeds Sheffield Exeter Walsall Worcester Carlisle Lincoln (7)	Stockport Wallasey Blackpool (3)
26—30	Bolton Bristol Oxford Stoke Manchester Leicester (6)	Derby Portsmouth Blackburn Ipswich Smethwick Newport (6)	Doncaster Birmingham Wolver- hampton York Halifax Swansea (6)	Southampton Coventry Dudley Gt Yarmouth Newcastle Tynemouth Plymouth W. Bromwich Nottingham Gateshead (10)	Huddersfield Sunderland Bury Burton (4)
31—35	Rotherham Dewsbury Burnley (3)	Warrington (1)	Oldham Rochdale Salford Bradford Barnsley (5)	St Helens Liverpool Middlesboro' Birkenhead Preston East Ham (6)	W. Hartlepool S. Shields (2)
36—40	(0)	(0)	West Ham (1)	Grimsby Kingston upon Hull (2)	Wigan Merthyr (2)
41—45	(0)	(0)	(0)	(0)	Bootle (1)

Table A.11. **Frequency distribution of per cent population living in Urban Districts and Metropolitan Boroughs by nursery places per 1,000 child population aged 2—4. County boroughs**

Pop. density \ Nursery provision	121 and over	91—120	61—90	31—60	Under 31
10 and under	Wakefield Dewsbury Rotherham Bolton Southport (5)	Barrow Eastbourne Hastings (3)	Rochdale Doncaster Canterbury Halifax Swansea Barnsley (6)	Exeter Lincoln (2)	Huddersfield Bury Merthyr (3)
11—15	Oxford Stoke Reading Darlington (4)	Chester Blackburn Ipswich Norwich Brighton (5)	Gloucester Bradford York Cardiff Newport (5)	St Helens Leeds Bournemouth Bath Coventry Sheffield Gt Yarmouth Walsall Worcester Carlisle W. Bromwich Dudley Tynemouth (13)	W. Hartlepool Burton (2)
16—20	Leicester Burnley Bristol Northampton (4)	Derby Warrington (2)	Oldham Croydon Wolver- hampton Southend (4)	Southampton Grimsby Plymouth Birkenhead Nottingham Preston (6)	Stockport Wigan Wallasey Blackpool (4)
21—25	Manchester (1)	Portsmouth Smethwick (2)	Birmingham (1)	Newcastle Middlesboro' Kingston upon Hull Preston (4)	Sunderland S. Shields (2)
26—30	(0)	(0)	(0)	Liverpool (1)	Bootle (1)
31—35	(0)	(0)	Salford West Ham (2)	East Ham (1)	(0)

Table A.12. Frequency distribution of proportion of day nursery places per 1,000 child population by nursery places per 1,000 child population aged 2—4. County boroughs

Day nursery places \ Nursery provision	121 and over	91—120	61—90	31—60	Under 31
0	Burnley Rotherham Northampton (3)	Derby Barrow Chester Newport Hastings Norwich (6)	Rochdale Swansea Canterbury Barnsley Southend Gloucester Cardiff (7)	Tynemouth Grimsby Gt Yarmouth Worcester W. Bromwich Dudley East Ham (7)	Bootle Burton Merthyr (3)
0·1—5	(0)	(0)	Croydon (1)	St Helens Southampton Walsall Plymouth Kingston upon Hull (5)	Blackpool (1)
6—10	Reading (1)	Portsmouth Ipswich Brighton (3)	Oldham Doncaster (2)	Bournemouth Sheffield Exeter Birkenhead Lincoln (5)	Stockport Sunderland (2)
11—15	Oxford Darlington (2)	(0)	West Ham (1)	Leeds Bath Liverpool Carlisle (4)	Bury S. Shields (2)
16—20	Stoke Bristol Bolton (3)	Eastbourne Warrington Smethwick (3)	Birmingham Bradford Wolverhampton York (4)	Middlesboro' Nottingham (2)	Wigan W. Hartlepool (2)
Over 20	Wakefield Leicester Dewsbury Manchester Southport (5)	Blackburn (1)	Salford Halifax (2)	Coventry Newcastle Preston Gateshead (4)	Huddersfield Wallasey (2)

Table A.13. **Frequency distribution of per cent over-size classes by nursery places per 1,000 child population aged 2—4**

Over-size classes \ Nursery provision	121 and over	91—120	61—90	31—60	Under 31
5 and under	(0)	Norwich (1)	Gloucester (1)	Dudley (1)	Merthyr (1)
6—10	Leicester Dewsbury Bolton (3)	Ipswich Hastings (2)	Oldham Rochdale York Swansea (4)	Bath Carlisle Lincoln East Ham (4)	(0)
11—15	Wakefield Oxford Stoke Reading (4)	Derby Chester Eastbourne Portsmouth Blackburn (5)	Doncaster Croydon Southend Barnsley (4)	Bournemouth Exeter Worcester Preston (4)	Wigan Bury (2)
16—20	Burnley (1)	Warrington Brighton (2)	Salford Canterbury Bradford Wolver-hampton (4)	St Helens Coventry Walsall Gateshead (4)	Bootle Huddersfield Burton (3)
21—25	Darlington Rotherham Manchester Southport Northampton (5)	Barrow Smethwick Newport (3)	West Ham Halifax (2)	Leeds Southampton Nottingham Tynemouth (4)	W. Hartlepool Wallasey S. Shields Blackpool (4)
26—30	Bristol (1)	(0)	Cardiff (1)	Sheffield Gt Yarmouth Plymouth Birkenhead Kingston upon Hull (5)	Sunderland (1)
31—35	(0)	(0)	Birmingham (1)	Liverpool W. Bromwich (2)	Stockport (1)
36—40	(0)	(0)	(0)	Grimsby Newcastle (2)	(0)
41 and over	(0)	(0)	(0)	Middlesboro' (1)	(0)

Appendix 4: Pre-school education in each local authority in 1965 (all categories)

PRE-SCHOOL EDUCATION, 1965

	1	2	3	4	5	6	7	8	9	10	11	12	13
	Day Nurseries		Maintained Nursery Schools and Classes						Independent (Education)			Independent (Health)	
	Day nurseries	Children	Nursery schools	Full-time places	Part-time places	Nursery* classes	Full-time places	Part-time places	Nursery† schools	Full-time places	Part-time places	Registered premises places	Child‡ minders places
Bedfordshire	1	40	3	152	–	3	73	3	2	16	13	33	273
Berkshire	–	–	14	399	275	2	32	11	6	74	93	470	118
Buckinghamshire	1	35	10	281	516	18	495	77	8	166	85	912	563
Cambridgeshire and Isle of Ely	1	43	5	193	109	11	295	2	2	38	25	341	36
Cheshire	13	574	2	49	18	21	579	2	5	72	76	945	673
Cornwall	–	–	1	40	–	1	26	2	1	11	1	227	107
Cumberland	–	–	1	40	–	2	29	–	–	–	–	45	105
Derbyshire	5	225	2	62	42	24	595	94	1	13	4	50	33
Devon	1	–	–	–	–	2	49	12	9	260	66	522	298
Dorset	1	50	–	–	–	2	58	2	2	15	2	111	118
Durham	4	220	19	804	48	28	712	134	1	8	–	139	32
Essex	20	956	4	183	166	16	485	77	8	151	20	2,041	2,042
Gloucestershire	3	115	1	40	–	4	121	23	3	20	11	108	154
Hampshire	2	100	1	40	–	–	–	–	11	238	73	1,486	585
Herefordshire	1	35	1	35	–	–	–	–	–	–	–	133	68
Hertfordshire	8	395	18	688	585	6	153	68	5	94	12	2,036	824
Huntingdon and Peterborough	–	–	2	74	40	2	56	–	–	–	–	–	8
Isle of Wight	–	–	–	–	–	–	–	–	–	–	–	65	–
Kent	3	–	3	97	84	9	250	88	13	327	81	3,358	990
Lancashire	53	2,506	43	1,518	614	53	1,489	12	3	96	–	1,624	214
Leicestershire	2	90	–	–	–	1	18	1	2	27	18	334	–
Lincs (Holland)	–	–	–	–	–	–	–	–	–	–	–	26	–

Lincs (Kesteven)	1	40	2	85	–	–	–	–	–	–	–	72	58
Lincs (Lindsey)	–	–	2	52	–	1	32	6	1	7	5	55	41
Norfolk	–	–	3	119	–	5	144	14	2	14	7	253	166
Northamptonshire	1	29	2	58	22	4	74	47	–	–	–	34	137
Northumberland	4	115	–	–	–	11	311	–	5	88	–	197	305
Nottinghamshire	1	35	2	77	–	5	130	3	1	27	14	322	217
Oxfordshire	–	–	2	42	42	1	22	–	–	–	–	257	130
Rutland	–	–	–	–	–	–	–	–	–	–	–	–	–
Shropshire	3	90	3	119	24	1	16	7	2	38	2	192	–
Somerset	5	230	2	71	12	4	111	12	3	43	7	453	139
Staffordshire	–	–	16	596	187	17	433	60	1	15	–	655	–
Suffolk (East)	–	–	–	–	–	1	20	1	1	10	–	142	38
Suffolk (West)	–	–	–	–	–	2	46	–	2	25	11	184	–
Surrey	13	543	15	651	221	20	517	10	28	610	325	3,909	–
Sussex (East)	1	51	1	–	–	3	76	29	4	82	13	840	154
Sussex (West)	–	–	4	100	173	2	44	–	4	27	15	884	145
Warwickshire	–	–	9	359	15	22	662	–	4	51	29	239	156
Westmorland	–	–	1	58	–	4	91	14	1	8	3	40	–
Wiltshire	1	25	–	–	–	9	207	12	3	43	5	325	376
Worcestershire	–	–	1	39	–	4	101	–	–	–	–	410	175
Yorks (East Riding)	–	–	1	37	–	8	188	–	2	26	25	173	161
Yorks (North Riding)	–	–	1	43	–	4	111	–	–	–	–	482	172
Yorks (West Riding)	5	220	11	437	155	100	2,517	37	–	–	–	182	93
Total, Administrative Counties	150	6,752	209	7,638	3,348	433	11,368	870	146	2,740	1,041	25,246	9,904

* No data were available for 1965 therefore that given is the mean of the 1964 and 1966 figures. Where an authority was abolished in 1965, 1964 figures were used.

† Includes schools recognized as efficient and other schools. There were nine of the former.

‡ Includes only those in registered groups of eight or more children.

	Day Nurseries		Maintained Nursery Schools and Classes						Independent (Education)			Independent (Health)	
	1	*2*	*3*	*4*	*5*	*6*	*7*	*8*	*9*	*10*	*11*	*12*	*13*
	Day nurseries	Children	Nursery schools	Full-time places	Part-time places	Nursery* classes	Full-time places	Part-time places	Nursery† schools	Full-time places	Part-time places	Registered premises places	Child‡ minders places
Barnsley	–	–	3	40	155	12	294	26	–	–	–	–	–
Barrow-in-Furness	–	–	1	105	–	7	181	–	–	–	–	48	20
Bath	1	55	–	–	–	3	76	59	1	24	1	20	63
Birkenhead	2	50	–	–	–	8	223	53	–	–	–	46	–
Birmingham	20	955	26	1,233	280	59	1,481	–	2	55	8	740	–
Blackburn	5	221	3	120	–	17	480	–	–	–	–	–	66
Blackpool	1	22	–	–	–	–	–	–	–	–	–	–	8
Bolton	4	190	2	179	–	29	838	1	–	–	7	42	–
Bootle	–	–	–	–	–	4	107	–	1	16	–	73	73
Bournemouth	1	45	–	–	–	3	101	–	–	–	–	–	–
Bradford	6	280	3	178	80	26	663	169	–	–	–	173	104
Brighton	1	36	2	41	80	13	368	113	1	5	3	199	–
Bristol	7	290	15	852	369	19	396	156	3	92	50	351	351
Burnley	–	–	10	404	77	7	174	–	–	–	–	–	–
Burton-on-Trent	–	–	–	–	–	2	34	–	–	–	–	–	–
Bury	1	38	1	40	–	1	13	–	–	–	–	–	18
Canterbury	–	–	–	–	–	1	28	–	–	–	–	60	19
Carlisle	1	50	–	–	–	–	–	–	–	–	–	93	–
Chester	–	–	2	80	–	5	104	–	–	–	–	111	–
Coventry	9	435	1	63	2	22	594	80	1	15	36	224	62
Darlington	1	50	5	259	140	4	83	–	1	66	–	–	–
Derby	–	–	2	113	–	16	454	–	–	–	–	67	–
Dewsbury	4	180	4	186	284	–	–	–	–	–	–	–	–
Doncaster	1	25	–	–	–	8	237	–	–	–	–	64	48
Dudley	–	–	2	145	–	–	–	–	–	–	–	–	–
Eastbourne	1	60	–	–	–	2	37	–	1	–	23	222	39

Exeter	1	40	1	26	34	1	14	29	1	46	–	85	10
Gateshead	1	116	1	40	–	2	60	–	–	–	–	55	–
Gloucester	–	–	–	–	–	6	158	123	–	–	–	20	–
Gt Yarmouth	–	–	–	–	–	3	85	–	–	–	–	–	10
Grimsby	–	–	1	46	–	6	159	–	–	–	–	20	20
Halifax	2	113	1	65	–	8	247	–	–	–	–	133	45
Hastings	–	–	1	–	–	2	53	–	–	–	–	130	–
Huddersfield	3	137	–	–	–	–	–	–	–	–	–	263	251
Ipswich	1	60	1	39	–	2	30	1	1	10	30	163	20
Kingston upon Hull	1	48	2	114	78	12	299	–	–	–	–	765	215
Leeds	7	350	1	27	–	13	330	1	–	–	–	330	129
Leicester	6	275	1	14	–	70	2,003	684	–	–	–	36	–
Lincoln	1	40	2	91	–	2	43	–	–	–	–	465	278
Liverpool	13	724	6	370	60	27	794	14	–	–	–	35	–
Luton	3	140	2	137	53	3	74	54	3	108	31	276	84
Manchester	24	1,156	4	228	–	128	3,415	479	–	–	–	108	10
Middlesborough	3	180	1	–	–	8	237	–	–	–	–	173	98
Newcastle upon Tyne	6	261	1	90	–	7	165	28	–	–	–	130	64
Northampton	–	–	5	214	1	5	149	–	1	44	35	67	55
Norwich	–	–	1	90	–	8	217	1	2	50	5	132	–
Nottingham	7	269	4	98	126	19	446	419	–	–	–	108	–
Oldham	1	42	3	101	–	9	267	–	–	–	–	50	74
Plymouth	1	35	–	–	–	4	119	–	3	109	39	440	340
Portsmouth	2	70	1	42	–	4	108	8	1	–	–	–	24
Preston	3	143	–	100	–	4	180	–	–	–	–	158	140
Reading	1	50	6	191	118	6	246	–	1	68	43	–	140
Rochdale	–	–	4	314	–	1	19	–	–	–	–	20	–
Rotherham	–	–	4	95	6	16	452	–	–	–	–	–	–

* No data were available for 1965 therefore that given is the mean of the 1964 and 1966 figures. Where an authority was abolished in 1965, 1964 figures were used.

† Includes schools recognized as efficient and other schools. There were nine of the former.

‡ Includes only those in registered groups of eight or more children.

	Day Nurseries		Maintained Nursery Schools and Classes						Independent (Education)			Independent (Health)	
	1	2	3	4	5	6	7	8	9	10	11	12	13
	Day nurseries	Children	Nursery schools	Full-time places	Part-time places	Nursery* classes	Full-time places	Part-time places	Nursery† schools	Full-time places	Part-time places	Registered premises places	Child‡ minders places
St Helens	1	30	—	—	—	5	137	—	1	—	—	40	—
Salford	58	235	6	175	113	12	326	—	—	121	—	16	—
Sheffield	4	190	3	259	40	14	416	—	—	—	—	160	221
Smethwick	1	35	1	81	—	7	195	1	—	—	—	—	55
Solihull	—	—	—	—	—	2	54	1	2	30	25	73	37
Southampton	1	20	—	—	—	9	261	9	1	5	8	250	97
Southend-on-Sea	—	—	—	—	—	5	95	2	—	—	—	262	—
Southport	2	100	1	20	40	10	300	61	—	—	—	35	—
South Shields	2	80	—	—	—	—	30	60	—	—	—	40	—
Stockport	2	87	5	264	—	2	43	—	—	—	—	47	45
Stoke-on-Trent	5	210	14	790	1	43	1,084	—	—	—	—	40	40
Sunderland	2	100	1	20	39	2	45	119	—	—	—	75	—
Tynemouth	—	—	2	7	222	2	47	—	—	—	—	30	—
Wakefield	1	47	1	—	—	14	442	—	—	—	—	12	—
Wallasey	3	130	1	25	30	—	—	1	—	—	—	40	—
Walsall	1	29	3	115	25	1	25	—	—	—	—	70	—
Warrington	1	50	—	—	—	14	315	86	—	—	—	—	—
West Bromwich	—	—	2	86	—	7	155	67	—	—	—	—	—
West Hartlepool	1	80	—	—	—	—	—	—	1	12	13	—	8
Wigan	1	67	—	—	—	3	80	—	—	—	—	—	8
Wolverhampton	2	115	1	20	41	11	280	19	—	—	—	42	40
Worcester	—	—	—	—	—	3	68	—	—	—	—	46	—
York	2	90	1	40	—	6	164	—	—	—	—	—	90
Total, County Boroughs	192	8,926	173	8,772	2,504	816	21,897	2,924	29	876	357	7,973	3,379

Anglesey	—	—	—	—	—	1	28	—	—	—	—	90	—
Breconshire	—	—	1	30	—	14	325	—	—	—	—	176	—
Caernarvonshire	—	—	—	—	—	22	483	23	—	—	—	—	—
Cardiganshire	—	—	—	—	—	6	120	6	—	—	—	221	—
Carmarthenshire	—	—	1	41	—	20	464	1	—	—	—	—	—
Denbighshire	—	—	—	—	—	21	600	—	—	—	—	40	—
Flintshire	—	—	1	30	—	17	438	—	1	19	3	—	—
Glamorgan	—	—	12	480	67	123	3,233	—	1	13	13	382	235
Merioneth	—	—	—	—	—	4	83	—	—	—	—	—	—
Monmouthshire	—	—	10	432	68	12	251	3	—	—	—	182	8
Montgomeryshire	—	—	—	—	—	8	150	—	—	—	—	—	—
Pembrokeshire	—	—	—	—	—	5	112	—	—	—	—	15	9
Radnorshire	—	—	—	—	—	—	—	—	—	—	—	—	—
Cardiff	—	—	8	409	100	5	130	—	—	—	—	392	171
Merthyr Tydfil	—	—	1	27	—	—	—	—	—	—	—	—	—
Newport (Mon.)	—	—	5	159	68	7	144	173	—	—	—	121	—
Swansea	—	—	2	229	—	13	335	—	—	—	—	76	—
Total, Wales	—	—	41	1,837	303	278	6,896	206	2	32	16	1,695	423
Metropolitan Area													
London	76	4,003	31	1,156	1,592	132	3,827	5,870	10	359	93	2,723	1,160
Middlesex	34	1,630	12	580	200	133	3,863	477	13	430	201	3,108	920
Croydon	1	50	1	20	40	7	234	—	1	9	12	336	225
East Ham	—	—	—	—	—	7	201	10	—	—	—	—	—
West Ham	2	105	5	179	280	6	146	72	—	—	—	22	26
Total, Metropolitan Area	113	5,788	49	1,935	2,112	285	8,271	6,429	24	798	306	6,189	2,331
Total, England and Wales	455	21,466	472	20,182	8,267	1,812	48,432	10,429	201	4,446	1,720	41,103	16,037

* No data were available for 1965 therefore that given is the mean of the 1964 and 1966 figures. Where an authority was abolished in 1965, 1964 figures were used.

† Includes schools recognized as efficient and other schools. There were nine of the former.

‡ Includes only those in registered groups of eight or more children.

§ In addition four playgroups are run by the health department.

Appendix 5: Provision of nursery education in the regions: number of places per 1,000 child population aged 2-4

	Maintained	Independent	Total
Northern region			
Cumberland	5·9	12·8	18·7
Durham	31·0	3·9	34·9
Northumberland	12·5	20·2	32·7
Westmorland	53·4	17·6	71·0
Yorkshire (North Riding)	6·8	28·8	35·6
Carlisle	—	32·2	32·2
Darlington	116·4	16·0	132·4
Gateshead	20·4	11·2	31·6
Middlesbrough	24·2	12·1	36·3
Newcastle	21·9	22·0	43·9
South Shields	10·4	7·0	17·4
Sunderland	13·2	7·0	20·2
Tynemouth	42·1	7·6	49·7
W. Hartlepool	17·8	5·5	23·3
Total	376·0	203·9	579·9
Average	26·8	14·6	41·4
Yorkshire (East and West Ridings)			
Yorkshire (East Riding)	20·0	33·1	53·1
Yorkshire (West Riding)	36·0	2·6	38·6
Barnsley	86·7	—	86·7
Bradford	60·2	17·3	77·5
Dewsbury	125·2	—	125·2
Doncaster	52·8	24·9	77·7
Halifax	67·1	—	67·1
Huddersfield	—	19·5	19·5
Kingston upon Hull	20·8	11·2	32·0
Leeds	15·7	38·8	54·5

	Maintained	*Independent*	*Total*
Rotherham	118·8	4·3	123·1
Sheffield	30·6	16·8	47·4
Wakefield	158·9	4·3	163·2
York	45·0	19·2	64·2
Total	837·8	192·0	1,029·8
Average	69·8	13·7	83·6
North Midland			
Derbyshire	19·1	2·6	21·7
Leicestershire	0·7	15·1	15·8
Lincolnshire (Holland)	—	5·6	5·6
Lincolnshire (Kesteven)	—	18·3	18·3
Lincolnshire (Lindsey)	4·7	5·8	10·5
Northamptonshire	6·1	6·3	12·4
Nottinghamshire	6·4	19·5	25·9
Rutland	—	—	—
Derby	104·2	12·3	116·5
Grimsby	36·7	7·2	43·9
Leicester	199·4	37·3	236·7
Lincoln	32·8	8·8	41·6
Northampton	74·0	48·4	122·4
Nottingham	52·0	8·4	60·4
Total	536·1	195·6	731·7
Average	38·3	14·0	52·3
Eastern			
Bedfordshire	15·4	22·4	37·8
Cambridgeshire	70·5	55·5	126·0
Essex	7·8	42·0	49·8
Hertfordshire	22·8	58·0	80·8
Hunts and Peterborough	21·4	0·9	22·3
Norfolk	14·1	22·7	36·8
Suffolk (East)	1·8	17·4	19·2
Suffolk (West)	6·7	31·2	37·9
Great Yarmouth	38·3	4·5	42·8
Norwich	60·2	34·5	94·7
Southend	13·4	49·9	63·3
Total	272·4	339·0	611·4
Average	24·7	30·9	55·6
Southern			
Berkshire	22·4	28·1	50·5
Buckinghamshire	34·6	54·4	89·0
Hampshire	0·8	49·4	50·2
Isle of Wight	—	17·6	17·6
Oxfordshire	6·9	23·0	29·9
Bournemouth	20·6	33·3	53·9
Oxford	124·1	89·3	213·4

H

	Maintained	Independent	Total
Portsmouth	17·2	87·7	104·9
Reading	81·7	63·8	145·5
Southampton	25·6	28·5	54·1
Total	333·9	475·1	809·0
Average	33·4	47·5	81·1

South-western

	Maintained	Independent	Total
Cornwall	4·6	23·7	28·3
Devon	2·3	47·2	49·5
Dorset	3·9	16·3	20·2
Gloucestershire	6·0	10·0	16·0
Somerset	7·7	25·3	33·0
Wiltshire	8·5	29·8	38·8
Bath	21·2	29·9	51·1
Bristol	82·2	44·3	126·5
Exeter	15·8	31·4	47·2
Gloucester	56·2	5·1	61·3
Plymouth	12·2	26·0	38·2
Total	220·6	289·0	509·6
Average	20·1	26·4	46·3

Metropolitan

	Maintained	Independent	Total
London	68·6	33·7	102·3
Middlesex	49·9	47·6	97·5
East Ham	46·5	10·8	57·3
West Ham	67·6	—	67·6
Croydon	22·6	47·5	70·1
Total	255·2	139·6	394·8
Average	51·0	28·0	71·0

Wales

	Maintained	Independent	Total
Anglesey	7·6	24·5	32·1
Brecon	153·0	—	153·0
Caernarvon	93·6	34·1	127·7
Cardigan	59·0	—	59·0
Carmarthen	72·1	3·0	75·1
Denbigh	74·5	—	74·5
Flint	62·3	8·0	70·3
Glamorgan	100·4	17·1	117·5
Merioneth	44·1	—	44·1
Monmouth	40·0	10·6	50·6
Montgomery	78·9	—	78·9
Pembroke	22·8	4·8	27·6
Radnor	—	—	—
Cardiff	42·7	40·8	83·5

	Maintained	Independent	Total
Merthyr Tydfil	9·3	–	9·3
Newport	72·3	20·7	93·0
Swansea	68·9	9·3	78·2
Total	1,001·5	172·9	1,174·4
Average	58·9	10·2	69·1

Midlands
	Maintained	Independent	Total
Hereford	5·1	29·2	34·3
Shropshire	1·0	15·2	16·2
Staffordshire	30·8	11·7	42·5
Warwickshire	33·9	34·2	68·1
Worcestershire	6·4	25·5	31·9
Birmingham	53·2	14·7	67·9
Burton on Trent	12·4	–	12·4
Coventry	36·4	16·7	53·1
Dudley	56·4	–	56·4
Smethwick	92·6	–	92·6
Stoke on Trent	161·1	7·0	168·1
Walsall	24·8	11·4	36·2
West Bromwich	38·5	–	38·5
Wolverhampton	50·9	12·7	63·6
Worcester	20·9	14·1	35·0
Total	624·4	192·4	816·8
Average	41·6	12·8	54·4

North-west
	Maintained	Independent	Total
Cheshire	12·1	32·8	44·9
Lancashire	27·3	23·2	50·5
Barrow	85·8	23·5	109·3
Birkenhead	32·6	5·9	38·5
Blackburn	99·6	–	99·6
Blackpool	–	11·8	11·8
Bolton	120·0	1·0	121·0
Bootle	19·0	7·5	26·5
Burnley	157·5	–	157·5
Bury	16·3	–	16·3
Chester	65·7	39·6	105·3
Liverpool	23·6	14·6	38·2
Manchester	117·3	10·9	128·2
Oldham	69·1	19·2	88·3
Preston	51·9	5·0	56·9
Rochdale	82·0	–	82·0
St Helens	27·4	32·2	59·6
Salford	69·5	2·0	71·5
Southport	113·1	10·6	123·7

	Maintained	Independent	Total
Stockport	22·9	6·9	29·8
Wallasey	7·6	7·6	15·2
Warrington	114·4	–	114·4
Wigan	23·8	2·4	26·2
Total	1,358·5	256·7	1,615·2
Average	59·1	11·2	70·2
South-east			
Kent	4·9	53·7	58·6
Surrey	18·6	68·1	86·7
Sussex (East)	5·6	65·1	70·7
Sussex (West)	11·3	52·2	63·5
Brighton	78·1	31·7	109·8
Canterbury	19·9	55·3	75·2
Eastbourne	12·5	92·2	104·7
Hastings	21·9	73·9	95·8
Total	172·8	492·2	665·0
Average	21·6	61·6	83·1

Appendix 6: Four different approaches to the establishment of nursery classes under the Addenda to Circular 8/60*

The Department of Education and Science found that the response to the first Addendum to Circular 8/60 was poor, but after the circulation of the second Addendum it improved somewhat. Nevertheless, there were still a large number of authorities who made no use of the new opportunities offered them under these Addenda. The following paragraphs may help to illustrate why this is.

The two authorities with less provision, that is Kent and Burton, have been able to make use of the Addenda more easily than Hertfordshire and Smethwick. This is not surprising since the latter both gave teachers' children top priority in the queue for places already, and therefore did not have such a large group of teachers, if any, ready to jump at the opportunity to return to teaching once a nursery class was established. Therefore, they have found it less easy to satisfy the Department's regulations, which require that a certain number of teachers should be released before a class is set up. (Under Method I four qualified teachers must be released by the provision of each new class. Under Method II a nursery class can be set up, provided that after this the number of women teachers, whose service is facilitated by the provision of nursery classes, is twice the number of women teachers employed in the authorities' nursery schools and classes as a whole.) On investigation the officers in Hertfordshire found that they would have to greatly increase the number of teachers released by their current provision before being able to make use of Method II. However, they quickly made further inquiries about the possibilities under Method I in several places, including Stevenage, where the staffing problems in the infant schools were particularly acute. One of the problems they have faced is that such areas also tend to have no spare accommodation in the infant schools, which can be used for nursery classes. Initially, the officers were pessimistic.† However, after further inquiries they found that there were one or two areas where a sufficient number of teachers would come forward. This was recorded in the minutes of the primary sub-committee of December 1965, which also noted that the 'appreciable number of teachers' authorities have to reach to set up nursery classes was likely to be relaxed by the Department. Therefore provision was made in the 1966/7

* For a detailed description of these Addenda see Chapter 4, p. 68.
† See Primary Sub-Committee, June 1965.

budget for a maximum of six such classes to be set up, which would involve additional expenditure of £21,000. The value of such forward planning was lost, however, since the expectation that the regulations would be relaxed proved over-optimistic. However, during the year 1966/7 two classes were set up under Addendum I. Meanwhile the officials have continued to investigate other methods in the spirit of the Addenda, but have so far not been successful in persuading the Department to accept them. Both officers and members appeared to welcome the Addenda as a way of increasing the amount of nursery education in the county rather than simply as a method of recruiting more teachers.

This contrasts sharply with the attitude of the chief education officer in Smethwick who believed that no teacher with a child aged 3 to 5 would be deterred from returning to the profession if she wished to do so, since there were accessible nursery classes in every part of the borough. Nor did he contribute to the local campaign for the recruitment of married women, which consisted of a joint advertisement by the surrounding local education authorities, since he believed it produced nothing. He did not see the Addenda as an opportunity to increase the number of nursery places either. As already stated, there was a strong feeling that the creation and operation of a new nursery class would make more work for everyone in a situation where staff in the education department and the schools had too much work.* Since all the nursery classes in Smethwick were staffed entirely by nursery assistants, owing to the chronic shortage of teachers, 43 per cent of the infant school teachers were unqualified in 1966, there would have been no difficulty in satisfying the Department's regulations under Method II, had any teachers who could make use of the facilities been found. The situation in Smethwick was almost the reverse of that in Hertfordshire. The latter authority wished to make use of the Addenda but could not satisfy the regulations, the former authority could satisfy the regulations, but did not wish to make use of the Addenda.

In Kent the situation was different again. The county was 200 under quota for full-time qualified teachers in 1966, and although it makes much of this up with part-timers, the authority was anxious to recruit as many extra teachers as possible. Consequently it grasped at the Department's relaxation of Circular 8/60 with enthusiasm. Between September 1964 and January 1965 it established seven new classes, which released 43·5 full-time equivalent

---

* The chief education officer's somewhat hostile attitude to the Addenda is illustrated by the following correspondence. An infant school head teacher wrote to him asking if the timetable of a grammar school teacher whose son she had just accepted into the nursery class could be arranged so that the boy could be picked up by his mother at 3.30 p.m. each day. He wrote back saying that he inferred that the Secretary of State envisaged that teachers would not have to remove their children by 3.30, and inquired why the head teacher could not arrange this. She replied that all the children were promptly picked up at 3.30 p.m. The chief education officer then wrote that the case 'reveals clearly that nursery classes in Smethwick are not in a position to carry out the functions which the Secretary of State thinks a nursery class should carry out, namely to look after the children of teachers undertaking full-time appointments who could not do so without the advantages of a nursery class'. The Addenda were designed largely to aid the recruitment of infant school teachers but where teachers of older children have made use of the classes, arrangements with other parents to collect their children have been successful.

teachers. Two of these classes in Gillingham between them released as many as twenty-two full-time equivalent teachers, a remarkably high number. Four more classes opened during 1967 and the divisional executives were asked for further submissions.* Owing to the extraordinary success of some of the classes in releasing teachers, Kent has remained well within the Department's regulations. Consequently, the only constraint on the establishment of further classes is the availability of accommodation. Although the officers saw the release of teachers as the major purpose of the new class, they were glad of the opportunity to re-establish a nucleus of nursery education in the county and were concerned about the fact that those areas where it was easiest to find teachers tended to be the areas which needed nursery education least.

The officers at Burton-on-Trent also regarded the Addenda to the circular primarily as a useful way of recruiting extra teachers, and they have found the class which they set up in 1965 under Method I very useful in terms of staffing. They had no difficulty in finding teachers with children in the relevant age group who wished to return and one woman travelled all the way from Derby to leave her child in the class and teach in a Burton School. Priority was also given to welfare cases and to the children of women in other short-staffed professions such as medicine and nursing. The latter priority is not national policy and has not been adopted generally, therefore it would be interesting to know how many authorities have initiated this. Given the success of the class in achieving what the authority regarded as its prime aim − the release of qualified women for work − it seemed surprising that only one class had been set up, particularly since there had been no opposition at all from members of the education committee to the establishment of the first class. In fact, there were definite plans to start another one in 1967 but unfortunately the finance committee, through the borough council, demanded cuts in educational expenditure during that year. The education bill had been rising rapidly and the borough treasurer had found that certain items of expenditure, such as the salaries of primary school teachers, were much above the national average.† The Tories, who had a small majority in the council, were determined that the rates should not go up again and in the ensuing conflict their superior numbers won the day and the cuts went through.‡ The argument was over educational expenditure in general and no particular cut was singled out either by those attacking the level of expenditure or those defending it. The director of education had decided informally which cuts were to be made in consultation with the chairman of the education committee and these were then discussed in the committee. The vulnerability of nursery education is revealed once again by these cuts in expenditure.

* The intention was also to open a class at a day training centre for teachers, in order to recruit the prospective teachers earlier.

† The explanation for this is that the authority has many small schools with small classrooms and consequently has a low pupil−teacher ratio.

‡ In the same year the Education Committee's plan for secondary school reorganization into a two-tier comprehensive scheme was thrown out by fifteen votes to thirteen.

Appendix 7: Smelser's model of structural differentiation

Part I*

Smelser applied this model to two empirical examples: technical changes in the Lancashire cotton industry during the late eighteenth and early nineteenth centuries; changes in the working-class family economy; that is, roles that are relevant to production and consumption during the same period.† Here it is applied to changes in family socialization in twentieth-century Britain.

The model of structural differentiation is an abstract theory of change. When one social role or organisation becomes archaic under changing historical circumstances, it differentiates by a *definite and specific sequence of events* into *two or more* roles or organisations which function more effectively in the new historical circumstances. The new social units are structurally distinct from each other, but taken together are functionally equivalent to the original unit. . . . Any sequence of differentiation is set in motion by specific disequilibrating conditions. Initially this disequilibrium gives rise to symptoms of social disturbance which must be brought into line later by the mechanisms of social control. Only then do specific ideas, suggestions and attempts emerge to produce the more differentiated social units (p. 2).

Structural differentiation with reference to the family begins when there is dissatisfaction over the performance of familial roles. Such dissatisfactions are frequently generated by industrial pressures. They are given extra weight when legitimized by the dominant family values of the time, and under such conditions differentiation becomes possible. Thus

the family may become under specific pressures, inadequate for performing its defined functions. Dissatisfaction occurs when it is felt either that performance of roles or utilisation of resources falls short of expectations. The symptoms of disturbance resulting from these pressures are first handled by mechanisms of social control. Gradually as the energy is harnessed, it is directed to the more positive tasks of legitimising and specifying ideas for social action, and transforming these ideas into social experiment. If successful, these experiments produce one or more new social units (Smelser, 1959, p. 3).

The specific pressures on the family are associated with the similar process of industrial differentiation, whereby the industrial structure becomes in-

---

adequate to meet industrial requirements. The model is thus concerned with a particular kind of social change. The theoretical model of differentiation occurs typically when the system increases in complexity, and consists of a series of seven stages or steps. These are as follows:

(1) The expression of dissatisfaction with the existing system, which may take the form of concern with role performance, utilization of resources, or both.

(2) The immediate responses to the dissatisfaction. 'Undirected or misdirected symptoms of disturbance − phantasy, aggression and anxiety.'

(3) These are brought into line by mechanisms of social control.

(4) More satisfactory means of solving the original dissatisfactions are encouraged which results in a proliferation of ideas at the general level.

(5) These are then specified. The new institutional forms are outlined.

(6) The new and more specialized forms are then implemented.

(7) Finally these are assimilated into the social system and thereby routinized.

This is the ideal form of the model of change but Smelser stresses that the sequence need not be complete, nor does each stage necessarily follow the previous one in neat order. They may occur simultaneously or overlap. There may be regression. For example, symptoms of disturbance may reappear until the system is remodelled. Indeed they are likely to reappear, as are the methods of handling them, since the dissatisfaction that caused them is still present if the new system is incomplete. Not only may regression take place, the sequence may also be truncated. 'If the initial dissatisfactions are minor the more explosive steps 2 and 3 may not appear at all. Further, if channels for expressing disturbance are well institutionalised for the purpose of initiating change, dissatisfaction is often conveyed directly to the incumbents of these roles; only if they fail to establish new methods are symptoms of disturbance likely to appear' (Smelser, 1959, p. 31). Furthermore, several sequences of structural differentiation may occur simultaneously. Lastly, not all sequences of structural differentiation are completed successfully. All the above considerations are of importance in applying this model to the development of pre-school education.

This briefly summarizes the theoretical model. Although a few criticisms will be made this study is not concerned with refining this model but with illustrating and explaining a series of facts, and if possible seeing these in terms of a wider context into which they may be fitted. That context is the advancing industrial society with the accompanying complexity of the organizations of a highly developed economy. The model must be judged on the basis of its relevance and suitability for this purpose. At the same time, a further empirical justification of the model would give more strength to the advocacy of regularities in the processes of change involved in the growing industrial society.

It is not intended to describe Smelser's 'detailed functional breakdown' of the family, and in particular of the family economy, or his confusing system of boxes, boundaries and the relationships between the various parts of the system and the external situation, which he calls boundary interchanges and boundary relationships. The theory used will be strictly limited to the notion of structural differentiation and the sequence of stages already outlined.*

Pointing out that the family is a multi-functional unit, Smelser identifies the following functions of the family.

It is a relatively permanent face-to-face group (integrative function); it allocates authority within this group (political function); it allocates economic goods and services among its members (economic function); it is the seat of much expressive behaviour (pattern-maintenance function). The family, however, like an industry has a *primacy* of function. All the functions of an industry, authority, integration, production, etc. are subordinate to its primary goal of adding economic value to products. The family's primary function is to transmit cultural values through socialisation (pattern-maintenance) and to manage individual tensions within a small face-to-face group (tension-management). In particular, its economic functions are subordinated to these latency functions. This proposition is fundamental. (Smelser, 1959, p. 159.)

It is with change in the primary function of the family that this study is concerned.

'Because it involves socialisation and emotional expression at the deepest psychological levels' (p. 212), the family as a social organization is inflexible. Structural change in the family is therefore likely to be a long-drawn-out process. Attitudes towards the family and its roles are clung to and deeply held, which results in resistance to the change which will be apparent in this study of pre-school education. The change under consideration is thus long-term; in this case it has been taking place over half a century and is still not complete. It is change which involves 'the disappearance, recreation and re-organisation of the social system's roles' (p. 14), rather than more minor adjustments, which do not require any such re-organization.

* The theory is based on the Parsonian model of the social system and some of the terms used in the sequence cannot be defined without prior reference to this. To begin with the central concept of the social system, the definition put forward is as follows: 'A social system is a number of concrete *units* which specialise according to certain *dimensions* and which utilise certain *resources*' (p. 16). There are three different kinds of units (see Parsons and Shils, 1951), but only the collective term roles, which describe these will be introduced here. They contribute at the more concrete levels to the functioning of a social system. They are the activities and the collectivities or groups organized to undertake them. These roles fulfil certain functions in the system. Parsons's theory of action (see Parsons, Bales and Shils, 1953, Chapters 3 and 5) specifies four:

(1) Latent pattern-maintenance and tension management. This concerns the values which support any social system and methods for ensuring adherence to and conformity with the accepted value-system.

(2) Goal-attainment – the system will have a particular set of goals, directed towards the external environment, given a particular value system.

(3) Adaptation – the organization of facilities to achieve the desired goals.

(4) Integration – the attempt to maintain harmony amongst the units in the pursuit of different goals.

'They are on the one hand, *dimensions* by which the behaviour of units is classified, described and analysed. They are second *functions* which these units must perform if the social system is to operate with any degree of efficiency and effectiveness' (Smelser, 1959, p. 12).

Having described the model, it is necessary to stress that the explanation of the growth of pre-school education in terms of structural differentiation in the family is only an underlying theme of this study. Most of its content is concerned with an analysis of the more immediate influences on the development of nursery education, such as the need for women in the labour force during wartime. Much of the analysis will be speculative, because dealing with historical material of this kind it is possible only to assume relationships between economic and political changes, such as war or depression, and simultaneous changes in the dependent variable pre-school education, rather than to demonstrate them with certainty. It is difficult to say what would have happened had the event not taken place. It is possible that some other undiscovered factor, rather than the one inferred, may be related to the change. To summarize, it is suggested that the family system of socialization, whereby the child under compulsory school age remains in the family household receiving care and training from kin, is undergoing structural differentiation. The child is spending part of its time outside the home, under the care and training of adults, who are not related to him, in a new system of pre-school education. New roles and organizations which are structurally distinct but functionally equivalent to the original unit — the family system of socialization — are being implemented. The term socialization will be used in its widest sense, and by the family system of socialization, roles of education, instruction, care and training are implied. At the same time, it should be noted that the inculcation of technical know-how and cognitive skills is largely indirect at this age and of secondary importance in comparison with the teaching of cultural beliefs and norms which it is believed serve to regulate, control and integrate the community.

Part II. Some limitations of the model

First, it has not been possible to demonstrate the sequence at the detailed level. For example, stage two, which consists of 'undirected or misdirected symptoms of disturbance — phantasy, aggression and anxiety', occurs only in very mild forms. Consequently, stage three, consisting of mechanisms of social control to bring them into line, is not apparent at all. It is possible that in addition to the social phenomena described as symptoms in this study, for example, anxious or aggressive letters to the press bemoaning the position of mothers, there are other symptoms which have not been considered. It is possible that the higher incidence of mental illness among women, compared with men in similar social classes and age groups, is related to dissatisfaction with role performance within the family. However, there is not enough evidence on the causes of differing rates of mental illness between men and women to argue this with confidence. This illustrates the difficulty of finding statistical data providing adequate illustration of the changes outlined. In this respect Smelser also faced difficulties with his example of the family economy, although that of the cotton industry presented less of a problem.

There are two more specific questions to raise with respect to stage two. How often will the violent outbreaks described in his own examples occur? It would seem that a sequence of structural differentiation will normally occur without obvious symptoms of disturbance of the kind Smelser described, such as rioting.* Should stage two vanish or possibly be incorporated into stage one, as a response to dissatisfaction which may *sometimes* occur? Secondly, it is difficult to decide whether a reaction to dissatisfaction such as a demand for full-time communal care of young children on kibbutzim lines is to be classified as step five, 'the outlining of new institutional forms' or as 'misdirected phantasy' under step two. In an article on feminism as a social movement Banks and Banks raise this question with reference to Smelser's suggestion that the slogan 'women's place is in the home' was a realistic response to the need for mothers to care for their children, when the latter were excluded from the factories, and as such took place at stage six. They argue that it was 'an unjustified negative, emotional reaction' which referred to single women who were never likely to marry anyway, and as such it belonged to stage two.

Clearly, whether an ideology is to be classified as positive rather than negative, as realistic rather than fantastic and hence placed on steps four or six of a sequence, rather than step two, depends on a prior decision about the nature of the new institutionalised forms which are 'consolidated as permanent features of the institutionalised family' (J. and O. Banks, 1955, p. 565).

They argue also that the new family system is one which accommodates, however badly, the combination of women as mothers and workers.

The chronology of the stages has also been difficult to demonstrate in the subject matter of this study. This is particularly true of stages four, five and six; sometimes it has been hard to separate proliferation of ideas from their specification or their specification from their implementation. An example is the development of the playgroup in the 1960s, which has taken place astonishingly-quickly. On the other hand, the nursery school or class has been developed so slowly that although stage six, that is implementation, was reached with the setting up of the first nursery schools over fifty years ago, instances of stages one to five are still occurring today.†

Over such a long period there are problems arising from changes in values. The nature of the family value-system, which plays such an important part in the way the change is received and the degree to which it is accepted, must be examined. It defines the conditions for the expression of approval or disapproval with the way the system is operating. Thus the specific dissatisfactions are generated and legitimized by certain value criteria. The crucial

---

* An exception to this are the current disturbances in the Universities. Dissatisfaction with, amongst other things, the education they provide has led to extreme forms of protest. One of the ideas being considered as a result of this is that separate research institutes should be set up, leaving teaching as the main task of the universities. It remains to be seen whether this sequence of structural differentiation will be implemented.

† Smelser also has a tendency towards teleological explanation. This is apparent in 'in order to' – 'to' statements. He implies that action was the result of conscious planning by those concerned, when frequently this is not obvious. The model appears to encourage this tendency, in that it sets up a sequence which tends to require conscious planning on behalf of those involved to move from one stage to the next. This is particularly true of the later stages (4, 5 and 6). In cases where there genuinely is conscious planning the criticism of teleology of course ceases to apply.

place of the value system involves describing its contents, but this has many problems. To quote Smelser, 'because its elements are complex and frequently implicit, to outline the appropriate value-system poses extremely delicate interpretative problems' (Smelser, 1959, p. 16). In studying the values behind the family system of socialization, there is difficulty in identifying the dominant value system. There is not unanimity and uniformity in values, but a whole range of attitudes. No comprehensive study of such values and attitudes exists to help in deciding which are the most widely held and which can, therefore, be regarded as dominant. A vital assumption made by Smelser is that although the value system is of such significance, it does not itself initiate change in the absence of other conditions. 'There must also be an actual or perceived situational pressure and the promise of facilities to overcome this pressure' (Smelser, 1959, p. 16). This assumption has been made here. Secondly, he assumes that within any one sequence of structural differentiation the major value system remains constant, that is the criteria for evaluating the units' performance will not vary. Although analysis may be made easier by making this assumption, it has not been made here since it is not tenable in the case of such long-term change. The values regarding the needs of young children have changed during the period and have played a part in furthering the sequence of structural differentiation. At the same time the assumption that values generally change more slowly than other aspects of the social structure is not disputed. Other conditions have also changed. After all, Smelser argues that the model only applies to growing social systems.* This is illustrated by the fact that the inability of the family to cope with the education of young children has replaced its inability to protect their health as the major argument for providing pre-school education.

The model is limited in that its functional emphasis on the needs of society leads to the undervaluing of the conflict aspects and the interplay between norms and power, which in this case concerns the competition for resources to provide social services and the allocation of these resources amongst the different services. This study has tried to emphasize the importance of the traditional conflict between those who emphasize freedom and responsibility and those who emphasize equality when priorities are decided upon, as in the fight for nursery education in Kent in the early 1950s.

Finally there is an even more fundamental criticism of the model than this, which is highlighted by the attempt to use it as an explanatory theory in the exposition of certain social changes, as here. This is that it is not a theory at all. It outlines a sequence of stages, which is empirically conceivable. Thus B follows A, C follows B, D follows C. But a series of provisions is then built in: the chronology of the stages may be reversed; the sequence may be truncated or cut off before completion; and stages may be missed out altogether. Since it makes no statements about the conditions under which these situations occur, the position is reached where anything which is observable would be consistent with the theory. Therefore it is non-refutable, and as such cannot

---

* It is not clear what he means by growing systems. It would appear that they are systems which can differentiate structurally, in which case what he says is true by definition.

claim to be a theory. There is also no adequate theory of moving from one stage to another in the model which, linked to the fact that stages may be missed, makes empirical demonstration difficult. All this detracts from the degree to which it enables the structuring of empirical examples in such a way as to demonstrate simple inter-relationships.

List of tables

Bibliography

Adamson, J. W., *English Education, 1709–1902* (Cambridge: C.U.P., 1964) (rev. edn).

Albrecht, Ruth, 'The Family Responsibilities of Grandparents', *Marriage and Family Living,* Vol. 16, August 1954.

Association of Childhood Education, *A Brief Historical Outline of Childhood Education* (Washington, D.C., 1957).

Banks, Olive, *Parity and Prestige in English Education* (London: Routledge and Kegan Paul, 1955).

Bathurst, K., 'The Need for National Nurseries', *Nineteenth Century,* May 1905.

Benedict, Ruth, 'Continuities and Discontinuities in Cultural Conditioning', *Psychiatry,* I, No. 2, 1938.

Benjamin, Joe, *In Search of Adventure; A Study of Play Leadership* (London: National Council of Social Service, 1966).

Bereiter, Carl and Englemann, Siegfried, *Teaching Disadvantaged Children in the Preschool* (New Jersey: Prentice Hall, 1966).

Bernstein, Basil, 'Class and Linguistic Development; A Theory of Social Learning', in A. H. Halsey, Jean Floud and C. Arnold Anderson (eds.), *Education, Economy and Society* (New York: The Free Press of Glencoe, 1961).

Blackstone, Tessa, *Preschool Education in Europe,* Council of Europe Series on Education Permanente, 1970.

Blood, Robert O. and Wolfe, Donald N., *Husbands and Wives, the Dynamics of Married Living* (Glencoe: Illinois Free Press, 1960).

Bloom, Benjamin S., *Stability and Change in Human Characteristics* (New York: Wiley, 1964).

Bloom, Benjamin S., Davis, Allison and Hess, Robert, *Compensatory Education for Cultural Deprivation* (New York: Holt, 1965).

Blyth, W. A. L., *English Primary Education* (London: Routledge and Kegan Paul, 1965), 2 vols.

Board of Education Educational Reconstruction, White Paper, HMSO, 1943.

—— Circular 1495 (1930), 1444 (1936), 1495 (1940), 1533 (1941).

—— Report of the Consultative Committees upon the School Attendance of Children Below the Age of Five, 1908.

—— Report of the Women Inspectors on Children under Five Years of Age in Public Elementary Schools, 1905.

—— Annual Statistics.

—— Codes and Instructions, Circulars 1405, 1054, 1929.

—— Nursery Schools and Nursery Classes, 1936a.

—— The Health of the School Child, 1936b.

—— Nursery Centres for Children in Reception Areas, 1940.

Bombas-Smith, H., 'A National System of Nursery Schools', *The Athenaeum,* July 1917.

Boskoff, Alvin, 'Functional Analysis as a Source of a Theoretical Repertory and Research Tasks in the Study of Social Change', in G. K. Zollschan and W. Hersch, *Explorations in Social Change* (Boston: Houghton Mifflin, 1964).

Bossard, James H. and Boll, Eleanor, *The Sociology of Child Development* (New York: Harper and Row, 1944), 4th edn.

— 'Personality Roles in the Large Family', *Child Development*, Vol. 26, March 1955.

Bossard, James H., 'The Law of Family Interactivity', *American Journal of Sociology*, Vol. 50, January 1945.

Boswood-Ballard, Phillip, *The Changing School* (London: Hodder and Stoughton, 1925).

Bott, Elizabeth, *Family and Social Network, Roles, Names and External Relationships in Ordinary Urban Families* (London: Tavistock, 1957).

Bowlby, J., *Child Care and the Growth of Love* (Harmondsworth: Penguin, 1964).

Bradford Independent Labour Party, Report of the Commission on Education, Part I, 1928.

Bronfenbrenner, Uri, 'Socialisation and Social Class Through Time and Space', in E. E. Macoby, T. M. Newcomb and E. L. Hartley (eds.), *Readings in Social Psychology* (New York: Holt, 1958).

Bruner, Jerome, *Towards a Theory of Instruction* (Cambridge, Mass.: Harvard University Press, 1966).

Buehler, Charlotte, *The Child and His Family* (London: Kegan Paul, 1940).

Burgess, Ernest W., 'Trends in the Psychological Study of the Family', *Transactions of the World Congress of Sociology*, 1956, Vol. IV, International Sociological Association.

Burton, W., 'The Influence of John Dewey in English Official Reports', *International Review of Education*, Vol. III, No. 3, 1961.

Cambridge Association for the Advancement of State Education, *A Survey of Nursery School Participation in Cambridge*, 1965.

Central Advisory Council of Education (England), *Children and their Primary Schools*, 2 vols., HMSO, 1967.

Chapman, Dennis, 'Changing Values in the British Family', *Case Conference*, Vol. 3, February 1957.

Coale, Ansley, Levy, Marion, *et al.*, *Aspects of the Analysis of Family Structure* (Princeton: Princeton University Press, 1965).

Cochin, J. D. H., *Manuel des Salles d'Asile* (Paris, 1853).

Collier, Virginia M., *Marriage and Careers; A Study of 100 Women who are Wives, Mothers, Homemakers and Professional Workers* (New York: Channel Bookshops, 1926).

Comenius, J. A., *The School of Infancy* (London, 1958).

Committee of Council Minutes, *Report on the British and Foreign School Society*, Vol. II, 1845.

Cotgrove, S., *Social Change and Technical Education* (London: Ruskin House, 1958).

Cottrel, Leonard S., Jr, 'The present status and future orientation of research on the family', *American Sociological Review*, Vol. 13, April 1948.

Cousin, Victor, *On the State of Education* (trans. Leonard Horner) (London, 1838).

Creech-Jones, V., *Nurseries and Nursery Schools*, Fabian Pamphlet (London, 1945).

Cusden, Phoebe, *The English Nursery School* (London: Kegan Paul, Trench and Trubner, 1938).

Davies, B. P., *Social Needs and Resources in Local Services; a study of variations and standards of provision of personal social services between local authority areas* (London: Michael Joseph, 1968).

Davies, E., 'Nursery Classes in Elementary Schools', *Education*, 28 February 1936.

Day, Kathleen, *Britain's Nursery Schools* (London: Day and Mason, 1949).

Dent, H., *Education in Transition, 1939–1943; A Sociological Analysis of the Impact of War on English Education* (Oxford: O.U.P., 1944).

Department of Education and Science, Statistics of Education.

Derby Association for the Development of State Education, Report on Nursery Schools, 1964.

Deutsch, Martin, 'Facilitating Development in the Preschool Child: Social and Psychological Perspectives', *Merill-Palmer Quarterly of Behaviour and Development,* Vol. 10, July 1964.

Dewey, John, *Democracy and Education* (New York: Macmillan, 1916).

Donnison, D. V. and Chapman, V., *Social Policy and Administration* (London: Allen and Unwin, 1964).

Douglas, J. W. B., *The Home and the School: a study of ability and attainment in the primary school* (London: MacGibbon and Kee, 1964).

Douglas, J. W. B. and Blomfield, J. M., *Children under Five* (London: Allen and Unwin, 1958).

Douglas, J. W. B. and Ross, J. M., 'Subsequent Progress of Nursery School Children', *Educational Research,* Vol. 7, 1964, pp. 83–94.

Drummond, M., 'The Nursery School: An Educational Problem', *The Contemporary Review,* April 1919.

Duvall, Evelyn M., 'Conceptions of Parenthood', *American Journal of Sociology,* Vol. 52, November 1946.

Education Act, 1918.

Education Act, 1944.

Education Enquiry Committee Report, *The Case for Nursery Schools* (Chairman: R. F. Cholmeley), (London: Phillip, 1929).

Ellis, Havelock, *Essays of Love and Virtue,* 2nd Series (New York: Doran, 1922).

van der Eyken, Willem, *The Preschool Years* (Harmondsworth: Penguin, 1967).

Fediavevsky, Vera and Smith Hill, Patty, *Nursery School and Parent Edvcation* (New York: Dutton, 1936).

Feldman, Shirley, 'A Pre-School Enrichment Program for Disadvantaged Children', *The New Era,* Vol. 45, 1964.

Fisher, H. A. L., *Educational Reform* (speeches delivered), (Oxford: Clarendon Press, 1918).

Fletcher, R., *Family and Marriage* (Harmondsworth: Penguin, 1962).

Floud, Jean and Halsey, A. H., 'The Sociology of Education: A Third Report and Bibliography', *Current Sociology,* Vol. VII, No. 3, 1900.

Foote, Nelson, 'New Roles for Men and Women', *Journal of Marriage and Family Living,* Vol. 23, November 1961.

Forest, Ilse, *The School for Children from Two to Eight* (Boston, Mass., 1935).

—— *Pre-School Education: a historical and critical study* (New York: Macmillan, 1927).

Foster, Josephine C. and Mattson, Maria L., *Nursery School Education* (New York: Appleton, 1939).

Froebel, Friedrich, *Autobiography* (trans. C. W. Burdeen), (Syracuse, 1889).

—— *The Education of Man* (1826) (trans. W. N. Hailmann), (Appleton, 1906).

Froebel Society, *Types of School for Young Children* (London, 1913).

Fuller, Elizabeth, 'Early Childhood Education', *Encyclopaedia of Educational Research* (ed. W. S. Monroe) (New York: Macmillan, 1952) (rev. edn).

Gavron, Hannah, *The Captive Wife* (London: Routledge and Kegan Paul, 1966).

Geddes Report, British Parliamentary Papers, 1922 (ii).

Gesell, Arnold, 'Pre-School Development and Education', *Annals of the American Academy,* Vol. LXXI, September 1925.

—— *The Guidance of Mental Growth in Infant and Child* (New York: Macmillan, 1943).

Gesell, Arnold *et al.,* *Infant and Child in the Culture of Today* (London: Hamish Hamilton, 1943).

Glick, Paul C., 'The Family Cycle', *American Sociological Review,* Vol. 4, April 1947.

Goldthorpe, J., 'The Development of Social Policy in England, 1800–1914', *Transactions of the 5th World Congress of Sociology*, 1962, Vol. 4.

Goode, W., 'The Process of Role Bargaining in the Impact of Urbanisation and Industrialisation in the Family System', *Current Sociology* (UNESCO), Vol. 12, No. 1, 1963–4.

Grande, Elaine, 'Miserable Married Women' (3 articles), *Observer*, May 1961.

Greenfield, Sydney, 'Industrialization and the Family in Social Theory', *American Journal of Sociology*, Vol. 67, November 1961.

Gundry, Elizabeth, 'Breaking Out of Purdah' and 'The Way Back to Work', *Sunday Times*, July 1963.

Haden-Guest, L. (ed.), *The New Education* (London: Hodder and Stoughton, 1920).

Hadow Report, Consultative Committee of the Board of Education, 195⁵.

Halsey, A. H., Floud, Jean and Anderson, C. Arnold, *Education, Economy and Society: a reader in the Sociology of Education* (New York: Free Press of Glencoe, 1961).

Hawtrey, F., *French Nursery Schools* (London: Dent, 1936).

Hechinger, Fred M. (ed.), *Pre-School Education Today* (New York: Doubleday, 1966).

Heinicke, C. M. 'Some Effects of Separating Two-Year Old Children from Their Parents: A Comparative Study', *Human Relations*, Vol. 9, May 1956.

Hentig, Hans Von, 'The Sociological Function of the Grandmother', *Social Forces*, Vol. 24, May 1946.

Herbinière-Lebert, Suzanne, *Les écoles maternelles et l'éducation pré-scolaire en Europe* (Repères, 1964), pp. 10–24.

Herzog, John D., 'Deliberate Instruction and Household Structure: A Cross-Cultural Study', *Harvard Educational Review*, Vol. 32, No. 3.

Hill, Reuben, 'A Critique of Contemporary Marriage and Family Research', *Social Forces, Vol. 33, March 1953.*

Hoeflin, Ruth, 'Child Rearing Practices and Child Care Resources used by Ohio Families with Children', *Journal of Genetic Psychology*, Vol. 34, June 1954.

House of Lords, debate on 'Education of the People', 21 May 1835.

Howe, Elspeth, *Under Five: A Report on Nursery Education* (London: Conservative Political Centre, 1966).

Hubert, Jane, 'Kinship and Geographical Mobility in a Sample from a London Middle Class Area', *International Journal of Comparative Sociology*, Vol. VI, No. 1, March 1965.

Hughes, E. and Roberts, R., *Children of Pre-school age in Gary, Indiana* (Washington, D.C., 1922).

Hunt, Audrey, A Survey of Women's Employment, Government Social Survey, HMSO, 1968, Vol. I, Report.

Hunt, J. McV., *Intelligence and Experience* (New York: Ronald Press, 1961).

Ingleby Report, Report of the Committee on Children and Young Persons, HMSO, 1960.

International Bureau of Education, The Organisation of Pre-Primary Education: Research in Comparative Education, I.B.E. Publication No. 230, Geneva, 1961.

Isaacs, Susan and De Lissa, Lillian, 'Principles and Practice in Nursery School Education', Address to the 18th Annual Conference of Education Associations, 1930.

Jacobson, Alver, 'Conflict of Attitudes Toward the Roles of the Husband and Wife in Marriage', *American Sociological Review*, Vol. 17, April 1952.

Jensen, Arthur R., 'The Culturally Disadvantaged, Psychological and Educational Aspects', *Educational Research*, Vol. 10, November 1967.

Jephcott, Pearl, *Married Women Working* (London: Allen and Unwin, 1962).

Jerman, Betty, 'Living in Suburbia', *Guardian*, February 1960.

Joint Parliamentary Advisory Council, Report on Nursery Education (London, 1923).

Klein, Viola, *Britain's Married Women Workers* (London: Routledge and Kegan Paul, 1965).

Kohlberg, Laurence, 'Early Education: A Cognitive-Developmental View', *Child Development,* December 1968, Vol. 39, No. 4.
Kolb, William L., 'Sociologically Established Family Norms and Democratic Values', *Social Forces,* Vol. 26, May 1948.
Komarovsky, Mirra, 'Cultural Contradictions and Sex Roles', *American Journal of Sociology,* Vol. 15, 1957.
König, René, 'Family and Authority: The German Father in 1955', *Sociological Review,* Vol. 5, 1957.
— 'Changes in the Western Family', *Transactions of the Third World Congress of Sociology,* 1956, Vol. 4, International Sociological Association.
Kooy, G. A., 'Urbanisation and Nuclear Family Individualisation: A Causal Connection?', *Current Sociology* (UNESCO), Vol. 12, 1963–4.
Labour Party and TUC, From Nursery School to University, Report of the Educational Advisory Committee of the Labour Party and TUC, London, 1926.
Lambert, Royston, *The State and Boarding Education* (London: Methuen, 1966).
Lawrence, Evelyn, *Friedrich Froebel and English Education* (London: University of London Press, 1952).
Linton, Ralph, 'Age and Sex Categories', *American Sociological Review,* Vol. 7, October 1942.
London Women's Parliament, Report of a Deputation to the Ministry of Health, 1945.
Lowndes, G. A. N., *Margaret McMillan – The Children's Champion* (London: Museum Press, 1966).
McMillan, Margaret, *The Nursery School* (London: Dent, 1930) (rev. edn).
— *Life of Rachel McMillan* (London: Dent, 1927).
Maizels, Joan, Two to Five in High Flats, An Enquiry into Play Provision for Children Aged 2–5 Living in High Flats (Pamphlet), (London, 1961).
May, Dorothy E., *Children in the Nursery School: Studies of Personal Adjustment in Early Childhood* (London: University of London Press, 1963).
Mead, M. and Wolfenstein, M. (eds.), *Childhood in Contemporary Culture* (Chicago: University of Chicago Press, 1955).
Miller, Daniel and Swanson, Amy E., *The Changing American Parent* (New York: Wiley, 1958).
Miner, Jerry, *Social and Economic Factors in Spending on Public Education* (New York: Syracuse University Press, 1963).
Ministry of Education, *Not Yet Five,* HMSO, 1946.
— Circulars 175 (1948), 153 (1947), 210 (1949), 242 (1951), 334 (1958), 280 (1954), 313 (1956), 8 (1960), 75 (1945), 125 (1946), 292 (1955).
— Annual Reports.
Ministry of Health Circulars 1954 (1929), 1936 (1940), 2388 (1941), 221 (1945).
— Annual Reports 177 (1946).
Mitchison, Lois, 'The Price of Educating Women', *Guardian,* January 1960.
Murdock, G. P., 'Family Universals', *Marriage and Family Living,* Vol. 9, May 1947.
Musgrove, F., *Youth and the Social Order* (London: Routledge and Kegan Paul, 1961).
Myrdal, Alva, 'Factors in Changing Family Patterns', Symposium on the Family, *Transactions of the Third World Congress of Sociology,* 1954.
Myrdal, Alva and Klein, V., *Women's Two Roles* (London: Routledge and Kegan Paul, 1956).
National Society for the Study of Education, *28th Yearbook* (Bloomington, Ill., 1929).
— *46th Yearbook,* Part II (Bloomington, Ill., 1947).
National Union of Teachers, *Nursery and Infant Education* (London, 1949).
Newcastle Commission, Royal Commission on English Education, 1861.
New Era, Editorials, November 1930; November 1938.
Newman, Sir George, *The Health of the School Child,* HMSO, London, 1930.

Newsom, Sir John, 'The Education of Women', *Observer*, September 1964.

Newson, John and Elizabeth, *Infant Care in an Urban Community* (London: Allen and Unwin, 1963).

—— *Four Years Old in an Urban Community* (London: Allen and Unwin, 1968).

Nimkoff, M. F., 'The Increase in Married Women in the Labour Force', *Transactions of the Third World Congress of Sociology*, 1954.

Nursery School Association, The Educational Needs of Children under Seven Years of Age, Memorandum to the Board of Education, 1936.

—— Annual Reports, 1924, 1929, 1933, 1935.

—— A Historical Record of the Nursery School Association of Great Britain, 1923–44, Pamphlet No. 60, 1945.

—— *Playgroup Facilities for Young Children* (London, 1964).

—— *The Under Fives in the Welfare State* (London, 1964).

—— Historical Record of the N.S.A. of Great Britain, Pamphlet No. 60, 1945.

—— *Nursery Schools in Relation to Public Health* (London, 1926).

—— A Statement of Policy, 1927.

—— The First Step in Education, 1943.

—— Variations Within the Nursery School Movement, 1932.

Nye, F. Ivan and Bayer, Alan E. 'Some Recent Trends in Family Research', *Social Forces*, Vol. 41, March 1963.

Nye, F. Ivan and Hoffman, Lois W. (eds.), *The Employed Mother in the United States* (Chicago: Rand McNally, 1963).

Ogburn, William F., *Social Change with Respect to Culture and Original Nature* (New York: Viking Press, 1950).

Ogburn, William F., and Nimkoff, M. F., *Technology and the Changing Family* (Boston: Houghton Mifflin, 1955).

Ottoway, K., 'The Educational Sociology of Emile Durkheim', *British Journal of Sociology*, Vol. 6, September 1955.

Owen, Grace, *Nursery School Education.*

Owen, Robert, *Life of Robert Owen by himself* (1858) (London: Bell, 1920), p. 145.

—— *Journal*, Vol. IV (London: Watson, 1852).

Packman, Jean, *Child Care: Needs and Numbers* (London: Allen and Unwin, 1968).

Parliamentary Debates, House of Commons, Official Reports, Vol. 209, No. 108, 27 July 1927.

Parsons, Talcott and Bales, Robert F., *The Family, Socialisation and the Interaction Process* (Glencoe: Illinois Free Press, 1954).

Parsons, Talcott, Bales, Robert F. and Shils, Edward A., *Working Papers on the Theory of Action* (Glencoe: Illinois Free Press, 1953).

Parsons, Talcott and Shils, Edward A., *Towards a General Theory of Action* (Cambridge, Mass.: Harvard University Press, 1961).

Peschek, David and Brand, J., *Policies and Politics in Secondary Education, Case Studies in West Ham and Reading*, Greater London Papers No. 11, LSE, 1966.

Pinchbeck, Ivy, *Women Workers in the Industrial Revolution, 1750–1850*, London School of Economics and Political Science, Studies in Economic and Social History No. 1 (London, 1930).

Plaisted, L., *The Early Education of Children* (Oxford, 1909).

Political and Economic Planning, *Planning*, March 1943.

Pollard, Hugh M., *Pioneers in Popular Education, 1760–1850* (London: Murray, 1956).

Pratt, Lois and Whelpton, P. K., 'Social and Psychological Factors Affecting Fertility: extra-familial participation of wives in relation to interest and liking for children, fertility planning and actual desired family size', Milbank Memorial Fund, *Quarterly*, Vol. 34, January 1956.

Pre-school Playgroups Association, 'A Breakdown of Supervisor Qualifications for 200 Playgroups', October 1965.

Priestman, Barbara, *Froebel Education Today* (London: University of London Press, 1946).

Pringle, M. L. K. and Tanner, M., *Deprivation and Education* (London: Longmans, 1965).

Ramsey, C. E. and Nelson, L., 'Values and Attitudes Towards the Family', *American Sociological Review*, Vol. 21, October 1956.

Rapoport, Rhona and Roscow, Irving, 'An Approach to Family Relations and Role Performance', *Human Relations*, Vol. X, No. 3, 1957.

Raymont, T., *A History of Young Children* (London: Longmans, 1937).

Registrar General, Quarterly Returns, 4th Quarter, 1964, 1965.

Ritchie, O. W. and Koller, M. R., *The Sociology of Childhood* (New York: Appleton-Century-Crofts, 1964).

Robbins Report, Higher Education, Appendix I, 'The Demand for Places in Higher Education', HMSO Cmnd. 2154-1.

Ronge, Johanns and Bertha, *English Kindergarten* (London: Hudson, 1855).

Rosser, C. and Harris C., *The Family and Social Change: A Study of Family and Kinship in a South Wales Town* (London: Routledge and Kegan Paul, 1965).

Ruderman, Florence, *The Day Care of Children*, Child Welfare League of America (New York, 1968).

Rusk, Robert F., *A History of Infant Education* (London: University of London Press, 1933).

Russell, Bertrand, *Education and the Good Life* (New York: Boni and Liverwright, 1926a).

—— *On Education Especially in Early Childhood* (London: Allen and Unwin, 1926b).

School and Home, Number on Nursery Schools, Vol. II, November 1927.

Selvin, Hannan C., 'Durkheim's Suicide and Empirical Research'.

Seward, G. H., 'Cultural Conflict and the Feminine Role: An Experimental Study', *Journal of Social Psychology*, Vol. 22, November 1945.

Sheridan, A., 'Variations in Secondary School Provision', unpublished Ph.D. thesis.

Slight, Jeanice D., 'The Froebel Movement in England', *National Froebel Foundation Bulletin*, No. 76, June 1952.

Smelser, N., *Social Change in the Industrial Revolution: an application of theory to the Lancashire Cotton Industry, 1770–1840* (London: Routledge and Kegan Paul, 1959).

—— 'Notes of Functionalism and Scientific Analysis', *Transactions of the 5th World Congress of Sociology*, 1962, Vol. 4.

Smieton, Dame Mary, 'Problems of Women's Employment in Great Britain', *International Labour Review*, January 1954.

Sretzer, R., 'The origins of full-time compulsory education at 5', *British Journal of Educational Studies*, November 1964.

Standing, E. M., *Maria Montessori: Her Life and Work* (London: Hollis and Carter, 1957).

Stevinson, Emma, *The open-air nursery* (London: Dent, 1923).

Stewart, Burgess J., 'The Study of Social Movements as a Means for Classifying the Process of Social Action', *Social Forces*, Vol. 22, 1943–4, pp. 269–75.

Stewart, C. M., 'Future Trends in the Employment of Married Women', *British Journal of Sociology*, Vol. 14, No. 2, 1965.

Sussman, Marvin B., 'The Help-Pattern in the Middle Class Family', *American Sociological Review*, Vol. 18, February 1953.

—— 'Needed Research on the Employed Mother', *Journal of Marriage and Family Living*, Vol. 23, November 1961.

Thompson, B. and Finlayson, H., 'Married Women who Work in Early Motherhood', *British Journal of Sociology*, Vol. 14, No. 2, March 1963.

Titmuss, R. M., *Essays on the Welfare State* (London: Allen and Unwin, 1958).

Townshend, Mrs, *The Case for School Nurseries*, Fabian Trust, 145 (London, 1909).

Tropp, Asher, *The School Teachers: the growth of the teaching profession in England and Wales from 1800 to the present day* (London: Heinemann, 1957).

Trouillet, Bernard, *Die Vorschulerziehung in neun europäischen Ländern* (Weinheim: Julius Beltz, 1967).

Turner, P., *Something Extraordinary* (London: Michael Joseph, 1962).

Turner, Ralph H., 'Children and Women's Work', *Sociology and Social Research*, Vol. 36, July–August 1952.

UNESCO, *Pre-school Education: Statistical Survey* (Paris, 1963).

Vaizey, John, *The Costs of Education* (London: Allen and Unwin, 1958).

Wallin, Paul, 'Cultural Contradictions and Sex Roles: A repeat study', *American Sociological Review*, Vol. 15, April 1950.

Wendell-King, C., *Social Movements in the United States* (New York: Random House, 1956).

Wesley, John, *The Works of John Wesley*, Vol. III, first American edn (Philadelphia, 1826).

Wilderspin, Samuel, *The infant system for developing the intellectual and moral power of all children from one to seven years of age* (London, 1840).

Wilson, F. M. G., *Administrators in Action* (London: Allen and Unwin, 1961).

Wiseman, Stephen, *Education and Environment* (Manchester: Manchester University Press, 1964).

Wood, Grace, 'The History and Development of Nursery Education in Manchester and Salford', M.Ed. Thesis, University of Manchester, 1934.

World Health Organisation, *The Care of Well Children* (Geneva, 1963).

Wynn, Margaret, *Fatherless Families* (London: Michael Joseph, 1964).

Young, M. and Wilmott, P., *Family and Kinship in Bethnal Green* (London: Routledge and Kegan Paul, 1957).

Yudkin, Simon, *0–5, A Report on the Case of Pre-school Children*, National Society for Children's Nurseries (London, 1967).

Yudkin, Simon and Holme, Anthea, *Working Mothers and Their Children* (London: Michael Joseph, 1963).

Index

rates, 139
Raymont, T., 13
reform in education, 30
Regent Street Polytechnic, 21
registered child minders, *see* child-minders
registered premises, *see* premises, registered
  for day care
regression analysis, 97–109, 116–19, 121
  in Plowden Report, 119
Report of the Women Inspectors, 29–30
requisitioned property, 126, 127, 128, 130,
  132, 137
resources
  allocation of, 123–4, 155, 166, 211
  manipulation of, 128, 147–8, 150, 157
Revised Codes, 23, 26
Robbins Report, 96
role learning, 29
Ronge, Johanne and Bertha, 24–6
Ross, J. M., 112
Rousseau, J.-J., 12, 16
Ruderman, Florence, 154
rural areas and levels of nursery provision,
  99, 102, 108, 117, 166
Rusk, Robert F., 12
Russell, Bertrand, 43, 50, 168–9

Sadler, Sir Michael, 43
salle d'asile, 16–17
Save the Children Fund, 49, 78
school building
  control over, 120
  costs of, 41
  and minor works programme, 128, 150
school governing bodies, 124
school management committees, 124
school meals, 35, 61
Schools Council, 164
schools of industry, 18–19
secondary education
  schools, 21, 30, 147, 168
  and standards, 41
selectivity, 168
Shaw, B., 39
Sheridan, A., 96
Shils, Edward A., 208
sibling rivalry, 55
  development of, 124
Smelser, N., 4, 16, 47, 158, 159, 206–12
Smethwick, pre-school education in, 123,
  143–5, 203–5
Smith Hill, Patty, 14
social class, 35, 58, 71, 80, 98, 99, 102,
  108–9, 115, 116, 158, 167
social mobility, 157
social services
  development of, 124, 157
  needs for, 119–20, 159

spending on, 139
  state provision of, 82, 96
social system, 208, 211
socialization, 9, 12, 34, 71, 165, 209
  see also family, and socialization
special schools, 120, 155
Spitz, 159
Sretzer, R., 23
state responsibility for education, origins
  of, 21–2
statistical sources, 83–4, 93–5, 110,
  170–78
statistics of education, *see* Department of
  Education and Science, statistics of;
  statistical sources
Stewart, C. M., 70
structural differentiation, 4, 5, 9, 47, 64,
  79, 149, 157, 159, 206–12
structured programmes, 162–3
student protest, 210
Sunley, R., 8
Swanson, Amy E., 8

teachers
  married women released to teach, 64, 68,
    203–5
  quotas of, 120
  shortage of, 65–6, 67, 150, 159, 168
teachers' salaries, 120
teaching methods, 30
technical education, 21
territorial justice, 166
The Times, 50, 142, 156
Thompson, B., 70
Thorndike, 16
Titmuss, R. M., 40, 159
Trades Union Congress, 46–7
tripartism, 30
Tropp, Asher, 42
Turner, P., 78

ultra vires, 152
unemployment and the demand for nursery
  education, 49
UNESCO, 19, 75
urban programme, 162
urbanization
  and the family, 4
  and levels of nursery education, 49, 108
USSR and nursery education, 48

Vaizey, John, 82, 155, 159

Wales, nursery provision in, 103, 106, 108
Wendell King, C., 76
Wesley, John, 8
Whitley scales, 132
WHO, 75

Books from the
Higher Education Research Unit

Allen Lane The Penguin Press 'L.S.E. Studies on Education'

Published
Decision Models for Educational Planning by Peter Armitage, Cyril Smith and Paul Alper (1969).
The Causes of Graduate Unemployment in India by Mark Blaug, Richard Layard and Maureen Woodhall (1969).
Paying for Private Schools by Howard Glennerster and Gail Wilson (1970).
Policy and Practice: The Colleges of Advanced Technology by Tyrrell Burgess and John Pratt (1970).
A Fair Start: The Provision of Pre-school Education by Tessa Blackstone

In the Press
Qualified Manpower and Economic Performance: An Inter-plant Study in the Electrical Engineering Industry by P. R. G. Layard, J. D. Sargan, M. Ager and D. J. Jones.

In preparation (1971) (provisional titles)
A Model of the British Secondary School System
Higher Education and the State
Educated Manpower for India's Industrial Development
Academics in an Age of Change

Published by Penguin Books

The Impact of Robbins: Expansion in Higher Education by Richard Layard, John King and Claus Moser (1969).

Published by Oliver & Boyd

Graduate School: a Study of Graduate Work at the London School of Economics by H. Glennerster with the assistance of A. Bennett and C. Farrell (1966).
The Utilization of Educated Manpower in Industry by M. Blaug, M. Peston and A. Ziderman (1967).
Manpower and Educational Development in India (1961–1986) by Tyrrell Burgess, Richard Layard and Pitamber Pant (1968).
Educational Finance: its Sources and Uses in the United Kingdom by Alan Peacock, Howard Glennerster and Robert Lavers (1968).
Education and Manpower: Theoretical Models and Empirical Applications by Tore Thonstad (1969).

Published in collaboration with the
Directorate for Scientific Affairs, O.E.C.D.

Statistics of the Occupational and Educational Structure of the Labour Force in 53 Countries (1969).